ACHIEVE MORE WITH ∞ GREAT KIT ∞

◢SPORTPURSUIT

FROM THE EDITOR

Running is now a mainstream activity – there's no two ways about it. The days of the odd furtive soul in tiny split shorts running a gauntlet of good(ish) natured taunts from builders and white van men have thankfully mostly been consigned to history. Everywhere you look on the streets there are brightly clad runners of every shape, size and ability doing their stuff with barely an eyebrow being raised. Of course, it's one of the easiest sports to take up: it's just left foot right foot, right? But if you want to improve or have a specific goal in mind it's worth getting some decent advice. And that's where this book comes in. It's a compilation of the best tips, most hard-won wisdom, and cutting edge scientific opinion from our international network of experts on the world's biggest selling running magazine.

There are common-sense training plans (from 5K to marathon); fad-free weight loss tips; and sage advice on how to improve your form, buy the right kit, fuel your body, avoid injury and much, much more.

Beginner or club vet, speed demon or back-of-the-packer, keen bean or weekend warrior – there's something in here for you. Say hello to the runner you're about to be.

Kerry McCarthy
Editor

Editor-in-Chief Andy Dixon
Editor Kerry McCarthy
Associate Editor Tom Stone
Art Director Graeme Sapsed
Sub Editor Thom Atkinson

Creative Development Director Morgan Rees
Group Publishing Director Alun Williams
Sales Director of Hearst-Rodale
Duncan Chater
Senior Sales Executives James Fricker,
Katherine Kendall
Sales Executive Andreia Rola
Classified Sales Executive Oliver Brierley
Production Manager Roger Bilsland
Marketing Director Claire Matthews

CEO, Hearst Magazines UK Arnaud de Puyfontaine
HEARST-RODALE JOINT BOARD OF DIRECTORS
President and CEO, Hearst Magazines
International Duncan Edwards
Finance Director, Hearst Magazines UK
Andy Humphries
Senior Vice President, Rodale International
Robert Novick

HEARST MAGAZINES UK
Director of Consumer Sales & Marketing
Sharon Douglas
HR Director Rachel Stock
Business Manager Sarah Hammond
Head of Newstrade Marketing Jennifer Caughey
Circulation Manager Lyndsay Macdonald

RODALE INTERNATIONAL
Rodale Inc, 33 East Minor Street, Emmaus,
Pennsylvania 18098, USA

Editorial Director John Ville
Deputy Editorial Director Veronika Taylor
International Content Manager Karl Rozemeyer
Editorial Assistant Samantha Quisgard
Business Development Director Kevin LaBonge
International Business Manager Seana Williams
Business Coordinator Hannah Roshetko

RUNNER'S WORLD
THE NEW COMPLETE GUIDE TO RUNNING
©2013, Hearst-Rodale Ltd, 33 Broadwick Street,
London, W1F 0DQ
Tel: 020 7339 4400 **Fax:** 020 7339 4420

For annual subscription rates for the UK, please call our enquiry line on 0844 848 5203. Back issues, customer enquiries, change of address and orders to: Runner's World, Hearst Magazines UK Ltd, Tower House, Sovereign Park, Lathkill Street, Market Harborough, Leics LE16 9EF (0844 848 5203; Mon to Fri, 8am to 9:30pm and Saturday, 8am to 4pm). Credit card hotline: 0844 848 1601. Runner's World is published in the United Kingdom by Hearst-Rodale Limited – a joint venture by Hearst Magazines UK, a wholly owned subsidiary of The Hearst Corporation, and Rodale International, a division of Rodale Incorporated.

CONTENTS

RUNNER'S WORLD

THE NEW COMPLETE GUIDE TO RUNNING

1 GETTING STARTED

12 49 REASONS TO LOVE RUNNING
Here's why you should be lacing up soon

18 READY TO START
Prepare to hit the roads for the first time

22 BEAT THE CLOCK
How to find time to train in your daily routine

27 ENJOY A SLOW LIFE
A walk can be as just as good for you as a run

30 BE A RUNNER
Turn your body into a running machine

36 BEST IN SHOE
Find out what your trainers can do for you

38 AMAZING FEET
A guide to picking the right footwear for you

40 YOUR FIT KIT
What to wear when you go out running

42 NEW TECH
The new kit to help you go that extra mile

2 TRAINING

48 12 TRAINING ESSENTIALS
Ready to run? Here's the basic know-how you need to hit your targets

52 YOUR ALL-YEAR PLAN
There is a run out there for all seasons. Learn how to map them out

54 5 RULES OF ACTION
The golden rules of training and how to make them work for you

56 IN THE LONG RUN
The best ways to cover long distances

58 WORK FAST, GO FASTER
Here the fundamental principles of speedwork are explained

60 20 WAYS TO SPEED
Quick tips for going faster, whether you're an experienced runner or a complete novice

62 HEIGHTS OF PASSION
Head to the hills for sessions that will make you stronger and fitter

66 PERFECT TEMPO
How to train to maintain race pace

68 THE UPSIDE OF RUNNING INSIDE
Tired of the road? Take to the treadmill

72 JOIN THE CLUB?
Become a team player and transform your training

76 FLIGHT TO THE FINISH
Ultimately the most important part of a race is the finish. Here's how to train for it.

3 CROSS TRAINING

80 CROSS ROADS
Swimming, cycling, weights... there are many different sports that will improve your running

84 CENTRE OF ATTENTION
Working your core will not only help you run stronger, it will make you look fantastic, too.

90 STRIKE A POSE
Yoga, Pilates and The Alexander Technique: different ways to stretch and strengthen your body.

94 X-FACTOR
An intense, outdoor circuit that will help you to hit the right note with your running.

4 NUTRITION

98 WHAT TO RUN ON
Put these super foods on your shopping list

102 PERFECT TIMING
Choose the right times to refuel during your day

108 POWER OF WATER
Know your H_2O: how much to drink – and when enough is enough

114 40 TASTY TIPS
Use these food tricks to power your body

120 FUELLING YOUR FIRE
What to eat and when you should tuck in while out on your run

126 SAFER EATING
Enjoy your favourite foods guilt-free with these healthy versions

138 LOSE 10LB IN A MONTH
A complete diet and exercise plan for guaranteed weight loss

142 RUN IT OFF
Slim yourself down by speeding up

144 PSYCH OUT FAT
Use the power of your mind to reduce your waistline

6 HEALTH & INJURY

152 RUNNER'S RELIEF
How to beat all your runner's woes

154 RECOVERY SCIENCE
The latest ways to recuperate

160 INJURY CLINIC
Common runner's ailments cured

172 DREAM RUNNING
Simply getting the right amount of shut-eye can help to improve your training and race times

176 JUST ADD WATER
Ever tried running in a swimming pool? Here's how you can use it in your training

5 WEIGHT LOSS

132 FAT-BURNING TIPS
You can run 100 miles, but you won't lose weight unless you eat right, too

Contents

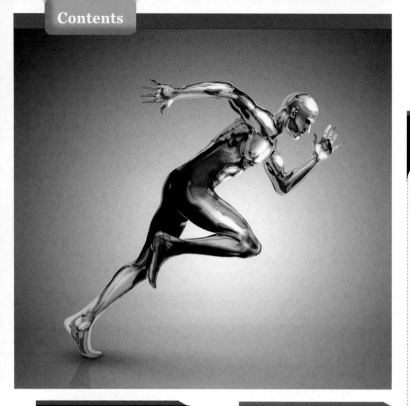

9 WOMEN'S RUNNING

222 WOMEN'S HEALTH
Common ailments that female runners need to consider before hitting the road

224 21 TIPS FOR WOMEN RUNNERS
Inspirational hints on how to put your mind to attaining peak fitness

228 BABY STEPS
Questions and answers on how you can adapt to pregnancy and parenthood. Plus the lowdown on the best buggies for running

236 COME BACK STRONG
A workout made for a post-pregnancy return to form – as designed and used by an Olympian. It also makes a great, any-time, full-body routine for all women

7 MINIMALISM & FORM

182 PIMP MY STRIDE
Changing the way you run can enable you to run further and faster

190 THE NAKED TRUTH
Get back to nature with barefoot running

8 MIND CONTROL

202 BREAK THE BARRIERS
Easy ways to smash through the negative thoughts and feelings that hold you back

206 48 WAYS TO KEEP GOING
Find yourself flagging? Keep on track with this list of tried-and-tested motivational tricks

212 QUICK THINKING
Sometimes your mind plays tricks on you. Here's how to short circuit pain and fight to the finish line

218 THE BRAIN-BOOSTING SERUM
The new science that proves running will make your cleverer

10 TRAIL RUNNING

240 OFF TRACK
Ready to off-road it? Here's a closer look at all that trail running can offer you that a life on the asphalt can't

242 TRICKS OF THE TRAIL
Head off road with this how-to guide to traverse up and down those trails without coming a cropper

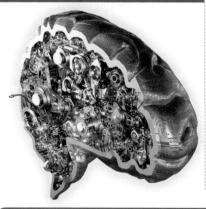

11 GUIDE TO RACING

254 NATURAL SELECTION
You were born to run, but are you a speed demon or a long-hauler? This quiz will help you work it out

260 YOUR BEST YEAR EVER
Get the most from your miles by mixing up your running over 12 months

266 MIRACLES IN A MILE
Here's why you should do this classic distance

268 TRAINING PLANS
Prepare for a 5K, 10K, a half or a full marathon

282 WHY LESS IS MORE
All your tapering questions answered

284 26 MILES LATER...
How to recover from a marathon

244 SUMMIT FOR THE WEEKEND
If you fancy a lofty challenge here's a guide to the best hills in the UK

250 RACING HOME
Trail running champion Scott Jurek reveals how he got the bug and revisits his home turf

Chapter

1

GETTING STARTED

Your guide to becoming a runner – whether you are new to the sport or you just want to know more

12   **49 REASONS TO LOVE RUNNING**
Why lacing up will cheer you up

18   **READY TO START**
How to prepare for the runner's world

22   **BEAT THE CLOCKS**
How to find the time to train

27   **ENJOY THE SLOW LIFE**
Why a walk can be as good as a run

30   **MAKE YOURSELF A RUNNER**
Turn your body into a running machine

36   **BEST IN SHOE**
What your shoes can do for you

38   **AMAZING FEET**
A guide to picking the right footwear

40   **YOUR FIT KIT**
What to wear for running

42   **NEW TECH**
The kit that could help you go further

PHOTOGRAPHY GLEN MONTGOMERY
MODEL: NIKKI LUPTON

**Sometimes
there's nothing
better than a run**

PHOTOGRAPHY SHUTTERSTOCK

49 REASONS TO LOVE RUNNING

Slipping on your trainers should be a delight, not a chore. A passion for running can be reached through any number of reasons, from the pounds you shed to its meditative qualities. Here's how to learn to love what you do

1 SAY GOODBYE TO YOUR BELLY

Dublin University researchers report that a 10-stone adult burns 391 calories in 30 minutes of running, compared with 277 calories while cycling, and 272 calories while playing tennis. Translation? You blitz your belly up to 40 per cent faster.

2 BULLET-PROOF BONES

Fifteen minutes of light jogging just three times a week is all it can take to reduce your risk of developing osteoporosis in later life by up to 40 per cent, according to research from the National Osteoporosis Society.

3 BLITZ BODY BLEMISHES

Running tones the buttocks and thighs quicker than any other exercise, which literally squeezes out the lingering fat," according to Dr James Fleming, author of Beat Cellulite Forever (Piatkus Books).

4 LAUGH AT THE WEATHER

It doesn't matter if the weather forecast shows rain, cold, wind – there's no excuse not to get out. Just layer up depending on how the skies look and see it as another challenge. It's an activity that is made bespoke for the rather unpredictable weather that we have in this country!

5 GET H-A-P-P-Y

"Mild to moderate exercise releases natural, feel-good endorphins that help counter stress," explains Andrew McCulloch, chief executive of the Mental Health Foundation. So if you want cheering up then it's time to lace up.

6 TAKE OVER THE WORLD!

Early-morning runs present truly beautiful experiences worth cherishing – while the rest of the world sleeps, you're the first to break the virgin snow over that field, the deserted streets are yours and yours alone, you see the glory of the sunrise and you don't have to share it with anyone. How smug do you feel?

7 JOIN THE ZZZ-LIST

Stanford University School of Medicine researchers asked sedentary insomnia sufferers to jog for just 20-30 minutes every other day. The result? The time required to fall asleep was reduced by half, and sleep time increased by almost one hour.

8 MEDALS ARE COOL

Silverware isn't just for Olympians. Enter a race, finish it, and you'll have your first medal to line up on your mantelpiece – perhaps the start of many – to prove what you've achieved.

9 GET REGULAR

According to experts from Bristol University, the benefits of running extend right down to your bottom. "Physical activity helps decrease the time it takes food to move through the large intestine, thus limiting the amount of water absorbed back into your body, leaving you with softer stools that are easier to pass," explains gastroenterologist Dr Ken Heaton.

10 KEEP THE DOCTOR AT BAY

"Moderate exercise makes immune cells more active, so they're ready to fight off infection," says Cath Collins, chief dietician at St George's Hospital in London. In US studies conducted at the University of North Carolina, candidates who jogged for just 15 minutes five days a week took half as many sick days as those couch potatoes who never lace up their running shoes.

11 SEE THE WORLD

What other sport is there where you get the chance to travel to all four corners of the earth in the name of fitness? From the New York to Rio de Janeiro marathons all the way to seeing parts of our own sceptred isle you never even knew existed, it's a veritable ticket to ride.

12 GUILT-FREE SNACKING

Upping your salt intake is seldom advice that you will hear from your doctor, but in the last few days before a marathon that's exactly what you should do – giving you the perfect excuse to munch on crisps. The salt in them helps protect against hyponatraemia, a condition caused by drinking too much water without enough sodium that can lead to disorientation, illness and, in rare cases, death.

13 YOU DON'T NEED INSTRUCTIONS

If you can walk, then you can run. Think back to your days of being a child and you will realise that running around or on track is actually one of the most natural instincts inherit to humankind.

14 PROTECT YOUR TICKER

Maintaining a healthy heart is vital for everyone and running is a great way to achieve this. Studies from Purdue University in America have shown that regular running can cut your risk of heart disease by 50 per cent.

15 GET TIME BACK ON YOUR SIDE

Whether loosely lodged in your mental schedule or typed into your BlackBerry, your daily workout should be a focal point of your day to day schedule. It helps you organise everything else you need to do, often into B.R. (Before Run) and A.R. (After Run) time frames, as well as giving you much needed time to yourself to be able to absorb and ponder the rest of your daily itinerary.

Turn globe trotting into globe running

18 YOU CAN BE AN ALL-ROUNDER

Whether you want to keep in prime shape like F1 champion Jenson Button, or go 12 hard rounds like boxer Amir Khan, running is the place to begin.

19 HILLS: THE ULTIMATE CALORIE-KILLER

Find a decent incline, take a deep breath (at the bottom, not the top) and incorporate it into your running programme. You'll burn up to 40 per cent more calories – the average 150lb runner will burn 1,299 calories running a 10 per cent incline for an hour, compared with 922 on the flat.

20 BOOST YOUR SEX LIFE

A study from Cornell University in the US concluded that male runners have the sexual prowess of men two to five years younger, while females can delay the menopause by a similar amount of time. Meanwhile, research carried out at Harvard University found that men over 50 who run at least three hours a week have a 30 per cent lower risk of impotence than those who do little or no exercise.

21 IT CAN REPLACE A HARMFUL DEPENDENCY...

...such as smoking, alcoholism, or overeating, says William Glasser, author of Positive Addiction (HarperPerennial Books). Result: you're a happier, healthier person getting the kind of fix that adds to, rather than detracts from, the good things in life.

22 END BOREDOM

Even the most mundane errand can be transformed into a training run, from returning a rental DVD to Blockbuster, posting a letter to taking the dog for some much needed exercise. Suddenly every journey has a double purpose – and will give you an activity.

23 THAT NEW-SHOE SMELL

You've tried on and sampled your top picks and made your choice. Now they're here, in your hands. It's the start of a beautiful and positive relationship.

24 THE JOY OF FINDING A NEW ROUTE

Today you took a left rather than a right and suddenly found amazing views and a piece of solitude you never knew existed before now. Then you imagine how many more runs there are out there just waiting to be discovered...

25 MAKE A DIFFERENCE

Millions of runners worldwide turn their determination to get fitter and healthier into fund-raising efforts for the less fortunate. The Flora London Marathon is the single largest annual fundraising event in the world, having brought over £400 million into the coffers of good causes to date. If that doesn't give you a warm glow inside, what will?

26 INDULGE YOUR WANDER-LUST

There's simply no better way of getting to know a new city than pulling on your trainers and hitting the streets. As well as giving you necessary orientation, it'll energise you after your

16 REACH CREATIVE BREAKTHROUGHS

Writers, musicians, artists and all other kinds of creative professionals use running to solve mental blocks and make must-do-it-today decisions. For this we can credit the flow of oxygen to your grey matter when it matters most, sparking your brain's neurons and giving you breathing space away 'real life'.

17 THINK FASTER

Researchers from Illinois University found that a five per cent improvement in cardio-respiratory fitness led to an improvement of up to 15 per cent in mental tests.

journey, reset your biological clock to any new time zone and give you the chance to meet locals in half the time. As well as giving you necessary orientation, it will energise you after your journey, reset your biological clock to any new time zone and give you the chance to meet locals quicker.

27 THAT KNOWING NOD FROM A FELLOW COMPETITOR

The race is about to start and you see the same face from the last meet. Out of mutual respect and an acknowledgement of the challenge to come, you both nod. Nobody else knows it, but the gauntlet has been thrown down and the race is on.

28 GET (A LEGAL) HIGH

Comparing the pre- and post-run scans of runners, neurologists from the University of Bonn, Germany, found evidence of more opiate binding of the happy hormone endorphin in the frontal and limbic regions of the brain, areas known to be involved in processing emotions and stress.

29 YOU'VE GOT A REAL FRIEND

We all go through phases in our lives, including times when we run less. You may get a job that demands more of your time. You may have to spend more time having and caring for a new baby. Maybe you simply go on holiday or take a sabbatical. That's fine. Running adapts itself easily to your ebbs and flows. Best of all, running is always there to take the strain when you need it most.

30 JOINING A RUNNING CLUB CAN SAVE YOUR LIFE

A nine-year study from Harvard Medical School found those with the most running friends in their lives would have their own risk of death cut by more than 60 per cent, by reducing their blood pressure and strengthening their immune system.

31 NUMBERS DO NOT LIE

There's no leeway for dishonesty with running, from distances you cover to times on the stopwatch. You get back what you put in.

32 EXCUSE FOR A MASSAGE

Post-race, nothing quite beats the indulgence of a professional massage and the relaxed, floaty feeling as you walk back to real life.

33 BOOST YOUR BELLOWS

When running, an adult uses about 10 times the oxygen they would need when sitting in front of the television for the same period. Over time, regular jogging will strengthen the cardiovascular system, enabling your heart and lungs to work more efficiently, getting more oxygen where it's needed, quicker. This means you can do more exercise for less effort. How good does that sound?

34 BURN MORE FAT

"Even after running for 20 minutes or half an hour, you could be burning a higher amount of total calories for a few hours after you stop," says sports physiologist Mark Simpson from the Loughborough University's School of Sports Science.

35 APPRECIATE THE ENVIRONMENT

The days of Bush Junior's denial are long gone, and with Barack Obama's new era came a dawn of awakening – the world needs your help. You crave fresh, clean air when you run. You long for soft trails, towering trees, pure water. You have plenty of time to ponder the big questions. You resolve: save the earth.

36 THAT PB FEELING

Note the 'P' here, standing for 'personal' – you set the goals, you put the work in, you get the results. Savour it.

37 SPEND QUALITY TIME AS A FAMILY

It's one of the few activities that the whole family can do together. The smallest tyke can clamber into his jogging buggy, fit parents and grandparents can take turns pushing, and Junior can follow along on his new two-wheeler. Hundreds of races include events for everyone in the family.

38 OUTRUN THE REAPER

Kings College London researchers compared more than 2,400 identical twins, and found that those who did the equivalent of just three 30-minute jogs a week were nine years 'biologically younger', even after discounting other influences including body mass index (BMI) and smoking.

39 TEACH YOURSELF DISCIPLINE

Practise makes perfect, in running and in life. The most successful people are the ones with a modest amount of talent and a huge amount of discipline.

40 IT'S NOT ELITIST

You're struggling in last in the race but get the biggest cheer. You deserve it. After all, you've been running for longer than anyone else. What other sport is there where last place receives as much applause as the winners do?

Get some target practice out on the road

HIT THE MARK

44 Some runners set distance or time goals, many will instead focus on improving their health or on weight loss; others run simply to unwind, relax or have a place to think freely. Running can help you in achieving any goal that you choose to set your mind to.

41 SIZE DOESN'T MATTER

Running can be a great activity and good way to stay in shape for every single body type. No matter when you choose to start there are no barriers to just getting out there and giving it a go.

42 YOU'RE IN CONTROL

Whatever the pressures of your daily life, be it your work or personal life, you have the final say in how much or little running you choose to do.

43 HELP BABY

Mums-to-be who regularly do exercise during their pregnancy can have an easier, less complicated labour, a quicker recovery and even a better overall mood throughout the nine months, according to researchers at Michigan University in the US. Also a strong case study would be mother and marathon record holder Paula Radcliffe.

45 IRON OUT THE CREASES

Regular running can reduce the signs of ageing. "Exercise creates the ideal environment within the body to optimise collagen production to support the skin, helping reduce the appearance of wrinkles," explains Dr Christopher Rowland Payne (thelondonclinic.co.uk).

46 YOU CAN KEEP ON GOING FOREVER

Just ask 71-year-old legend Ron Hill, who hasn't missed a day's running since December 1964.

47 TAKE A JOURNEY

You never know what you'll find. You don't know whom or what you'll see. Even more interesting, who knows what thoughts might flash into your mind. Today's run could change your life in a way that you could never have imagined when you laced up your shoes.

48 YOUR PERSONAL THERAPIST

There's no greater escape from the pressures and stresses of modern life than slipping on your trainers and just getting out there. It's just you and the road – giving you time to organise your life, think things through and invariably finish in a better place than when you set off.

49 IT'S FREE

You don't need to join a club straight away. All you need are running shoes, shorts and a shirt to get started. So lace up and head out of the door.

READY TO START

Thinking about taking up running for the first time? Or simply want to brush up on the basics? Here's all you need to know...

Anybody can be a runner. The sport's inclusiveness is part of its appeal. But how do you actually become a runner? Tie your shoes and go? In essence, running is that simple. But as you get going, questions arise: should I run for 20 minutes or 30? Is walking okay? If I've been a runner before, do I need to start right back at the beginning? Over the following pages, you'll find the answers, along with everything else you need to get started on a running programme.

① PREPARATION
What to do before you set out on your first run

Many new runners are reluctant to spend money or time on the sport before they get started because they don't know if they'll stick with it. But getting started will be easier if you commit some time and do a bit of planning first. It may be overwhelming to begin with – thoughts of new shoes, training plans and races can get too much, so we've made it really simple for you to get started

GET A CHECK-UP
You may feel fine, but if you're a man over 45 or a woman over 55, and especially if you have risk factors for heart disease (obesity, family history of hypertension, high cholesterol) get your doctor's clearance to start exercising. If you have cardiovascular disease, which you may not know about, you could be at greater risk of suffering a heart attack. A plan to start running is a good reason to get a check-up scheduled.

SET A GOAL
"Your goals become incentives," says coach Nick Anderson (fullpotential.co.uk). "If you don't set a target, you'll get bored. A target might be to run for 30 minutes continuously, or it might be a 5K race that you want to do without having to walk." Choose a realistic goal while you build your base levels of fitness.

TAKE IT EASY
Beginners can be enthusiastic, but don't push too hard. "I always start new runners gently," says coach Richard Holt (momentumsports. co.uk). "It's vital not to let eagerness lead to early injuries through over-training, but to build a platform from which to make progress later."

BUY RUNNING SHOES
"Often beginners are reluctant to buy a pair of running shoes in case they decide not to keep it up," says Ben Noad, runner and marketing manager for specialist shop Runner's Need. "Shoes are the most important piece of kit – you can start in any clothes, but you must wear decent trainers. They'll pay for themselves in keeping you injury-free." Cross-trainers, tennis shoes and other athletic footwear don't have enough cushioning to handle running's impact – nor does the pair of running shoes you last wore two years ago, so buy new ones. We'll tell you how later in the chapter.

PHOTOGRAPHY 101 WEST PHOTOGRAPHY
MODELS ADRIANA NELSON, JEREMY NELSON

Run your way
to a fitter,
healthier body

2 HIT THE ROAD

Taking you through your first three weeks of running

Your old self will soon be left behind

First-run horror stories are common, but avoidable. "Starting or returning to a sport is going to be a little uncomfortable because you're not conditioned to it," says coach Greg McMillan. Having been a runner before or being fit doesn't exempt you from this reality. Elizabeth Hufton, 29, who recently returned to running after more than a year out, says, "At first my legs gave out with a few minutes' jogging. I'd cross-trained, but it was a shock to find how much running fitness I'd lost." Minimise discomfort by taking walk breaks and keeping your pace slow. Use the following guidelines to make running a positive experience.

WALK FIRST

Start with three 30-minute walks a week for two to three weeks. You could even build these in to your regular commute by getting off your bus a stop or two early.

THEN RUN/WALK

Interspersing walk breaks into your running lets you catch your breath and protects your joints and muscles. "Even if you've run before, and especially if you're returning from an injury, walk breaks are smart," says top coach Jeff Galloway.

GO FOR TIME OVER DISTANCE

Runners love ticking off the miles, but don't worry about that at first. Running by time de-emphasises pace, and allows you to adjust to how you feel that day.

TAP THE POWER OF THREE

"People who do not run regularly are more likely to quit," says Galloway. Run three days a week: you can only achieve running fitness if you do it consistently.

AIM FOR THE NINTH

The end of the third week is the turning point for many new and returning runners. "Your metabolism's changed, you've got more energy, you've probably improved your diet – everything starts happening for you," says Anderson. "But you start to feel unfulfilled, so you need a new target."

GO FOR ENDURANCE OVER SPEED

Faster running puts a much greater demand on all of your muscles, connective tissues and cardiovascular system than jogging. Build to 30 continuous minutes before you work on speed.

WHEN YOU REACH YOUR MILESTONE GIVE YOURSELF A TREAT – IT WILL HELP YOU TO ACHIEVE MORE

FLEX PLAN

It's likely that you'll wake up after your first run with sore, stiff muscles. You can minimise the 'morning after' effect by walking for a few minutes and stretching after your run. As well as improving flexibility, it flushes the muscles with blood and oxygen, which promotes recovery. At the very least, focus on these three areas...

HAMSTRINGS

WHY? They're your main propulsion muscles.
HOW? Place your heel on a step and bend slowly at the waist until you feel a stretch in the back of your thigh. Avoid rounding your back. Hold for 30 to 60 seconds. Do four or five on each side.

PHOTOGRAPHY 101 WEST PHOTOGRAPHY,
CATHERINE WESSEL. MODELS ADRIANA NELSON,
JEREMY NELSON

"Whether it's a cake or a trip to the Bahamas, it doesn't matter. It is the 'carrot' that can help people achieve," says Holt. Rewards don't need to be physical, either. "You might want to simply set a new targets as a reward," says Anderson.

ENLIST FAMILY

Support is vital. If you are being nagged every time you go for a run it can soon become a chore, says Holt, but "most runners' families and friends can see the benefits". They may need a crash course when you start though. "Educate your family so they understand what you do," says Anderson.

ADD VARIETY

A new route can enliven your running regime. Find a trail, a different area to try, or if you normally run a loop do it in reverse.

ACCEPT BAD RUNS

If you acknowledge that every run is not going to feel great, you'll reduce your frustration. On tough days, slow your pace, take walk breaks or shorten your run. "Runners think that once they've built up, they can't go back," says Galloway. "You can."

ACCENTUATE THE POSITIVE

A big mistake is to start to compare yourself to others. "Don't put added pressure on yourself," says McMillan. "Instead, focus on the accomplishment of every workout."

③ MAKING IT STICK

Avoid the guilt of missing a session any way you can

SEEK PEER PRESSURE

Run with someone else. It's a great motivator. You can find groups in your area at runnersworld.co.uk.

RACE

A race is a good way to focus your mind and help you to plan ahead, says Holt. "You need to know what you are aiming for, whether it be completing a race or losing weight."

REWARD YOURSELF

When you reach a milestone – that ninth run or completing your first race – give yourself a treat.

CALVES

WHY? They help propel you and absorb impact.
HOW? Place both hands on a tree and step back with one leg. Keep your heel on the ground and lean into the wall. Repeat four times a side. Bend your back knee slightly to stretch the lower calf.

QUADS

WHY They are your legs' shock absorbers.
HOW Bend one leg behind you, and grab your foot; pull it towards your bottom until you feel the stretch in the front of your leg. Hold for 30-60 seconds. Release and repeat four times on both legs.

BEAT THE CLOCKS

You have the motivation to run but find you don't have the time – or so you think. These tips will help you squeeze running into the busiest of schedules

With so much to do in everyday life running can get squeezed out. Lack of time – whether actual or perceived – is the biggest barrier to running as much as you might like. We're here to help.

Time problems will fall into the three categories below: Making Time (questions of when, where and how); Saving Time (little dos and don'ts that add up to serious savings); and Re-thinking Time (adjusting the relationship between your running and the time you need to do it).

Here's the plan: below are 25 time-management tips in these three categories. Pick any three of the strategies – one from each section – and try them for a month. If any work, great; if not, pick three more. If you try them all and still can't find time to run, you probably don't want to. Which is a shame. Chances are, however, you'll find some that work every time. So stop making excuses and get your kit on!

MAKING TIME
Here are tips you can action yourself along with ways to rope in a little help from those around you

① PLAN YOUR WEEK
Sit down with your diary on a Sunday and draw up a training schedule, before the blank spaces start filling up with other priorities.

② THINK QUALITY, NOT QUANTITY
Take the most out of what you have. Finding time for a 20-minute run is easy. Just make every minute count. Alternate one minute a little faster than your normal pace with one-minute recoveries. Do a two-to four-minute warm-up first and a similar cool-down afterwards.

③ GET UP 30 MINUTES EARLIER
Run before anyone else is even out of bed, because there are no

A MORNING RUN INVIGORATES YOU FOR THE DAY AHEAD

appointments to get in the way of an early morning run, and it will invigorate you for the day ahead.

④ IF YOU POSSIBLY CAN, BUY A DOG
Not everyone has the space or hours at home to make one practical, but if your circumstances allow canines make great training partners. There's no way to ignore a snout in your face telling you, "now, now, NOW!" You'll be literally dragged out of the door.

⑤ SWAP YOUR DUTIES
One morning, afternoon or evening, let your other half look after the children while you run. The next day, reverse the roles. Or...

⑥ TAKE THE KIDS WITH YOU
Many gyms now offer in-house nurseries. In 90 minutes, you can squeeze in an hour on the treadmill and a 20-minute circuit-training session on the weight machines — an excellent all-round workout that will improve strength and endurance. And your children should get a bit of exercise into the bargain as well.

⑦ GIVE 'EM THE RUNAROUND
While the children are playing football (or whatever), run loops around the field. I do this twice a week," says mother-of-two Judie Simpson. "Once as a steady one-hour run. The second time I'll pick it up on the long side of the field and jog the short side for 45 minutes." Don't forget to cheer if your offspring scores, though.

⑧ BEAT THE RUSH HOUR
Take your kit to work and run home while everyone else is stuck in gridlock. By the time you're home you'll be de-stressed from the rigours of the day and can allow yourself to feel slightly smug.

Fitting in your run requires careful planning

9 SET SHORT-TERM GOALS

Too many runners think too far ahead when laying out their training. "Instead, set a fortnightly goal, and make it specific: run three times a week for the next two weeks." says Dave Scott, six-time Ironman Hawaii winner.

10 PLACE YOUR BETS

People who bet £25 that they could stick with their training programme for six months had a 97 per cent success rate in a study at Michigan State University in the USA. Bet against a friend, and the first to give up pays up.

11 THINK LITTLE AND OFTEN

If you're new to it, aim for frequency, not duration. Instead of trying to find time for a 45-minute run two or three times a week, do shorter sessions of 15-20 minutes.

SAVING TIME

Fifteen seconds here, a minute there. It doesn't seem like much, but watch how fast it all adds up.

14 THINK AHEAD

Get your kit ready the night before. Even loosen your laces so your feet slide straight into your shoes. That way, you sit down and dress for battle quickly. No back-and-forth from bedroom to laundry and back to bedroom, tracking down something clean to wear before you go.

15 GET READY FOR BREKKIE

Plop your smoothie ingredients in a blender the night before an early morning run and put it in the fridge. After your run, hit the switch and eight seconds later... breakfast is served. We tried this

Sunday	Monday	Tuesday
1	2	3
		10
15	16	17
22	23	24
29	30	31

BUSY DAY? BEAT THE CLOCK BY BREAKING UP YOUR RUN INTO SHORTER SESSIONS

12 GO LONGER TO GET STRONGER

Veteran runners should focus on two "key" runs a week, sessions where they really push. Try a one-hour interval session (or hills or fartlek) in the week and then long run at the weekend. Fill in around them with short, easy runs, cross-training and rest days.

13 FIND A FRIEND

If someone is expecting you to show up, you're less likely to make excuses.

ourselves: assembling from scratch in the morning took 1:53, meaning we saved a total of 1:45.

16 HOLD OFF ON THE STRETCHES

Don't spend time stretching cold muscles before you train. Instead, walk briskly for a few minutes, then jog slowly to start your run.

17 RUN BEFORE YOU TALK

You meet your running partners and start talking while doing some

lame trunk twists as a warm-up. Don't do it. Say hello (it's only polite), and start jogging slowly. Talk then, before the pace picks up. Do all four of these tips from 14 to 17 and you save up to 10 minutes – enough time to turn a five-mile run into a six-miler. Over the course of a week, you net at least 35 minutes of extra running time.

18 KEEP YOUR SHORTS ON

"Wear shorts as underwear," says US running guru Jeff Galloway, so you're run-ready the instant your antennae pick up a 10-minute block of free time. "Accumulate enough short runs and they add

ILLUSTRATION: FREDRIK BRODEN

ay	Thursday	Friday	Saturday		
	5	6	7	8	9
	12	13	14		
	19	20			
	26	27			

Shift your week around to make room for running

RE-THINK TIME
Some attitudes toward running and/or ourselves stop us working out. Think differently to get ahead.

22 BE REALISTIC
Cut back on your running if you need to. But don't throw in the towel because life gets busy. Ride these periods out, and fit in a run of some kind — 15 minutes, 10 minutes — every second or third day. Then resume a more intense routine when you can. When your schedule implodes, short-term changes can stop you fretting your way into being a sofa sloth.

23 BE A BIT SELFISH
By giving your run a high priority — not just in your day but in your life also — you boost your physical and emotional health, and live up to your obligation to your family to be healthy and happy.

24 BE FLEXIBLE
If circumstances change, don't make excuses to ditch your planned run. If a surprise meeting cancels the lunchtime jog, do it after work. If you miss the alarm, take your kit to work and run at lunch. And "I don't feel like it" doesn't wash. "If you really want to run, you'll find time," says former 2:09 marathoner Ron Hill. "It's really no different than finding time to shave, eat or read the morning paper."

25 HAVE FUN!
Enjoying a run greatly increases the likelihood that you'll want to — and will — find time for the next one. Run a new route; run an old one backwards. If you usually run on roads, head for the park and run through the trees. Variety really is the spice of life, so mix it up when you are pounding out the miles.

up," he says. A Stanford University study found multiple bouts of moderate exercise produce significant effects. Leading us to...

19 DIVIDE AND CONQUER
On busy days, beat the clock by breaking up your run into two shorter sessions. Instead of a single 40-minute run, maybe do 20 in the morning and again at lunchtime, or whatever fits your schedule.

20 TURN DOWN THE VOLUME
Runners clocking up 50 miles a week had marathon times no faster than those who logged 40,

in a study at the University of Northern Iowa in the USA. More isn't always better, so don't scramble to find time for miles simply to pad out your weekly total.

21 THE 10-MINUTE MIRACLE
"Run faster-than-normal training pace (but don't sprint) for 10 footfalls of your right foot. When you reach 10, do 10 more steps of easy jogging," says exercise physiologist Jack Daniels. Then do 20-20 and so on up to 60-60. Then work back to 10-10. This is a good way to warm up, cool down and throw in some intensity in a short space of time.

PARTICIPATE

Run one of the World's top marathons with Sports Tours International

As the UK's leading running tours company we can ensure you a guaranteed place in most of the big races run around the world today.

We cater for runners of all abilities and our race packages are tailored to your exact needs and include a guaranteed starting place, travel and accommodation.

Walt Disney World Marathon Weekend	Jan
Barcelona Half Marathon	Feb
Land Rover Malta Marathon and half marathon	Feb
Tokyo Marathon	Feb
Paris Half Marathon	Mar
Barcelona Marathon	Mar
Los Angeles Marathon	Mar
Rome Marathon	Mar
NYC Half Marathon	Mar
Two Oceans Marathon	Mar
Paris Marathon	Apr
Rotterdam Marathon	Apr
Boston Marathon	Apr

Virgin London Marathon	Apr
Geneva Marathon	May
Edinburgh Marathon	May
Great Wall Marathon	May
Stockholm Marathon	June
Comrades Marathon	June
Lanzarote Wine Run	June
Medoc Marathon	Sept
BMW Berlin Marathon	Sept
Bank of America Chicago Marathon	Oct
Music Marathon Festival Lanzarote	Oct
Marine Corps Marathon Washington	Oct

Venice Marathon	Oct
Frankfurt Marathon	Oct
Dublin Marathon	Oct
French Riviera Marathon	Nov
ING New York City Marathon	Nov
Behobia San Sebastian 20km	Nov
Athens Classic Marathon	Nov
San Sebastian Marathon	Nov
International Running Challenge, Lanzarote	Nov
Honolulu Marathon	Dec
Lanzarote Marathon	Dec

BOOK NOW ONLINE

 www.sportstoursinternational.co.uk

running@sportstoursinternational.co.uk

+44 (0) 161 703 8161

Join the conversation
@sportstoursint

Going slowly could
supercharge your
fitness levels

ENJOY A SLOW LIFE

There's no shame in adding a little walking to your running, reckons 1968 Boston Marathon winner Amby Burfoot. In fact, it could help you go faster

PHOTOGRAPHY STEVE BATESON

Shhhh. I have a secret to share with you. You see, I used to be a fairly fast runner. In fact, I won the Boston Marathon in the USA at the age of 21. And there's a certain amount of honour among Boston winners — a sort of "pain is my friend" ethic — that we're sworn to uphold. Now, about that secret. I wouldn't want anyone to think I've gone soft or anything but... this is hard to get out... I often take walking breaks during my daily runs.

There, that feels much better. Though I don't know why it was hard to say in the first place. After all, it makes perfect sense to mix running and walking. Think about it: when new runners start off, they often follow a run-walk routine; they run for maybe 30 seconds,

walk until they feel recovered, then repeat the process for 20-30 minutes. This system has proved successful a thousand times over.

THE ON/OFF WINNERS

When world-class runners peak for the Olympics, they concentrate on "interval" training — the still unsurpassed method for achieving maximum results. They run hard for one to five minutes, then walk or jog very slowly until they're ready to run hard again.

When ultra-distance runners participate in those seemingly crazy races of 100 miles or more, they inevitably alternate running and walking. It's hard to imagine any other way to cover the mega-mile distances. You, on the other hand,

probably view walking as the enemy. The thinking is that you run, and this is good. You are proving and improving yourself; you are a moral person. Whereas when you walk, it is bad. You are lazy; you are a loser; you don't deserve to be loved (not even by your mother).

Mental-health therapists have many words for this sort of inflexible thinking, and I have one, too. I call it "stupid". (None too elegant, but it has the benefit of clarity.) The goal of a session is not to avoid walking. The goals are to feel better, get in shape, reduce tension, lose weight, train for an race and so on. Take your pick. They're all worthwhile goals.

Run/walk training (R/W training) is a simple, common-sense approach to conditioning. It

can help you train more; it can help you to train healthier; and it can even help you to get faster. Enough talk. Let's be more specific.

WALK TO SUCCESS

Olympic marathoner Jeff Galloway has pioneered the idea of walking breaks during marathons. He advocates this programme not only for many first-timers, but also for those who have previously hit the wall and experienced the crushing fatigue and depression of those last few miles. By walking early and often, Galloway has found, most runners survive the final miles in much better shape. They feel better, and often run faster as a result. You can run/walk a marathon anyway, but the simplest is to run the first mile, then walk for 60 seconds. Run the second mile, then walk for 60 seconds (and have a sports drink). Repeat 24 more times, then hold your head high and sprint.

The method has been used successfully by thousands of marathoners. Several have dipped below 3:30 this way, but fast times aren't the point. The point is that you can finish the marathon, feel good, run strong to the end, and admire that gleaming finisher's medal for the rest of your life.

THE NEXT STEP

The Galloway programme has many converts, and I'm one of them. I've now run four marathons with walking breaks, in times ranging from 3:45 to 4:30. I'm a modest trainer these days, averaging 20-30 miles a week, so the marathon can easily intimidate me. A few years ago, I was starting to dread the thought of running 26.2-milers. Now, I don't even think of the marathon that way. I think of it as a one-mile run that I just happen to repeat 26 times.

R/W training has also made my daily training easier. It used to be that, much as I love running, I sometimes felt too tired to get through the door. I talked myself out of many sessions: when you're already tired, why drag yourself out on the roads for 40 minutes? I don't have this problem anymore, because I don't run for 40 minutes. I run for four minutes, then walk for a minute, then repeat the process until I've completed 40 minutes. All I care about is enjoying session and feeling energised afterwards. Now I always do.

A STEP BACKWARDS

Let's pause for a moment to consider some of the differences between running and walking.

THE RUN/WALK CHEAT SHEET

1 If you want to call yourself a runner, walking's out, isn't it? Not really. Running is good, but so is walking. It's a valid form of interval training employed even by elite runners.

2 R/W training can allow you to run longer, healthier and, yes, faster — even on marathon day.

3 Try this marathon day plan: run a mile, walk 60 seconds. Repeat 26 times until complete in good time and with no walls hit.

4 Incorporating walking into your routine reduces your chances of injury and assists injury recovery.

5 Ease the pain of those long runs with an R/W strategy that will deliver near-full endurance benefits.

Some are small, others more significant. Running and walking have much in common, with one big difference. Runners "jump" from foot to foot, walkers don't. When you run, your knee flexes more than in walking, your quadriceps contract, and you "toe-off" like a long-jumper, coming down forcefully on the other foot. This is the "impact shock" of running — said to be two to three times your body weight — that can lead to over-use injuries. Walkers don't jump, so they are less likely to get injured.

Because you jump when you run, you can cover ground much faster than a walker and burn many more calories. In other words, you get a superior session in less time,

PHOTOGRAPHY GETTY IMAGES

Running then walking? Take it all in your stride

and easier. The R/W system gives you a new tool to help achieve this. Does it come at a cost? Sure. Your overall session is slower, so you get slightly less training effect, but most of the time you do long runs to build overall endurance and increase your body's ability to burn fat and calories in general.

INCREASED VARIETY Far too many runners do the same session at the same pace every time they run. It's boring, and it's not a smart way to train. An R/W session has many small segments, which encourages you to experiment.

BETTER SPEEDWORK An R/W session is an offshoot of the classic

SOME HAVE CLOCKED SUB-3:30 MARATHONS BY WALKING 60 SECONDS AFTER EACH MILE

which is one of the major benefits of running in the first place.

Unfortunately, many potential runners never get into the rhythm of running. They set out to run around the block, but get out of breath at the first corner, so go back to the sofa and never leave it again. These people need to learn about R/W training. You won't get exhausted (thanks to the walking), and you'll get all the benefits that vigorous exercise brings (thanks to the running). There are many reasons for R/W training. Some are physical, some mental, but all will change (and probably improve) your running. Here are a few...

RUNNING FURTHER, EASIER All runners, from beginners to veterans, would like to run longer

interval session, so it's easy to make it a real gut-buster. Here's one of my favourites: jog for one minute, run hard for two minutes and jog for one minute. Then do the one-minute walk. Repeat this eight times, and you've come reasonably close to the 8 x 400m torture my college coach loved to inflict on us.

On the topic of intervals, exercise physiologist Jack Daniels had two groups of women run three times a week, either continuously or with walking breaks. After 12 weeks, the run/walk group was fitter. Why? "In effect, the walking breaks turned the sessions into interval session," says Daniels. "It allowed the women to go faster overall."

FEWER INJURIES Walking doesn't cause as many injuries as running, so R/W training shouldn't

either. Walking uses the leg muscles and connective tissues in a different way to running so it should reduce over-use injuries. Walk with a slow, elongated stride to feel other muscles coming into play.

MORE SIGHTSEEING What's the point of running in some beautiful location if all you see are the rocks and roots on the trail in front of you? With R/W you can drink in the views during your walking breaks.

SPEEDIER RECOVERY Some days you need to run slower than normal, particularly if you ran long or fast the previous day, or if you're busy at work or home. These are known as 'recovery' runs. R/W training is perfect for them.

FASTER COMEBACKS You've had a sore knee, a bad Achilles or a nasty cold. You're ready to get back into your training but don't want to overdo it and suffer a setback. Listen to your body, and don't run faster than what feels right.

FINAL THOUGHTS

The aspect of R/W training I find most appealing — the mental breaks provided by the brief walking periods — won't prove equally compelling to all runners. Many will staunchly resist. "I didn't start running to become a walker," they'll snort derisively. Old habits die hard, and R/W training isn't for everyone. Or for every session. I do it a couple of times a week, usually when I run by myself and often as a long run. However — and this is the most surprising thing about it — I've found that it has motivated me to do more speedwork. In fact, you say that R/W training is classic interval training that's been liberated from the track and allowed to roam wherever you want to take it. You just might discover an entirely new, enjoyable (and effective) way to run. It's worth a try, isn't it?

SHOULDERS

RUB SHOULDERS
Plans to run with others, and it'll be harder to skive off. Find running buddies in your area by posting on the forums at runnersworld.co.uk

MAKE YOURSELF A RUNNER

If you're a beginner, or coming back from a break, here are all the building blocks you'll need to transform your body into a lean, fit, injury-free running machine

✚ BODY ARMOUR
Extreme measures

Your hands, ears and nose get colder faster than your core, especially when exposed to winds. Cover them when it's chilly.

ARMS

GET INTO THE SWING "Set your cadence with the speed of your arm swing and your legs will follow their lead," says running coach John Loftus.
WORK THE ANGLES "Relax your shoulders and arms by keeping your hands at waist level, not pumping around your chest," says Dr Brian Hand, a running coach with a PhD in kinesiology. Bend your arms at a 90-degree angle and swing them straight.

EARS

LISTEN UP Recent research from the University of Southern Queensland in Australia found that listening to music can increase time to exhaustion by 19 per cent when running, and lower perceived exertion. So get some up-tempo tracks on your MP3 player to boost your performance. Check out the bespoke running playlists available for download by logging on to runnersworld.co.uk.

BRAIN

BORN TO RUN
Humans can run further than most animals, says Daniel Lieberman, professor of human evolutionary biology at Harvard. So a lap the park is within your reach.

NO EXCUSES
"New runners often see a minor mishap as a reason to stop running," says Burningham. If you falter, recommit by remembering your original motivations.

THINK SLOW
Walking isn't a cop-out when you're starting out. In fact, taking walk breaks improves your fitness by extending your exercise time, says Loftus.

DEFINE EFFORT
Running can be hard, but don't call it pain, says Loftus. "Pain is getting burned," he says. Some discomfort can lead to improved fitness.

BE FLEXIBLE
"Don't be bound by a rigid schedule," says coach Jennifer Burningham. "Instead, make a weekly plan that works for you. And if you miss a day, don't panic. Just run the next day."

DON'T PUSH IT
Forget about marathons. Just focus on getting out of the door. "Any exercise is better than none," says Burningham. "You'll break the negative mind set caused by inactivity"

TAKE THE LONG VIEW
"Your 40-year-old body won't respond like it did in your 20s," says Burningham. Whether you're making a comeback or a debut, be patient. You will get to where you want to be in time. Push too hard and you risk injury and getting demotivated.

EYES

LOOK AHEAD
One simple visual cue can correct many issues with your running form. "Relax your torso by focusing your gaze on the horizon," says Hand. Raising your eyes naturally straightens your posture, engaging stability muscles from your core to your hips.

LOG SOME SCREEN TIME
Time in front of your PC can be a valuable part of your training schedule. Sharing information online can help to keep you motivated and improve your running. Build your confidence – and get instant feedback – by posting your latest times and/or distances.

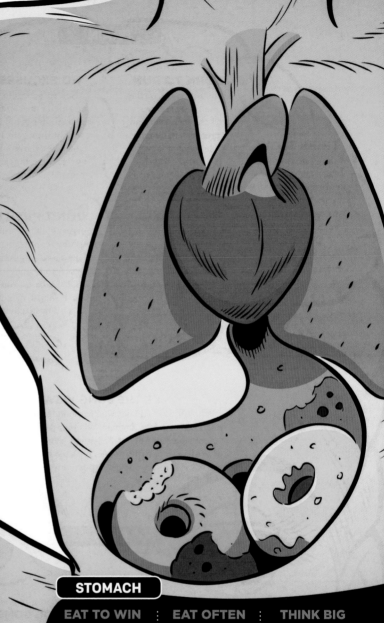

HEART & LUNGS

Danish researchers found sedentary men increased cardiovascular fitness by 11 per cent after exercising two or three times a week for 12 weeks. Use this simple plan to reap the same rewards safely and steadily.

WALK FIRST. . .

If you're a beginner, start with a 15-20 minute walk three times a week for two to three weeks. Walking increases your metabolism to encourage weight-loss, and strengthens running-specific muscles and tendons.

. . .THEN RUN

Add run segments to your walk. For example, alternate one minute easy running with two minutes walking for 20 minutes. This combo helps strengthen your heart muscles, lowers your blood pressure and increases your lung capacity. Begin and end each workout with five minutes of fast walking to warm up your legs and flush out toxins.

ADD TIME

Increase the length of your run segments each week. "After three weeks you should be running more than walking," says Loftus. After five weeks, aim to run for 20-30 minutes continuously. Run by time, not mileage. This encourages a steady pace.

HAVE FUN

"New runners won't stick at it if it isn't fun," says Hand. Keep runs fresh by changing your route, running with friends and setting micro goals, like running five more minutes than last time. Variation helps keep you motivated, says Roy Baumeister, author of *Willpower: Rediscovering the Greatest Human Strength*.

STOMACH

EAT TO WIN

"Willpower is sustained by your energy levels," says Baumeister, so food is essential for determination "Sugar provides a quick boost. Protein works over a longer period of time."

EAT OFTEN

Every four hours, eat a meal of 500-700kcal to maintain energy, says dietitian Nancy Clark. "If you stay fuelled all day, you won't be tempted to overeat at dinner."

THINK BIG

Focus on your diet over an entire week, says Clark, not on whether each morsel is good or bad. Quality calories should equal 85-90 per cent of your diet. Relax with the rest.

BODY ARMOUR
Freshen up

Look for apparel embedded with anti-odour properties such as silver fibres to stop synthetic fabrics from fouling your senses.

TORSO

STAY CENTRED

New runners tend to lean too far forward and take long strides that cause each footfall to act like a brake against the body's momentum. Run tall, look up, shorten your stride, and your feet will land beneath your centre of gravity. This saves energy and reduces impact forces on your knees and ankles.

GLUTES

BEEF UP YOUR BUM

The weakest muscles in a beginner's body are the gluteus duo of the maximus and medias. Curse your office chair, then strengthen the muscles with these moves:

WALKING LUNGES

Step forward with your right leg. Bend both knees until the left touches the floor. Thrust upward and step into the next lunge. Do 10-15 per leg.

THE CLAM

Lie on your left side, knees bent and together, head resting on your left arm. Keep your feet together; raise your right knee towards the ceiling. Do 10-20 reps. Over time, increase the number of reps.

BODY ARMOUR
Ditch the cotton

The wrong fabric will turn into a heavy, soggy, chafing suit. Invest in high-tech fabrics that wick sweat away, keeping you warm and dry on a run.

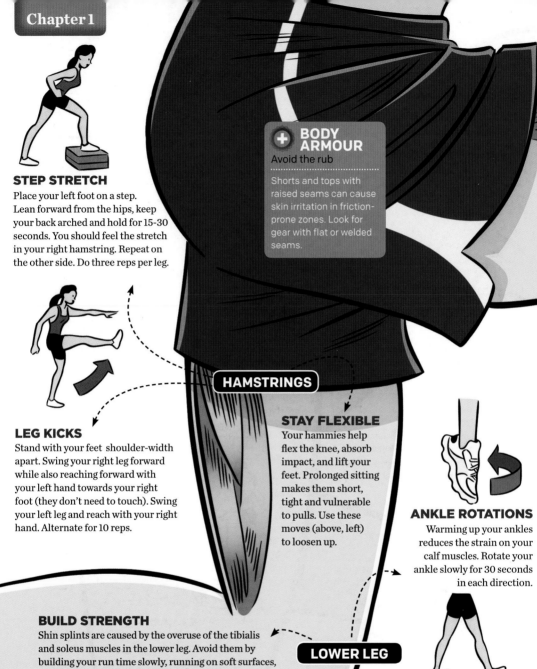

STEP STRETCH

Place your left foot on a step. Lean forward from the hips, keep your back arched and hold for 15-30 seconds. You should feel the stretch in your right hamstring. Repeat on the other side. Do three reps per leg.

➕ BODY ARMOUR
Avoid the rub

Shorts and tops with raised seams can cause skin irritation in friction-prone zones. Look for gear with flat or welded seams.

HAMSTRINGS

LEG KICKS

Stand with your feet shoulder-width apart. Swing your right leg forward while also reaching forward with your left hand towards your right foot (they don't need to touch). Swing your left leg and reach with your right hand. Alternate for 10 reps.

STAY FLEXIBLE
Your hammies help flex the knee, absorb impact, and lift your feet. Prolonged sitting makes them short, tight and vulnerable to pulls. Use these moves (above, left) to loosen up.

ANKLE ROTATIONS
Warming up your ankles reduces the strain on your calf muscles. Rotate your ankle slowly for 30 seconds in each direction.

BUILD STRENGTH
Shin splints are caused by the overuse of the tibialis and soleus muscles in the lower leg. Avoid them by building your run time slowly, running on soft surfaces, and doing these two daily exercises.

LOWER LEG

HEEL STEPS
Walking with your toes pulled up strengthens the tibialis muscles. Start with 30 seconds, twice a day. Work up to one minute.

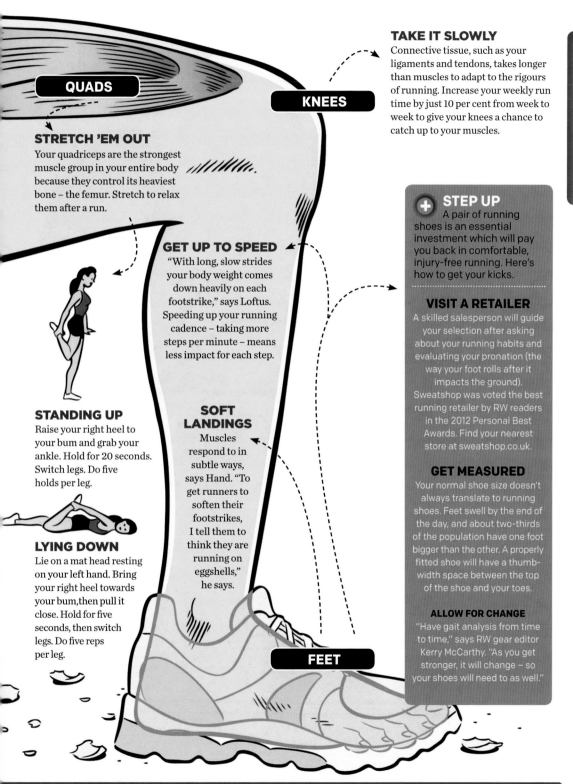

QUADS

KNEES

TAKE IT SLOWLY

Connective tissue, such as your ligaments and tendons, takes longer than muscles to adapt to the rigours of running. Increase your weekly run time by just 10 per cent from week to week to give your knees a chance to catch up to your muscles.

STRETCH 'EM OUT

Your quadriceps are the strongest muscle group in your entire body because they control its heaviest bone – the femur. Stretch to relax them after a run.

GET UP TO SPEED

"With long, slow strides your body weight comes down heavily on each footstrike," says Loftus. Speeding up your running cadence – taking more steps per minute – means less impact for each step.

➕ STEP UP

A pair of running shoes is an essential investment which will pay you back in comfortable, injury-free running. Here's how to get your kicks.

VISIT A RETAILER

A skilled salesperson will guide your selection after asking about your running habits and evaluating your pronation (the way your foot rolls after it impacts the ground). Sweatshop was voted the best running retailer by RW readers in the 2012 Personal Best Awards. Find your nearest store at sweatshop.co.uk.

STANDING UP

Raise your right heel to your bum and grab your ankle. Hold for 20 seconds. Switch legs. Do five holds per leg.

SOFT LANDINGS

Muscles respond to in subtle ways, says Hand. "To get runners to soften their footstrikes, I tell them to think they are running on eggshells," he says.

GET MEASURED

Your normal shoe size doesn't always translate to running shoes. Feet swell by the end of the day, and about two-thirds of the population have one foot bigger than the other. A properly fitted shoe will have a thumb-width space between the top of the shoe and your toes.

LYING DOWN

Lie on a mat head resting on your left hand. Bring your right heel towards your bum, then pull it close. Hold for five seconds, then switch legs. Do five reps per leg.

ALLOW FOR CHANGE

"Have gait analysis from time to time," says RW gear editor Kerry McCarthy. "As you get stronger, it will change – so your shoes will need to as well."

FEET

BEST IN SHOE

There's no such thing as the 'best shoe' – everyone has different needs

Running shoes can be divided into six main categories – neutral cushioned, motion-control, stability, performance, barefoot and minimalist – which, for all the bright colours and crazily named high-tech features, are basically designed to suit different people's biomechanical needs.

The full breakdown on the next page will give you a greater understanding of what the six different types on offer, and should start to give you some idea of what type that will suit you best. But you shouldn't buy your first pair before visiting a biomechanics expert or, more realistically, an experienced specialist running shop to get a "gait analysis" done. They look at how your foot strikes the ground to help choose a shoe with the right levels of support.

ONE FIT NEVER FITS ALL

Most runners will find it relatively easy to find at least a nearly ideal shoe with the right advice. Once you've determined which category you fall into, you have a wide range of shoes to choose from. All you have to do is decide which shoe within your category provides the best comfort, fit and performance for your needs – although that can be a daunting prospect for a beginner. Try out a range of shoes, listen to the advice and don't rush into a decision if you're unsure.

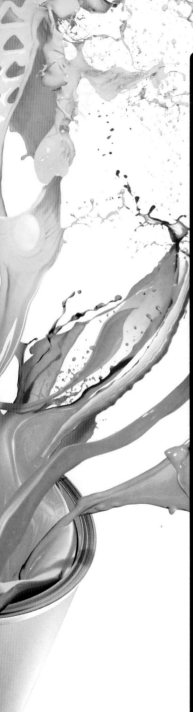

WHAT DO I NEED?

Before consulting an expert, here's an overview of what the different types of trainer have to offer

NEUTRAL CUSHIONED
This type of trainer is best suited to runners who need maximum midsole cushioning and minimum arch support. They suit biomechanically efficient runners and midfoot or forefoot strikers who have high or normal arches.

MOTION CONTROL
These are ideal for runners with low arches who are moderate to severe overpronators and who need maximum stability and support on the medial side of their shoes. Often bigger runners who need plenty of support find these are the ideal choice.

STABILITY
Recommended for runners who are mild to moderate overpronators (their feet roll inwards as they strike the ground) and have low to normal arches. These runners tend to need a shoe that has a combination of good support and midsole cushioning.

PERFORMANCE
Trainers in this category are ideal either for racing or, if you're biomechanically efficient, for training. They have varying degrees of support and cushioning but they're light (most weigh around 250-300g) and fit like a glove.

BAREFOOT
One of the newest shoe categories, these are particularly good for lightweight runners with good biomechanics or anyone looking to strengthen their lower leg and foot muscles, and improve their gait. Only use them occasionally to start with.

MINIMALIST
Another new category. These are good for biomechanically efficient runners who want a stripped-down shoe with a little cushioning. These are the mid point between neutral cushioned and performance in weight, support and general 'heft'.

Think carefully before splashing out on new shoes

AMAZING FEET

Make sure you step out of the shop with a perfect pair of running shoes by following our seven simple steps to sensible trainer buying

Arch locks? Medial posts? Decoupled SRC impact zones, anyone? There's enough shoe-related jargon out there to make buying a new pair of trainers a baffling experience. It's no wonder so many of us part with our hard-earned cash only to end up disappointed.

Before heading out on your quest for your ideal running shoes, here is our step-by-step guide – from experts with years of experience in specialist shops – to help you avoid the kind of pitfalls that can trip up even the most experienced of shoe shoppers.

① DON'T BE A FASHION VICTIM

"The most common error is that people pick a shoe off the display and ask for it because of its looks, particularly the colour. People go for dark colours, which are the trail shoes, when what they might really need is a high-mileage road shoe. Runners should start by looking at

The right footwear will help you to fly

not seem like quite such a good idea when you get physiotherapy bills for twice the cost of the trainers. We had one customer who had bought completely the wrong pair of shoes online after a knee operation. They could have done some serious damage, because the shoes gave too much support. Always get your shoes physically fitted whenever you need a new pair."

Jamie Halliday, Up and Running, London

What they don't realise is that doesn't mean it will be the best shoe for them – it's likely to be ill suited and cause discomfort or, worse, injury. And websites often manage to confuse people by using terms without explaining their meaning. I would say stick to a few trusted sources of advice, and be aware that you can always phone up a specialist shop."

Simon Royle, Sole Obsession, Salisbury

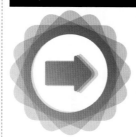

"A COMMON ERROR IS THAT PEOPLE PICK A SHOE OFF THE DISPLAY BASED ON ITS LOOKS"

the way they run, get a gait analysis and use that to decide which shoe they end up with."

David Newman, Runner's Need, London

② BE FLEXIBLE ON SIZE

"New runners ask for a size smaller than they actually need, especially women who are used to wearing fashion shoes and have been a size five all their life. Shoes that are too small can cause problems from black toenails and blisters to shin splints, so get properly fitted."

Gareth Long, The Derby Runner, Derby

③ STEER CLEAR OF THE INTERNET

"Sure, you can save loads of money, but the bargains you can find might

④ JOIN A CLUB TO CUT THE BILL

"Some people don't know that they can get a discount on shoes if they are a member of a running club. Obviously, the stores can't ask every single customer, but a lot of returning customers say they didn't realise they could have saved money. We offer 10 per cent off for members of an AAA affiliated club, as long as they bring along a club card or a fixtures list that proves membership."

Dipika Smith, Run and Become, London

⑤ KEEP AN OPEN MIND

"People shouldn't get too hung up on well meaning advice from friends and seemingly "expert" websites. Customers who have asked friends for guidance often come to us and request a particular brand of shoe, just because they know it worked for someone else.

⑥ KNOW YOUR SIZE CONVERSIONS

"The conversion rates between US and UK sizes can vary quite a lot between brands. Customers often come in to our store expecting a uniform size six, but these different conversion rates mean that an Asics six will not be quite the same as a Nike six. Customers should be aware of that when they're getting fitted out and trust what the expert has to say on the matter."

Jamie Smith, Sweatshop, Reading

⑦ WATCH THE TIME

"The foot expands towards the end of the day, so shoes you buy in the morning can start to feel too tight later on. We recommend that you leave a gap of between half a millimetre to a full millimetre around the foot to allow for this, or go shopping at the end of the day."

Steven Curtis, Running Bath, Bath

YOUR FIT KIT

You don't need much gear to run, so it's worth thinking carefully about what you do buy. Here are the useful features to look for

LEGGINGS

FEATURES YOU WANT...

- ⊕ **An elasticated waistband for added comfort**
- ⊕ Fluorescent piping for safer running at night
- ⊕ **Small pocket for holding change, keys, etc**
- ⊕ Panelling, which creates a comfortable ergonomic fit

T-SHIRTS

FEATURES YOU WANT...

- ⊕ **Flatback seams add comfort by reducing chafing**
- ⊕ Wicking material will transfer sweat away from your body
- ⊕ **A UV protective coating for running in the sun**
- ⊕ Anti-odour technology for whiff-free training

SHORTS

FEATURES YOU WANT...

- ⊕ **An elasticated waistband that won't dig in**
- ⊕ Reflective strips to make night running safer
- ⊕ **Small pocket for keeping money and keys safe**
- ⊕ Webbing inside to hold everything in place

PHOTOGRAPHY: STUDIO 33

JACKETS

FEATURES YOU WANT...

⊕ **Adjustable waistband and cuffs for added comfort**

⊕ Strong weather-resistant material for durability

⊕ **Soft, non-rubbing fabric to avoid chafing**

⊕ An ergonomic design to allow ease of movement

SOCKS

FEATURES YOU WANT...

⊕ **Elasticated arch lock to support your feet**

⊕ Padded soles provide comfort and help prevent blisters

⊕ **Seam-free toe section to avoid rubbing and nail snags**

⊕ Breathable, anti-chafe material will keep your feet cool

NEW TECH

New advances are constantly made in the world of running gear. Here's the latest kit to look out for

COMPRESSION KIT

In essence, compression wear is close-fitting clothing – from socks to base layers and T-shirts – with a high Lycra (or other elasticated material) content that squeezes and hugs the muscles that are key to efficient running. It is designed to help you train more efficiently, avoid common injuries and recover faster. The cost of such kit varies widely by brand and can be high, but here are the benefits you should expect to see if you decide to invest

COMPRESSION TOPS: THE BENEFITS

Core support Compression tops provide support around your stomach, sides and lower back, which can become fatigued on long runs. Although compression wear from the waist down (such as tights) will help both during and after exercise, compression tops only really help during a run.

Better breathing Tops train the breathing by gently squeezing the chest with each inhalation. This encourages a more focused breathing style and can even reduce the risk of a painful stitch.

Improved posture Support is delivered through the back for a more upright approach to the run. Better posture equals better breathing, and this in turn equals improved running.

COMPRESSION TIGHTS: THE BENEFITS

Increased recovery speed Used as part of the 'RICE' regime (Rest, Ice, Compress, Elevate), compression leggings – or tights – can rapidly reduce recovery time and minimise delayed onset muscle soreness.

Less cramp Lactic acid is flushed out by the squeezing of muscles and increased venous return – which may help reduce or even eliminate cramping on the run.

Decreased injury risk The force of impact is lessened, helping to support and stabilise injury-weakened areas such as the knee.

More oxygen Compression socks increase venous return (the flow of blood back to the heart) and help deliver oxygen to muscles with a tight fit around the foot and a squeeze up the calf.

TRAINING WATCHES

If you want to achieve a certain goal, or even simply keep a log of your progress as a runner, information is king. Investing in a sports watch need not break the bank and today there are watches to suit everyone, regardless of your budget or level of affinity with technology. Watches can range from £80 to £400 depending on the level of sophistication. Here are the key features you should expect to find in each price range.

BUDGET (£80-£150)

Clear visibility You should be clearly able to read the figures on the watch face while on the run

Chronograph You should at least be able to time the total length of your run and keep tabs on individual lap times if you're interval training

Data log You don't always have time to review your data after training so your device should be able to store the information from a number of training sessions.

Easy functionality Using your watch should not require a session consulting the manual before you set out on the run. It should be easy and intuitive to operate.

MID-RANGE (£150-250)

Heart Rate Monitor Training to a specific heart rate is a useful alternative to running within target speed zones. A decent mid-range watch should have be able to monitor your beats per minute.

Speed and distance How fast, how far, how long: these are the basic information requirements of someone training to hit a target time for a race. Your watch will either measure these things using a pedometer strapped to your foot or, if more high-spec, using GPS technology built into the watch itself.

Calorie counter If you are running to watch your weight, this is essential.

HIGH-END (£250-400)

Altitude counter A top-of-the range watch will measure how many metres you climb – useful if you're training for a hilly race.

Training zones Its useful to be able to set parameters for your run, whether speed, heart rate, pace or another gauge. On the best watches you can set alarms to go off if you stray outside of your target zone.

Data upload Top-end devices can upload your training stats (either through USB connection or wirelessly) to an online training log where you can analyse your performance in more detail and often share the information with friends through social media.

SPORTS BRAS

A good sports bra is as essential a piece of kit for female runners as the right shoes. But which one should you go for?

A BUYER'S GUIDE

"To ensure the right fit try several brands, styles and sizes," advises Amanda Brasher, senior buyer for Sweatshop. "Many women rush into buying a size or style only to find that it's unsuitable so don't be afraid to experiment to find your perfect fit." Here are Brasher's top tips:

The underband should be tight without digging in – no more than two-and-a-half centimetres' give.

Cups should encase each breast fully with no wrinkling or gaping, or flesh bulging.

Straps should have only two to two-and-a-half centimetres' give. They should be adjustable to fit each individual breast (most busts are slightly asymmetrical).

Underwires should sit behind the breast tissue and not rub or dig in.

Bras lose effectiveness with use so if you run three times a week or more for up to an hour, replace yours every eight to 12 months.

Chapter
2

TRAINING

Ready to go? Not sure how? Our expert tips will help you
from your first training session all the way to the finish line

48 **TRAINING ESSENTIALS**
Twelve top tips for better running

52 **YOUR ALL-YEAR PLAN**
How planning your runs makes them easier

54 **5 RULES OF ACTION**
Listen to your body for better results

56 **IN THE LONG RUN**
Cover that long distance more efficiently

58 **WORK FAST, GO FASTER**
A beginners guide to speedwork

60 **20 WAYS TO SPEED**
Handy tips to make you go faster

62 **HEIGHTS OF PASSION**
Head to the hills to improve your running

66 **PERFECT TEMPO**
How to train for race pace

68 **THE UPSIDE OF RUNNING INSIDE**
You can make treadmills a poweful ally

72 **JOIN THE CLUB?**
Being a team player could help you

76 **FLIGHT TO THE FINISH**
How to finish with a bang, not a whimper

PHOTOGRAPHY: GLEN MONTGOMERY
MODEL TABIE GREYLING

12 TRAINING ESSENTIALS

Running doesn't have to be complicated: arm yourself with some basic knowledge and you can start training with confidence. Here's how to make it through your first effort with flying colours

1 START WELL

This might be your first try at running, you could be a return visitor who's had a break, or you might be attempting to improve on what you already do. The less running you've done recently, the more you can expect to improve your distances and speeds in the first 10 weeks. On the other hand, the less you've run lately, the more likely you are to hurt yourself by doing too much, too soon. That's why it's so important to set two related goals as you start or restart your running programme — you need to maximise improvements, but also minimise injuries.

2 ALWAYS WARM UP

Don't confuse a little light stretching with a good warm-up. Stretching exercises generally don't make you sweat or raise your heart rate, which is what you really want from a warm-up. A proper warm-up begins with walking or running very slowly to ease your body into the session. Try walking briskly for five minutes (about a quarter of a mile), and then breaking into your comfortable running pace. (Don't count the warm-up as part of your run time or distance – that's cheating.) When you finish your run, resist the urge to stop. Instead, walk another five minutes to cool down more gradually. After you've

cooled down is the best time for some static stretching — this is when your muscles are still warm and at their most pliable.

3 MAKE A PLAN

As for finding places to run, anywhere that's safe for walking is also fine for running. Off-road routes (parks, footpaths, playing fields) are better than busy streets, while soft surfaces (grass and dirt) are better than paved ones, but any choice is better than staying at home and not running. Map out the best courses in your immediate area. This will save you time and solve the "place" issue, making it much more likely you'll execute your planned runs.

IT IS IMPORTANT THAT YOU START RUNNING AT AN EASY PACE. THINK OF YOURSELF AS THE TORTOISE, NOT THE HARE

4 EAT RIGHT

Sports nutrition is a huge and important topic, but, in general, the rules for good nutrition and fluid consumption are pretty much the same for runners as for every other athelete. There are three areas of special interest to runners: (1) control your weight, as extra pounds will slow you down; (2) eat lightly after training and racing; (3) drink 250-500ml of water or a carbohydrate drink an hour before running, as dehydration can be a dangerous enemy.

5 GET F.I.T.

Kenneth Cooper, a giant in the fitness field, long ago devised a simple formula for improving as a runner. Run two to three miles, three to five days a week at a comfortable pace. It's easier to remember as the F.I.T. formula: frequency (running at least every other day); intensity (keep at a comfortable pace); and time (about half an hour a run should do). Even with some short walking breaks thrown in if you tire, you could cover two miles in 30 minutes, and soon after you might be able to run three miles in that time. It is very important to run these efforts at an easy, comfortable pace. Think of yourself as the tortoise, not the hare. Make haste slowly.

ILLUSTRATION OSCAR GIMENEZ

Don't get caught
in traffic

6 RUN SAFELY

The biggest threat you'll face as a runner on the road, by far, is traffic. Cars, lorries and bikes zip past you. A moment's lapse in attention from either you or them can result in, at the very least, a bad case of road rage. The best way to lower this risk is to avoid running near roads, but for many of us this is a near impossibility, or it's an approach that adds time and complexity to our routine (if you have to drive sto and from a park, for example).

So most of us adapt and learn to be extremely cautious on the roads. Try to find quiet roads with wide pavements; if there is no pavement, run on the right side of the road, facing the oncoming traffic; obey traffic signs and signals; and follow every road rule your parents taught you. If you look out for cars, lorries and bikes, they won't have to look out for you.

7 FIND YOUR PACE

We've told you to keep your pace comfortable, which sounds simple. The problem is that most novice runners don't actually know what a comfortable pace feels like, so they tend to push too hard. As a result, they get overly fatigued and discouraged, or even injured, early in their training programme. As a result they either give up almost before they've started or face an injury lay-off.

Here are some more guidelines: a comfortable pace is one to two minutes per mile slower than your optimum mile time. Or you can use a heart-rate monitor and run at 65 per cent of your working heart rate (see runnersworldstore.co.uk for the best devices). Finally, as a low-tech alternative, just try listening to your breathing. If you aren't gasping for air, and you can talk while you're running, your pace is about right.

8 DECODE PAIN

Runners get hurt. We rarely hurt ourselves as seriously as skiers or rugby players, but injuries do happen. Most are musculoskeletal, meaning that it is possible to recover relatively rapidly — just so long as we take days off or other appropriate action (such as ice treatment). ▶

Keep your eyes on the prize

running neglects, and stretch those that running tightens, which means strengthening your upper body and stretching your legs. Always stretch out after running and also add a few classic upper body moves such as press-ups and chin-ups. Your muscles will be nicely warmed up after your run so these exercises will have the greatest benefit.

11 GO EASY

Most runs need to be easy. This is true whether you're a beginner or an elite athlete. (Of course, the definition of easy varies hugely; an easy mile for an elite runner would be impossible for many beginners or even experienced runners.) If you are a new runner, make sure you limit yourself to only one day of hard running per week. Run longer and slower than normal, or shorter and faster than normal, or enter a short (5K) race and maintain your best pace for the entire distance.

12 BE A WINNER

One of the great beauties of running is that it gives everyone a chance to win. Winning doesn't happen automatically; you still have to work for success and you'll risk failure, but in running, unlike in other sports, there's no need to beat an opponent or an arbitrary standard (such as "par" in golf). Runners are able to measure themselves against their own standards.

When you improve a time, increase a distance, or set a personal best in a race, you win — no matter what anyone else has done on the same day. You don't have to run very far or fast to outrun people who have dropped out by the wayside. It's the tortoise and the hare all over again. Slow and steady always wins the most important race.

◄ Most running injuries are self-inflicted — we bring them on by running too far, too fast, too soon or too often. Getting over an injury is more often than not as simple as changing your routine. If you can't run steadily without pain, mix walking and running. If you can't run-walk, simply walk. If you can't walk, cycle. If you can't cycle, swim. As you recover, climb back up this fitness ladder until you can run again.

ONE OF THE GREAT BEAUTIES OF RUNNING IS THAT IT GIVES EVERYONE A CHANCE TO WIN

9 TAKE A MILE TRIAL

Friends who hear that you've begun running will soon ask what your best mile time is — so you might as well get used to testing it. Before long, you'll be calculating your pace per mile on longer runs, but you should begin with a simple one-mile test run (four laps on a standard track) to determine your starting point.

Think of this run as a pace test, not a race. Run at a pace that is beyond easy, but isn't a massive struggle, and count on improving your mile time in later tests as your fitness improves.

10 BE BALANCED

Running is a specialised activity, working mainly the legs. If you're seeking total-body fitness you need to supplement your running with other types of exercise. These should aim to strengthen the muscles that

WINTER   SPRING   SUMMER

YOUR ALL-YEAR PLAN

If you want to keep running you'll need to set some goals

The trick to sticking to your running regime is knowing you aims. But running goals can be tricky. Set them too high, and they'll frustrate you. Set them too low, and they won't challenge you. Set them just right, and they'll be a powerful source of motivation, driving you to achievement. To set the perfect running goals, follow the six-step plan below. Don't forget, the paths you take to reach your running goals are just as important as achieving the goals themselves.

① MAKE A LIST

In order of importance, write down two to four running goals you'd like to achieve in the next six months. They can be as general as to run injury-free; to feel good on almost every run; or to balance your running with your family life and career, or they can be more specific, such as completing a particular race or achieving a certain time. You'll need to review this list every so often to make adjustments as needed. For example, as the date of a 5K goal race gets close, it will move higher on your list than when it was months away.

② PENCIL IT IN

With your list of goals in hand, you can begin to sort out how you'll achieve each one by plotting the key sessions you'll need in a training log, notebook or on a calendar. If one of your goals is to enjoy your runs more, you'll need to schedule social runs, runs in scenic locations or runs with your favourite four-legged friend.

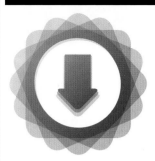

BIG GOALS ARE EASILY ACHIEVED IF YOU DIVIDE THEM INTO SMALLER GOALS

runnersworld.com/calculators that will calculate your predicted race time at a given race distance based on your actual time at another race distance. If your goals are more qualitative (e.g. to enjoy running more), look over the notes in your log every few weeks to see if you're on the right track. If not, make the training adjustments necessary to give you a realistic shot of reaching your goal.

6 PLANNING A RACE SEASON

Once you are used to running, you might want to plan the events you enter so you can make the most of your training, and maintain your interest as the months pass. Each year there are well over 5,000 running races in Britain, ranging from a mile to 100Ks and more, with options over trail, countryside, fell, track and road. Some people may manage 100 races in a year, including 30 marathons, but it isn't advisable if you want to maximise your performance and keep injury and boredom at bay. Variety and recovery should be your keywords. It's also valuable to decide what, for you, are going to be the three or four most important races of the year. This not only helps focus your training, but also affects the way you approach the other races in your year. April, of course, is when the London Marathon takes place, so if you're running it, the first months of the year will be largely about training. As the weather heats up during the summer it's a good time to enter a 5K or 10K race, especially if you're recovering from the rigours of London. But there are some great events throughout the year, even in winter when it's an ideal time to go cross-country. Go to runnersworld.co.uk/events for details on races.

Time-specific goals mean you'll need to chart a series of speedwork sessions, and if you're looking to complete a marathon or half-marathon, you'll need to map out your long-run strategy. Use a pencil to schedule these runs, just in case changes need to be made.

3 INK IT IN

After you've pencilled in all the sessions, you need to make sure you have time to achieve those goals – so take an overall look at your calendar to assess things. Do you have the time and the resources to follow through with your plan as you have scheduled it? Are you able to make the sacrifices necessary to achieve your specific race and time goals? If so, take out a pen and make your schedule permanent. If not, scale down your goals, and set up a new programme based on your time and energy constraints. Then put it in ink.

4 BREAK IT DOWN

Big goals are achieved more easily if you divide them into smaller ones. For example, instead of trying to make the "good-for-age" qualifying times for the London Marathon before you've even run a half-marathon, aim to finish a 10K in the next two months. As this goal approaches, plan your second goal of finishing a half-marathon.. Write down each intermediate goal in your training log, and fill in the long run and speed sessions needed to prepare for them. If any of these smaller goals become too stressful, add another stepping stone.

5 GET REAL

How do you know your time goals are achievable? By running a 5K, you can predict your potential finishing time in a 10K, half-marathon or marathon. There are a number of prediction charts around, such as those at www.

5 RULES OF ACTION

Discover the perfect training strategy for you by listening to the needs of your body — and following these five universal rules

Running isn't rocket science. But figuring out a training strategy can seem just as tricky. How many miles should you run? At what speed? What is VO2 max again? And lactate threshold? Is that related to glycogen stores?

The fact that every runner is unique further complicates matters. So it's crucial to learn the quirks and requirements of our own bodies and play by its rules.

Luckily, there are some principles that, regardless of individual mileage and pace, apply to almost every runner — whether you're slow or fast, training for a marathon or for life. Conceived by coaches and employed by elites, these time-tested rules will help you stay motivated, avoid injuries and run strong year after year.

① MINIMAL TRAINING, OPTIMAL RESULTS

If you've improved by running 25 miles a week, you could be so much better by running 50, right? Not exactly. Training isn't a matter of cramming in as many miles as you can. It's about finding the balance of miles, days per week, and types of workouts that get you to your goals without injury or exhaustion. Tim Noakes, in his book Lore of Running, describes this concept as the "individual training threshold". And that threshold is uniquely yours. One runner may excel on 55 miles

a week over six days with extra tempo running, while another runner may do well on 25 miles a week over four days, with a focus on short, fast repeats.

ACTION Experiment with different mileage levels. If you've been logging megamiles (50+ per week), back off for a while and see if you can still hit your goal times in workouts. If you've been doing the bare minimum (three days per week), try adding a day or two. Keep a detailed log, noting how both your body and your race times respond during the change.

MOST OF US SEE BIG IMPROVEMENTS EARLY IN OUR RUNNING CAREERS

② BALANCE WORK WITH REST

Imagine running as hard as you possibly can one day, then again on the next day, and then again on the next. Sooner or later, you'd barely be able to run at all. That's the scenario that exercise physiologist Jack Daniels uses to illustrate the necessity of the work-rest cycle. "The benefits of stressing the body come during recovery," he says. On easy or off days, your body is busy

repairing muscle fibres, increasing your ability to process nutrients and oxygen, building new blood cells and eliminating waste. If you don't give your body enough time to recover, sooner or later you will tear it down.

ACTION As a rule of thumb, put in one easy day between hard workouts (more if you happen to be feeling particularly fatigued) and make sure that you take at least one full day off a week. During training, reduce your mileage by 15 to 20 per cent every fourth week, and if you find that a certain week is

particularly difficult, keep training at that week's level until it becomes more comfortable.

③ EXPECT PEAKS AND PLATEAUX

You drop three minutes off your 10K time. The six-mile loop that used to feel impossible now feels easy. At some point, though, the improvements will slow, or stop. That's not necessarily a bad thing. It means you've adapted to your

The perfect runner keeps their regime varied

training and you've climbed to a higher plateau. But now is the time to change your workload so that you can push on through to the next level.

Most of us see the greatest improvements early in our running careers. Once you reach a certain level (predetermined by genes and influenced by age), you'll have to work harder, and perhaps rest more, in order to wipe extra seconds off your race times. **ACTION** Try adding some hills, increasing the time of your tempo run, or trying longer or faster repeats as new ways to intensify your training sessions and advance towards a new level. However, if you are already training at a high intensity – 50 or more miles a week with a mix of intervals, tempo miles, hills and long runs – then a plateau may be an indicator that you need rest.

④ BE CONSISTENT

Ask a coach what the single most important factor is in training, and most will answer "consistency". You won't improve if you run only once a week, or if you repeatedly run hard for a week, then take the next week off. Better running comes from regular running. Consistency, however, doesn't mean you need to train all-out year-round. Periods of structured training, paired with months of fewer miles, will help you avoid both physical and mental burnout.
ACTION Maintain a minimum, even if that's 30 minutes, two or three days a week, and run in the morning so you're sure to get it done. Plan your 'down' months for times you know it'll be harder to run — winter weather, big projects, life changes, and so on.

⑤ PRACTISE PATIENCE

Piling on the miles or pushing the intensity too soon won't get you in shape faster (your body needs time to adapt), but it might get you injured. So whether you're a new runner or returning after a break, increase quantity and quality gradually.
ACTION When we say to step up gradually, this translates into an increase in mileage or time by only 10 per cent a week. So say you put in 20 miles a week, including one long run and one speed session. You could add a mile to your long run and a half-mile to an easy run, while increasing your speed session by one 800m rep for a total of two additional miles across the whole week. Avoid increasing intensity and distance simultaneously. New runners should focus on going further before going faster.

IN THE LONG RUN

If you manage them right, your long runs will help you improve in covering the distance better, from 10K to marathons and beyond

Compared with other training sessions, the long run is fairly simple – put one foot in front of the other and stop when you've done 20 miles – but its simplicity is deceptive. "The long run is the single most important workout you can do," says coach Jeff Galloway, who ran the 10,000m for the USA in the 1972 Olympics, "but it's more complex than you'd think, and most runners don't do it right."

There are many questions about the long run, including the big four: Why do it? How long should you go for? How fast should you go? And how often should you do one? We'll answer those, and take a look at related issues such as nutrition, rest and recovery. So put your feet up and read on at a comfortable pace

WHY DO A LONG RUN IN THE FIRST PLACE?

Long runs give you endurance – the ability to run further. Yet they can help 10K runners as well as marathoners. Long runs do several things...
➡ They strengthen the heart.
➡ They open up capillaries, speeding energy into working muscles and flushing away waste from tired ones.
➡ They strengthen leg muscles and ligaments.

➡ They recruit fast-twitch muscle fibres to assist slow-twitch tasks – such as marathon running.
➡ They help burn fat as fuel.
➡ They boost confidence.
"If you know you can go that far in training, it gives you the confidence that with the

adrenaline of the race, you can do that too," says Danielle Sanderson, former European 50K champion.
➡ They make you faster.
"Increase your long run from six miles to 12 — change nothing else — and you will improve your 10K time," says Galloway.

HOW LONG SHOULD YOU RUN FOR?

It's not an exact science but there are two general rules you should follow to get it right:

Time is a much better gauge than distance "The duration of the long run will vary depending

on the athlete's age, fitness and the competitive distance they're training for," explains Norman Brook, Britain's former national endurance coach. "The run should be for a minimum of 45 minutes and can extend to anything up to three hours for elite athletes

THE LONG RUN IS THE MOST IMPORTANT WORKOUT YOU CAN DO, BUT IT'S MORE COMPLEX THAN YOU THINK

and those preparing to run a marathon or ultra-distance events (which are anything longer than a marathon)."

Measure your long runs by all means, if it helps, but for the most part, the goal of a long run is not covering a certain distance, but quality time spent on your feet.

You should gradually try to get your long-run time up to one-and-a-half to two hours. That's the minimum – roughly 10-16 miles — needed to maintain a high endurance level. Increase your long runs by no more than 15 minutes at a time. "Build up to the

ILLUSTRATION THOMAS FUCHS

long run gradually," Brook advises. "If the longest you're running for is 30 minutes, gradually build up to an hour by adding five minutes to your run each week." Just a few minutes of extra running makes a difference — but do too much and you're setting yourself up for injury or illness.

HOW FAST SHOULD I BE RUNNING?

You want to run a marathon in 3:30, which is eight-minute mile pace, so you do your long runs at that pace. Sounds logical, right? Wrong. "Running isn't always logical," says Benji Durden, a 2:09 marathoner who now coaches both elite and recreational runners. There are reasons for going easy on your 20-milers:

➡ Long runs at race pace may be training sessions in your mind, but they're races to your body. That can lead to overtraining, injury or illness. "Running long runs fast causes more problems than any other mistake," says Galloway. Marian Sutton, winner of many marathons, agrees: "There's no point pushing yourself too hard. You need to run at a pace that feels comfortable."

➡ Fast, long runs miss the point. "Long runs are for endurance," says Sanderson. "It's amazing how quickly they reduce your resting heart rate, making your heart more efficient."

➡ The ideal pace for long runs is at least one minute per mile slower than your marathon pace. "The intensity of effort is low, and you should ensure a steady state is maintained," says Brook. You should be able to conduct a conversation during the run without discomfort."

➡ You might even walk at points during longer runs – it works for Sanderson. "It's good to just plod round, walk a bit if you need to, or even stop for a break," she advises.

HOW OFTEN SHOULD I DO A LONG RUN?

Don't run long more than once a week. It is, after all, a hard session, requiring rest or easy days before and after. The other end of the scale is debatable. Some runners have no problem going two or three weeks between long runs. Others will come back with a midweek long run if a shorter race precludes the weekend session. Galloway recommends a simple formula: roughly one day's gap per mile of your long run. For example, if your long run is 12-17 miles, you can go two weeks between long runs without losing endurance; if it's 18-23 miles, three weeks. "That is, if you're running at least 30 minutes every other day in between," he adds. This rule can also be used to taper before a marathon. For instance, if your last long run is 22 miles, you'd run it three weeks before race day. If it's 16 miles, you get a two-week rest before the race.

WHICH DAY IS BEST?

Sunday is traditional, because that's when most people have most free time. Also, most marathons are at weekends. But there's no need to stick to a set day, though. "I'm not rigid about it," says marathon world record holder Paula Radcliffe, "because I never know when I'll be racing." Sanderson also plans her schedule around events. "I do my long run on a Sunday, unless I'm racing," she says.

DON'T GO SOLO

Contrary to popular opinion, long runs aren't boring. You just have to know how to run them – that is, with friends. Find a Saturday or Sunday morning group, or arrange to meet a training partner regularly. "I do some of my runs with friends," says Sanderson, "and the time always goes much faster."

WORK FAST, GO FASTER

It may be a cliché, but that's because it's true: the only way to run faster really is… to run faster. And speedwork is the best way to do it

Most of us can come up with plenty of reasons to avoid speedwork: it hurts; it increases our chances of picking up an injury; it makes us too tired for our other runs; we don't need it for running marathons… the list is endless. The thing is, they're all unnecessary fears. What's more, whether you want to beat an ancient 800m best set on the grass track at school, or out-kick the runner who always sprints past you in the local 10K, adding speedwork to your regime will be immensely rewarding.

Speedwork doesn't just make you run faster. It makes you fitter, increases the range of movement in your joints, makes you more comfortable at all speeds, and it will ultimately help you to run harder for longer. If you've already added a speed session or two to your schedule then you'll know all of this already. If you haven't, then here are a few things to remember.

EASE INTO IT

When you started running, you ran for just a couple of miles every other day, and gradually built up to your current mileage. You didn't suddenly start running 35 miles a week, so adopt the same approach to speedwork. Put at least three months of steady running behind you, then start with just one session every 10 days or so. Then go on from there.

NOT TOO HARD

Speed sessions aren't about sprinting flat out until you're sick by the side of the track. They're about controlling hard efforts and spreading your energy evenly over a set distance or time.

PHOTOGRAPHY MIKE KING

PACE YOURSELF

When you first start speedwork you may find monitoring your pace difficult. If you've run a 5K race you'll know how that pace feels, but don't panic if you haven't — you'll find the right pace through trial and error. Don't be afraid to make mistakes, but don't worry about being over-cautious at first — it's better to build up gradually than fail and hate speedwork.

WARM UP AND WARM DOWN

Before each session, jog for at least 8-10 minutes to raise your blood temperature, increase blood-flow to the muscles and psyche yourself up for the fast run ahead. Follow that with some gentle stretching and then run a few fast strides before getting down to the tough stuff. Afterwards, jog for another 5-10 minutes, and stret again.

FIND A PARTNER

Speedwork takes more effort and willpower than going out for a gentle jog. It's much easier and more fun to train with someone else — and if you want to improve, try running with someone just a bit quicker than you are.

QUALITY NOT QUANTITY

Speed training should not account for more than 15 per cent of your total mileage. So slot in your speed sessions around the regular work you've been doing all along.

THE DIFFERENT TYPES OF SPEEDWORK

➡ **REPETITIONS/INTERVALS**
Periods of hard running at 5K pace or faster, between 200m and 1200m in length, or 30 seconds and five minutes. Recovery periods can be short (30-90 seconds), or of an equal time or distance to the reps. Running at harder than race pace for short periods not only improves speed, but also allows you to work on your running form. When you're pushing hard, it's important to concentrate on things such as arm and hand motion, posture and stride length. If you can keep these together during a hard session of reps, it will be easier to do so during a race. Don't attempt reps until you've tried other types of speedwork for a couple of months.

➡ **TEMPO INTERVALS** These are longer than ordinary intervals in that they take between 90 seconds and 10 minutes (or between 400m and two miles) and are run a little slower than your 5K pace.

➡ **FARTLEK** Fartlek is Swedish for "speed play" and is the fun side of speedwork. Best done on grass or trails, you simply mix surges of hard running with periods of easy running with no set structure. Run fast bursts between phone boxes, lampposts or trees when you feel like it, and as hard you like. Great for newcomers to speedwork.

➡ **HILLS** Simple: find a hill that takes between 30 seconds and five minutes to climb at 85-90 per cent effort, and run up it. Jog back down the hill to recover.

20 WAYS TO SPEED

These tips will make you faster, especially when you want to kick for home at the end of a race

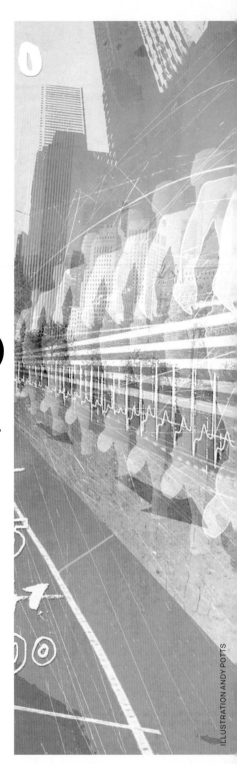

BEGINNERS

If you haven't tried speedwork before, here are some (relatively) gentle introductory sessions.

1 KEEP IT SHORT

You could start with a session of brisk efforts. Six minutes brisk, one-minute walk, six minutes brisk and so on.

2 ADD SOME FARTLEK TRAINING

To begin, add some quick bursts into your shorter runs. Each burst can be as little as 20 seconds or as much as a few minutes.

3 DO AN INTERVAL SESSION

6 x 1 minute, with three-minute jog/walk recoveries, or 5 x 2 minutes with five-minute jogs.

4 GO FOR SHORT REPS

After two months or so of speedwork, try your first session of short repetitions: 5 x 300m, with four-minute recoveries; 5 x 200m, with 3-minute rests; or try 10 x 200m with 3-minute recoveries.

5 GLIDE DOWNHILL

On down slopes during long runs, go with the hill and allow it to pick up your pace to around 80-85 per cent of flat-out, allowing gravity to power you downhill. Don't go any further than 150m. The idea is to speed up without using any extra energy.

ILLUSTRATION ANDY POTTS

INTERMEDIATES

Once you've tried a few sessions, you want to build up your efforts with these...

6 DO A PYRAMID SESSION

Start at 120m, add 20m to each rep until you reach 200m, then come back down to 120m. Run these at 400m pace, with a walk-back recovery.

7 TRY FAST REPS

For 200m or 300m: run 6-10 x 200m, with three-minute recoveries, or 5-8 x 300m, with five-minute recoveries. Start both at 800m pace, eventually running the last reps flat out.

8 DO A SIMULATION SESSION

This should replicate an 800m race. Run two sets of either 500m + 300m, or 600m + 200m, at your target 800m pace.

9 BUILD YOURSELF UP

Find an open area and mark out a circuit of 800-1,000m. Run a circuit at your 5K pace, jog for five minutes, then run a second circuit, aiming to do it about three seconds faster than the last. Speed up by three seconds until you've completed five circuits
.

10 KEEP GOING

Now try 5 x 800m at a pace 10 seconds faster per 800m than your usual 5K pace. Recover between intervals for the same amount of time it takes you to run them.

11 PILE ON THE MILES

Begin with a three-mile warm-up, then 4 x 1 mile at a pace faster than your 10K pace, with a three-minute jog between each.

12 BUILD YOUR PYRAMIDS

Try 1,000m, 2,000m, 3,000m, 2,000m, 1,000m at your half-marathon race pace, with a four-minute recovery between each.

13 OR DO A HALF PYRAMID

If you're short on time, try 400m, 800m, 1,200m, 1,600m, 2,000m, each run faster than your 10K pace but not flat out. Jog 400m between.

14 CARVE UP A 2K SPEED SESSION

Divide 2,000m into: 400m at 5K race pace, with a 400m jog; 300m at race pace, with a 300m jog; 200m slightly quicker than race pace, with a 200m jog; 100m slightly quicker, with a 100m jog.

15 GO LONGER

Run five miles, alternating three-minute bursts at 10K pace with 90-second recoveries.

16 GO OFF-ROAD...

Jog for 10 minutes, then run at your mile pace for 1:40; slow down to a jog (don't walk), and recover for three minutes, then repeat another 100-second burst. Try four of these sessions to begin with, and gradually work up to doing 10 altogether.

17 ...OR USE A TRACK

Run eight laps, alternating fast and slow 200s. The fast 200s should be hard, but not a full sprint.

18 BUILD UP TO 5K

5 x 1,000m. Run 800m at your 10K race pace, then accelerate to 3K pace for the last 200m, with three-minute recoveries.

19 BREAK UP THE LONGER RUNS

Run at marathon pace for five minutes, then increase your speed to 10K pace for one minute. Continue this for 30 minutes.

20 DIVIDE YOUR TIME

If you want to complete a marathon in three hours 27 minutes, run 800m reps in three minutes and 27 seconds.

TRAINING

Head out into
the great green
yonder

PHOTOGRAPHY STEVE BATESON

HEIGHTS OF PASSION

It's worth learning to love them — with the right approach,
hills can help you become a much better runner

Hills are hard. That is why many of us run round them rather than over them in training. It's not just training, either, it's possible to avoid hills at races if you always choose flat courses. But while running hills might be exhausting and demoralising if you're not used to them, with the right training and attitude, hills will make you not only faster but they will shap you into a stronger, tougher runner too, both physically and mentally.

"Hills are a challenge but bring huge rewards for those who regularly include them in their training mix," says Nick Anderson, British cross-country coach and runner. He ensures that all his athletes' training schedules include hills, even when they're racing on the flat. "Hills make you tough and give you confidence," he says. "If you can work for 10 minutes uphill, then 10 minutes on the flat will seem a lot easier."

Hills won't just make you faster and harder — they'll make you stronger too, which is good news if you're a runner who focuses on weekly mileage at the expense of improving muscular strength. "Running hills will make you physically stronger and improve both speed endurance and mechanical efficiency," says Anderson. In other words, if you skip circuit training or weights at the gym, hills will give you the strength to run faster for longer.

GOOD HEALTH

The strength you build when training on hills will also help you to run injury-free. Hills, especially when run off-road, provide a great total-body workout that will protect against stresses and strains. "I pick up fewer injuries when I train on hills," says Angela Mudge, who became the Buff Skyrunner World Champion in 2006 after completing a world-

wide series of trail races at altitude. "The ever-changing terrain means that each foot placement is subtly different, so you don't tend to develop the repetitive injuries experienced on roads." The ascents will make you a more powerful runner but the descents are just as helpful: the balance and need to constantly change stride length when you're coming downhill will make you more agile. **Try this** Train off-road as often as possible. The forgiving terrain protects against injury, while uneven surfaces improve your balance and core strength.

ON THE UP

You'll develop your own strategies for conquering hills, but borrowing tips from elite runners can help. As well as organising the Montrail Ultra-running Championships (runfurther.com) — a series of 12 mountain and trail races of over 30 miles — Mark Hartell is a former winner of the elite class of the Lowe Alpine Mountain Marathon, and the record-holder for the most Lake District peaks climbed during the 24-hour Bob Graham Round. He always prepares himself for an upcoming hill. "If you know there is a big ascent coming up, slow down a little, try to relax and prepare yourself mentally to 'float' up the hill," he says. "Running hills is about getting your breathing right too. It should be quite a meditative process. Try to breathe in time with your footsteps."

Try this Hartell suggests running three strides as you breathe in — making sure you pull air right into your lungs — and three strides as you exhale, forcing the used air out a little more quickly.

OVER THE TOP

When you're near the top of a hill, work your arms hard to maintain rhythm. "Always push for a point just beyond the summit," says Hartell, "and keep your faster breathing pace going for longer to help to expel built-up lactic acid." The oxygen you take in will speed up this process.

Try this Aim to maintain the same strong effort for at least one more minute when you've reached the summit, even if your body feels like it needs to ease off a little.

ROUTE MAP

Becoming fitter will help you to run quicker on both the ascents and descents, but there are other ways to save time tackling hills. "Learn to navigate," says Mudge. "Save time by following the best route rather than the runner in front."

Try this Think about investing in a pair of off-road shoes to help you on your way. These specialised models feature studs on the outsole for extra grip and a lower-slung sole so you're less likely to turn an ankle. Inov-8 and Walsh shoes are popular with fell runners.

⊕ HILL STARTS

Whether you're training for a 5K or marathon, these hill sessions will toughen you up

⊖ THRESHOLD

Hills run at threshold pace with a downhill recovery run at a similar effort will build endurance and strength. Find a gradual gradient you can run up for between 45 seconds and five minutes at 80 per cent of maximum heart rate.
TRY THIS Run one minute uphill followed immediately by one minute downhill. Repeat this 12 to 20 times.
BEST FOR muscular endurance.

⊖ SPEED

These hills increase power, strength, speed endurance and mechanical efficiency. They are run at speed (90 per cent of maximum heart rate) with the arms driving and pumping hard and with a long, bounding stride and high knees. These hills are tough and run above threshold.
TRY THIS Complete a session of 8 to 12 times 30 to 45-second hills on a good gradient, walk or jog back to the start.
BEST FOR 5K, 10K or half marathon runners.

⊖ OFF-THE-TOP

You wouldn't run hard up a hill in a race only to start walking when you reach the top, so train by running hard up the hill and to continue at a hard pace once you've reached the summit.
TRY THIS Find a route that has hills that take 30 to 90 seconds to climb and run these hard each time you hit them. Then run for the same time at the same effort after you reach the top.
BEST FOR Giving you confidence to put some time into your rivals at the top of hills during races.

What goes up must come down

LOCATION, LOCATION

"The perfect hill to train on is the one nearest to you," says Hartell, "because what matters is that you get out there and do it." Different gradients do suit different types of training though. Do short repetitions on steep slopes and longer repetitions on gradual gradients. If you only have a short hill to train on, you'll just have to run up and down it more times. In terms of the surface you choose to run on, grass and forest trails are easiest on the body, but the only hills that aren't suitable to train on are ones where you can't get a firm grip on the surface and you may stumble or fall.

PHOTOGRAPHY DAVE COX

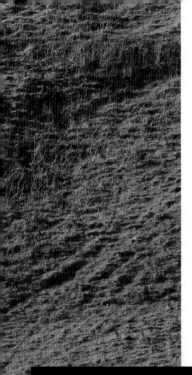

"THE PERFECT HILL TO TRAIN ON IS THE ONE THAT'S NEAREST TO YOU"

Try this Scout out your local area and look for a hill with a gradient of about 10 per cent, give or take. "That means not too steep and not too shallow," says Anderson. The most important thing to remember here is that you need to be able to maintain good form on the ascent up the hill. Too shallow, too easy. Too steep, too hard.

NEED FOR SPEED

Some runners choose to use hills as a substitute for speedwork but Anderson advises against this. True speedwork on the flat is conducted over distances of less than 50 metres, but hill running can be a good alternative to longer intervals on the flat. "If you spend time in an endurance phase of training, running lots of miles, putting in threshold runs and hill sessions, you will probably be able to run faster for sustained periods in longer intervals on the flat," says Anderson on the subject.

Try this Hills shouldn't replace short repetition training on the flat, but you can add them to your schedule if you're currently just focusing on longer interval sessions in your regimen.

THIS WAY UP

Proper form helps you power up any incline

➡ HEAD
"Keep your head upright and your neck relaxed," says running coach Richard Holt (momentumsports.co.uk). This will help you maintain a steady breathing pattern.

➡ EYES
"Keep your eyes focused about six metres directly ahead of you," says ex-British fell-running champion Keith Anderson (fullpotential.co.uk). "This will help keep your head straight and your eyes away from the task ahead."

➡ HANDS
"Keep your hands loose," advises Paula Coates, author of *Running Repairs: A Runner's Guide to Keeping Injury Free* (A&C Black). Loose hands help your whole body stay relaxed.

➡ LEGS
"Push your legs off and up, rather than into, the hill," says US Olympian Adam Goucher. This will aid you as it helps you feel as if you are "springing" up the hill.

➡ GOING UP
"If the gradient is constant, keep your pace constant," says Anderson. Otherwise, you should create your own a strategy to manage it. "If necessary, adopt a fell-runner's walk," advises Anderson. "Place your hands on your legs above the kneecap and below the quadriceps, and use them to push off."

➡ BRAIN
"You'll need to drive to reach the top. Remember that your training is evidence that you can beat the hill, so go for it." says Anderson.

➡ TORSO
"Lean into the hill slightly," says Coates. "This will keep your pelvis in position to drive through the legs and maintain momentum."

➡ ARMS
"Keep the motion of your arms in proportion to the effort that the hill requires," says Anderson. "Focus on driving the elbow behind you – it will come forward all on its own," says Holt.

➡ FEET
You need to stay on your toes – literally. "Push yourself off from your forefoot using your calves and your quads," Holt advises.

➡ GOING DOWN
Your feet should land beneath you, and a shortened arm swing helps shorten strides.

Hit the right speed to crank up your times

PERFECT TEMPO

The 'comfortably hard' run is the key to clocking your fastest time. Here's how to make it work for you

Pssst! Want to run like a world-beater? Okay, you might not make it to the very top, but your training regime can help you achieve new PBs, simply by incorporating the same method that helped propel the likes of Ethopian world-record holder, Haile Gebrselassie, and his Kenyan predecessor, Paul Tergat, to running greatness.

The secret? The tempo run — that faster-paced session also known as a lactate-threshold, LT or threshold run. One US-based coach championing this method is Toby Tanser. In 1995, when Tanser was an elite young track runner from Sweden, he trained with the Kenya "A" team for seven months. They ran classic tempos — a slow 15-minute warm-up, followed by at least 20 minutes at a challenging but manageable pace, then a 15-minute cool-down — as often as twice a week. "The foundation of Kenyan running is based almost

ILLUSTRATION: THOMAS EHRETSMANN

TEMPO RUNS HELP YOUR BODY TO USE OXYGEN MORE EFFICIENTLY

exclusively on tempo training," says Tanser. "It changed my view on training."

Today, Tanser and many running experts believe that tempo runs are the single most important session you can do to improve your speed for any race distance. "There's no beating the long run for pure endurance," says Tanser.

"But tempo running is crucial to racing success because it trains your body to sustain speed over distance." So crucial, in fact, that it trumps track sessions in the longer distances. "Tempo training is more important than speedwork for the half and full marathon," says Gale Bernhardt, author of *Training Plans for Multisport Athletes*. "Everyone who does tempo runs diligently will improve." However, you also have to be diligent about doing them correctly.

WHY THE TEMPO WORKS

Tempo running improves a crucial physiological variable for running success: metabolic fitness. Most runners train their cardio system to deliver oxygen to the muscles, but not how to use it once it arrives.

Tempo runs teach the body to use the oxygen for metabolism more efficiently.

HOW? By increasing your lactate threshold (LT), or the point at which the body fatigues at a certain pace. "During tempo runs, lactate and hydrogen ions — by-products of metabolism — are released into the muscles," says Dr Carwyn Sharp, an exercise scientist who works with NASA. The ions make the muscles acidic, eventually leading to fatigue. The better trained you become, the higher you push your threshold, meaning your muscles become better at using these by-products. The result is less acidic muscles — in other words, muscles that haven't reached their new threshold, so they keep on contracting, letting you run further and faster.

DOING IT PROPERLY

But to garner this training effect, you've got to put in enough time at the right intensity — it's easy to get it wrong with runs that are too short and too slow. "You need to get the hydrogen ions in the muscles for a sufficient length of time for the muscles to become adept at using them," says Sharp. Typically, 20 minutes is sufficient, or two to three miles if your goal is general fitness or a 5K. Runners tackling longer distances should do longer tempo runs during their peak training weeks: four to six miles for the 10K, six to eight for the half-marathon and eight to 10 for 26.2.

HOW SHOULD TEMPO PACE FEEL?

It should feel what we call "comfortably hard". You know you're working, but you're not racing. At the same time, you'd be happy if you could slow down. You'll be even happier if you make tempo running a part of your training schedule, and get results that make you feel like a champion.

⊕ GETTING YOUR TEMPO RUN RIGHT

A classic tempo or lactate-threshold run is a sustained, hard effort for two to four miles, with a decent warm-up before and cool-down afterwards. The sessions below are geared towards experience and goals

⊕ GOAL: Get Started
Coach Gale Bernhardt uses this four-week progression for tempo newbies. Do a 10- to 15-minute warm-up and cool-down.
Week 1 5 x 3 minutes at tempo pace, 60-second easy jog after each one (if you find that you have to walk during the recovery, you're going too hard).
Week 2 5 x 4 minutes at tempo pace, 60-second easy jog recovery.
Week 3 4 x 5 minutes at tempo pace, 90-second easy jog recovery.
Week 4 20 minutes steady tempo pace.

⊕ GOAL: 5K to 10K
Run three easy miles, followed by two repeats

of two miles at 10K pace or one mile at 5K pace. Recover with one mile easy between repeats. Do a two-mile easy cool-down for a total of eight or 10 miles.

⊕ GOAL: Half to Full Marathon
Do this challenging long run once or twice during training. After a warm-up, run three (half-marathoners) or six (marathoners) miles at the easier end of your tempo pace range. Jog for five minutes, and then do another three or six miles. "Maintaining that pace for so many miles will whip you into shape for long distances," says coach Toby Tanser.

⊕ THE RIGHT RHYTHM
To ensure you're running at the right pace, use one of these four methods to help to gauge your intensity:

RECENT RACE Add 30 to 40 seconds per kilometre to your current 5K pace or 15 to 20 seconds to your current 10K pace.
HEART RATE Run at 85 to 90 per cent of your maximum heart rate (use a heart-rate monitor).
PERCEIVED EXERTION An eight on a one to 10 scale (a comfortable effort would be five; racing close to a 10).
TALK TEST A few words should be possible, but not conversation.

THE UPSIDE OF RUNNING INSIDE

Millions of runners love the treadmill and millions more hate it. Yet this much is certain: running above the belt means more consistent training, less time in the cold and the end of wintertime blues

The treadmill can be more than a stopgap on days when the weather doesn't cooperate or the baby is taking a nap upstairs. Done right, treadmill training will help you maintain and improve your fitness throughout the winter so you're ready to race — or outpace your running buddies — by the time spring comes along.

"If you're doing a spring marathon like London, the treadmill gives you the option to take some of your training away from the cold of the British winter," says Nick Anderson, RW contributing editor and running coach (runningwithus.com).

On top of a friendlier temperature, you can tackle made-to-order hills and enjoy cushioning that protects your joints. Most importantly, you force yourself to stick to a pace. "You've got to keep up, or you'll fly off the back of the machine," says Rick Morris, author of Treadmill Training for Runners (£11.49, Shamrock Cove).

It may take a little experimenting to build a routine you enjoy. That's fine — just don't make it too much of a routine. "Be playful with your workouts," says Gregory Florez, CEO of Fitadvisor.com. "One day do a steady run, the next do intervals. Never get locked into the same pattern, otherwise your body will quickly adapt and you won't get as much out of your training." we have put together five workouts over the following pages that make the best use of a treadmill's programme features.

⊕ DREAD THE MILL?

Nine reasons to embrace it instead

1 It's the only way to do a tempo run on a cold, sleety morning without cursing your existence.

2 There's no need to obsess over your mile splits because the belt demands an even pace. You just can't get it wrong.

3 You can condition your legs to get used to running up hills, even if you live in Suffolk.

4 There's no more rushing out the door to squeeze in an evening run before it gets too dark.

5 You get to do less layering, less shivering and less laundry.

6 You don't have to shove a 20kg baby jogger up a steep hill.

7 You can do hill repeats without having to find steep gradients – or pound down them, for that matter.

8 A cushioned treadmill belt is kinder to your body if you're recovering from an injury.

9 It's the only time you can watch an *EastEnders* omnibus without feeling guilty.

RACE SIMULATIONS
Do it to train for the course

1 Wouldn't it be great if you could train for the hills you'll encounter in your upcoming race? You can: it's possible to get an elevation chart for many races so you can simulate its topography.

THE WORKOUT Mimic the course by using a race's elevation map to time your ups and downs on the treadmill. For instance, say you know there's a killer hill two-thirds of the way into a 10K you've entered. All you have to do is hit that 'up' button at the same point in your treadmill run.

INSIDE SCOOP On the day, when you get to that hill, you can console yourself that you've done it before — and that it felt much worse when you were stuck inside without the fresh air.

RANDOM INTERVALS
Do it to mix things up

2 Unpredictable changes in incline and speed provide a more complete workout than a steady pace on a flat surface because they force you to work different muscles.

THE WORKOUT Just a little variation in your run helps the time go by much faster. Try a 10-minute warm-up, 20 minutes of random intervals and a 10-minute cool-down.

INSIDE SCOOP If you don't have much time, this will give you a burst of intensity over a short period. Plus, it's a healthy change for obsessive runners who like to plot out every split.

3 SPEED INTERVALS
Do it to get faster
When you do intervals on the track, almost everyone slows down over the last few repeats because they're fatigued. "On the treadmill, you can only slow down when the belt does," says Morris.

THE WORKOUT Try three sets of three minutes at about 10 seconds per mile faster than 5K pace. It takes the treadmill a few seconds to get to your interval speed, so start timing once you've reached it. Do two minutes of easy jogging in between each rep. Add another set every two weeks.

INSIDE SCOOP It's a killer, but the results will definitely show.

4 TV TEMPO RUN
Do it to lock in your pace
Tempo runs are hard to get right. Runners without much experience tend to go too fast or too slow. Once you've entered your target pace, the treadmill ensures you stay at the right speed.

THE WORKOUT Find a treadmill at the gym with a TV attached and tune in to ITV 10 minutes before your favourite half-hour programme. Do a 10-minute warm-up, and move up to your tempo pace when the episode begins. Jog during the adverts, then resume your faster pace when the programme comes back on. Cool down for five minutes.

INSIDE SCOOP As you improve, try maintaining your tempo pace throughout.

5 HILL REPEATS
Do it to design your own terrain
You can control the gradient of the hill, and you don't have to run down it and place more stress on your quads. Instead, you can flatten the belt for a few minutes of recovery, then go back at it.

THE WORKOUT Try one-minute runs up a four per cent incline with two minutes of slow, flat jogging in between. Build up to 10 reps at six per cent. This gives you a cardiovascular challenge but is easier on your legs.

INSIDE SCOOP "You're doing the same intensity as you would be if you were running on a track, but on a track your legs have to move much faster," says US Olympic marathoner Magdalena Lewy-Boulet.

FATIGUE SLOWS EVERYONE DOWN. BUT ON THE TREADMILL YOU CAN ONLY SLOW DOWN WHEN THE BELT DOES

TREAD RIGHTLY
Expert advice for belting it out

TREADMILLS offer some benefits you may not get from the roads — as long as you adapt your workouts to match the conditions. Use these tips to get started.

1 LEARN TO ADJUST AS YOU GO
Whenever Magdalena Lewy-Boulet uses the treadmill, she whacks the elevation up by two per cent to counter the lack of wind resistance she would face outside. Because there's no hard science equating wind resistance to incline percentages, experiment with your own adjustments.

2 SHORTEN YOUR STRIDE
The constantly moving surface and extra cushioning of a treadmill makes most people adopt a shorter stride. "It's kind of like running on grass instead of a nice firm surface where you generate a lot of power," says Rick Morris. Listen to your body to find a comfortable pace. If what you normally find to be an easy pace outdoors feels hard on a treadmill, slow down.

3 DRINK UP
You're likely to sweat more on a treadmill. To avoid dehydration, drink two to four sips of water every 15 minutes while you're running.

JOIN THE CLUB?

Thinking about signing up with a running club?
Here's all you need to know before committing

The days when running clubs were the sole preserve of ultra-competitive elite racers hell-bent on crushing the opposition at all costs and putting in more hours than Haile Gebrselassie or Paula Radcliffe are thankfully long gone. With hundreds of clubs catering for runners up and down the country, there's something for everyone, from beginner fun-runners to serious pace-setters. Indeed, it's possible to join a running club without ever racing,

without being able to make it round the athletics track in under 90 seconds and without finding it fascinating to discuss the relative merits of control versus stability running shoes.

Not everyone feels the need to be coached as part of a group – after all, getting away from the crowds has always been one of the main pulls of our pastime. But with the help of the country's finest club coaches and input from regular runners, we've come up with the ultimate guide to help you decide

whether joining a club could help you reach your goals, or realise that you're better off flying solo.

HOW TO CHOOSE A CLUB

SUIT YOURSELF

If you're simply keen to get out there and meet other recreational runners, you need to know you're not joining a club packed with elite racers. "While everyone will change their goals over time as

Stevenage's award-winning Fairlands Valley Spartans

a runner, you need to make sure there's a group, at least at the start, that's on the same wavelength as you," says Fraser Smart from Kirkintilloch Olympians (kirkintillocholympians.co.uk). All clubs will claim to be "friendly", but that depends on your outlook. "Prioritise what it is you're aiming to get from your club, and email or call one of their coaches to see if it tallies with their approach – it's better to be upfront from the start than leave after a couple of months with a bitter taste in your mouth."

GO LOCAL

If the club's not convenient, you'll find your reasons not to go. "There'll be times when the last thing you want to do is go for a run, so it has to be easy to get to and from," says Clare Naden from Clapham Chasers (claphamchasers.co.uk). "If it takes you an hour to get home, it'll impinge too much on your stress levels, which defeats the point –

it's supposed to be enjoyable, not a strain." Add in the problem of commuting time and you're also less likely to make any post-run socials that are an integral part of any club's cohesion. "Mine's on my way home from work, so it's virtually impossible for me to justify not going – and I can enjoy a relaxing drink afterwards knowing I've got an easy 10-minute jog home." Find clubs by postcode and proximity at goodrunguide.co.uk.

FRINGE BENEFITS

As well as potentially reduced race costs, there are other extras you might want to ask about. "The £20 a year I pay is more than offset with discounts at local running shops, not to mention the contacts you make in terms of physios when you get injured, and massage therapists," says Lucy Colquhoun from City of Edinburgh AC (edinburghac.org.uk). "Any good club should at least be aware of local physios and other running-

specific professionals who can help you out, either with discounts or just priority treatment." And once you enter the circle of trust, you won't be simply relying on the first ad you see on yell.com to iron out any of those issues.

MAKE THE RIGHT FRIENDS

While being sociable is no doubt top of every runner's list, that probably stops short of drinking yards of warm lager out of dirty training shoes as part of Frat-party-worthy initiation rites. "The post-run environment is absolutely essential for you to make friends, determine running partners and discuss issues with coaches," says Rory McDonnell from Clapham Chasers. "I've known clubs that have really frowned on any post-run drinking, which I find as off-putting as compulsory drinking – you just have to know what you want first," he says. "You'll also be sharing cars to races, and helping each other through problems, so you have to know you're vaguely on the same page as your club mates." See if you can meet up for a couple of post-run sessions to get to know them.

MAKE CONTACT

While running is probably the oldest sport known to man, most clubs have moved with the times, with websites that provide information. "If there are lots of pictures of runners at a recent race or meet, you've got an idea that the club is run efficiently and for the runners," says Guy Regis from Serpentine Running Club (serpentine.org.uk). "Too many clubs stagnate under bureaucratic committees who've lost touch with what they're trying to achieve." But don't always judge a book by its cover. "There should be an email address on the site – if they don't get back to you in a few of days, I'd give it a wide berth, as you could be left similarly stranded once you join."

READ ALL THE SMALL PRINT

While some clubs only charge yearly subs of up to £20, which

Make new friends on the road

may seem reasonable, once you're in the club you might well get stung for some extra hidden costs. "Often you have to buy their club-branded running bibs and shorts, at prices that seem far from reasonable," explains Lesley Foster from Sunderland Strollers (sunderlandstrollers.co.uk). "Also ask if there are any monthly admin charges, or what you have to pay for each session throughout the year. "If money's an issue, say it is and see what reaction the club gives. "If they don't suggest they'll waive or cut costs if you're hard-up or unemployed, it gives you a pretty good indication of the people running the club."

GIVE IT A TRY

As well as asking questions of the coaches, see if you can trial a few sessions before signing up. "It often takes more than one session to get to really know a club, so don't base all your judgements on one evening," says Michael Morris from Morpeth Harriers (morpethharriers.co.uk). And don't try three Monday evenings in a row. "Different sessions and evenings often have different focuses and people, so dip your toe in several spots before making up your mind."

THINK THE WORST

While no runner goes out looking for injuries, they inevitably hit us all from time to time. "Ask the coaches their views on over-training and limiting sessions to see if they're generally aware of your long-term safety," says Rob Pullen from the Owls running club in Leicester (owlsac.org.uk). Ask what contingencies they have for injuries during runs, whether they have insurance, and ask if they have a group for runners who are coming back to fitness from injury.

PAY BACK

Clubs aren't just about running. "There's a whole load of other activities, from organising socials to marshalling races to helping out at water stations, which some clubs expect you to take part in," says Ken Rushton from Trentham Club in Stoke-on-Trent (trenthamrunningclub.co.uk). "With our club it's voluntary – I seem to have a right arm that shoots into the air every time someone mentions cross-country – but a lot of clubs have a strict rota that you might not want to get involved in, so always check first." Likewise, if you don't want to be part of a club where runners don't want to get involved in the dirty work, the same rule applies.

⊕ 'I THANK MY CLUB'

BEN MILLAR
Clapham Chasers
I'd been running for years, but thought that a club could help take my running up a gear. I decided to go for one that I could get to easily. They got back to me straight away and were really welcoming, which clinched it. We have coaches on hand to discuss our issues with. It's not just their qualifications, but also their willingness to help that make the difference to me.

I've found good local sports therapists through the club, something I'd never have considered as a lone

runner. I've also discovered good local routes for long runs. Principally, I've found that training with other runners has pushed me to my limits – and not beyond them, so I avoid injury.

Racing's another key draw for me – we have regular race fixtures that most of us attend. It makes a difference to the amount and type of races we do, often leading up to a big event like a marathon.

For me, the numbers speak for themselves: my marathon PB was 3:48, and after just four months with the club it went down to 2:56. I can't overstate how much I enjoy my running now and I have my club to thank for it.

PHOTOGRAPHY TOM MILES

Learn to cross the
line like a pro

FLIGHT TO THE FINISH

Getting a killer kick is about more than just running. You can leave the
competition behind with these five clever training disciplines

G o on, admit it: you've
dreamed about breaking
the tape at a race. At the
sharp end of a race, prizes and
pride hang on how you run the last
few metres, but learning to burst
over the line is just as useful for
everyone else. Finishing strong
puts on a great show and is a superb
confidence booster, but most
importantly, a sprint finish is the

difference between hitting and
missing your targets.

Some people are naturally
good at putting in a last spurt at the
end of a race. "Most good sprint
finishers are born, not made," says
Steve Smythe, a coach and distance
runner. "A runner with lots of
natural fast-twitch muscle fibres
will usually beat the one-paced
endurance runner, but there are

things that you can do to help to
redress the balance."

If you've taken up running
in adulthood, it can take time to
work out which camp you fall in
to, because nearly all recreational
runners are slow enough to have
something left for a final push. As
you become faster and race more
often, you'll soon learn when
and where to push the pace, but

even if you're lucky enough to be a naturally strong finisher, you can work on your overall race for a better time and placing.

1 BUILD THE FOUNDATIONS

A strong finish is the icing on your running cake, but you need to bake the cake first. Yes, that means building up mileage slowly and introducing new training elements gradually – especially intense speed sessions. "There's a lot to be said for running 200m or 400m intervals with short recovery periods in the build-up to a race," says Nick Anderson, British cross-country team coach. "But you need to put in the basic training first."

For a fast finish, your base shouldn't just include mileage, though. Include core training – working on your abdominal and back muscles – to develop good sprinting form, and strength training, which helps to develop the fast-twitch muscle fibres needed to go up a gear. One or two sessions per week should do the trick – try gym classes if you're not sure where to start. When you do start sprint sessions in training, think about your form from the outset: relax your face and neck and pull up tall. Pump your arms back and forth (not out to the sides), your leading knee should drive up high and your foot should be planted firmly in front of you.

2 BECOME FIT TO BURST

The strong finish is all about a sudden fast burst, especially at the front of a race where intimidating your rivals is almost as important as the speed itself. To learn this, you need some short, fast intervals. Smythe recommends a session of 100m sprints: warm up, then try five to eight reps of 100m (or 15 to 20

seconds very fast) with walking breaks. Time your efforts and try to run quicker each time.

3 RUN ON EMPTY

Running short sprints in training can be fun. At the end of a race, though, you'll be sprinting off the back of your very last reserves of strength. This isn't fun, but thanks to the good old rule of specificity (training as you want to race), you'll need to practise fast running when you're tired just as much as the sprinting. The best way to do this is to make your hard sessions slightly harder. "I always try to finish a speed session with a hard final effort, so my body does it automatically in a race," says Smythe.

Change your approach to your long runs: promise yourself you'll never trot down to your front door at the end, and pick a point – perhaps at the end of your street, or when you see a familiar landmark – to race home from.

4 PLAN FOR THE FINALE

In order to finish really well you need to know exactly what's coming. "To make sure you judge your effort at the right place, familiarise yourself with the end of the course before you actually take part in the race," says Smythe. If there's a nasty hill, narrow path or difficult ground in your way, you need to factor that in to your final approach.

INTIMIDATING YOUR RIVALS IS ALMOST AS IMPORTANT AS SPEED ITSELF

If you're in contention for a top-three place, try to suss out your competition. If you don't know who you'll be up against, it could be worth checking previous years' results – are there any regular winners? Is the finish usually close, or is the winner usually minutes ahead? Race standards change from year to year, but often particular events will have a reputation for being particularly fast or not, and this could help you to plan your tactics.

In the race itself, don't focus so much on the finish that you forget about your pace the rest of the time – your sprint can buy you seconds, but your overall pacing puts you in pole position for that sprint. Over long distances, it can be tempting to distract yourself from the passing miles, but research has shown that concentrating on your body and your performance has a better outcome, so make sure you're switched on from at least one-third in to the race.

5 THE FINAL PUSH

By the time you reach the end of the race, you'll know where your strengths lie and who you're racing for a place. For middle-of-the-pack runners, your task is simple and satisfying: speed up gradually to pick off runners as you approach the finish. Further up the field, you'll need to be more precise with your timing of the final big push. "If you don't have a killer kick and want to beat a rival, make your effort 400m to 800m from the finish to draw the speed out of your opponent," says Smythe.

For most of us, the sight of the finish line is enough to spur us on – but when you reach that point, remember that however unpleasant you feel physically, it won't last long. So give it everything you've got.

Chapter
3

CROSS TRAINING

Embrace other sports such as rowing, cycling and swimming – they can make you a better runner

80 | **CROSS ROADS**
Get on your bike, or in the pool

84 | **CENTRE OF ATTENTION**
How to work your core muscles

90 | **STRIKE A POSE**
The benefits of trying yoga

94 | **X-FACTOR**
Outdoor circuits for impressive form

PHOTOGRAPHY: NEALE HAYNES

CROSS ROADS

A good cross-training regime can be the best way to improve your running

C ross-training can be a tough concept for many who don't believe that a variety of workouts is good for us. It's just that we can't work out where the time is going to come from. A 30-minute run is often difficult enough to fit in, so how are you going to swim and bike and row and all that other stuff?

Maybe we feel under pressure to put more effort into cross-training because of the increasing interest in triathlons and other multi-discipline events. To be an elite triathlete, some people will spend many hours a day training. Who needs all of it?

Fortunately, no one but an elite athlete. The rest of us can benefit from more realistic doses of cross-training. Still, it's hard to work out how to begin, how much and what kinds of cross-training to do.

Life used to be simple. Runners ran, and swimmers swam. Cyclists pedalled and weight-lifters grunted. Then everything got mixed up. Runners started cycling, swimmers lifted weights and cyclists started running. Now, it's not unusual to see athletes climbing stairs that go nowhere, or cross-country skiing over a gym floor.

These activities may look odd but they're very good for you. You'll stretch certain muscles, strengthen others and burn plenty of calories, but what exactly can cross-training do for runners?

And, given all the cross-training choices, which of them are the best ones for you?

THE DO MORE, GET FITTER THEORY

Proponents of this position believe that runners should cross-train with exercises and activities that are as close to running as possible. **THE LOGIC** The stronger you make your running muscles, the better you'll run.

THE REST THEORY

According to this approach, runners should cross-train with sports that are as different from running as possible. **THE LOGIC** You can burn calories and get a good workout, and, at the same time, you'll be resting your running muscles and won't be creating the one-sport muscle imbalances that often can lead to an unfortunate injury.

THE SPECIFICITY THEORY

Specificity advocates believe that runners shouldn't cross-train – and that's the end of it. It's a waste of time and will only tire you for your next run. When you need a day off from running, take a day off from everything. **THE LOGIC** Training is specific to the sport it is aimed towards, so therefore the best way to train for running is to run.

No wonder so many runners are confused. Who are they supposed to believe, and which theory should they follow? "All of the approaches make sense and could work," says Dr Mike Flynn, an exercise physiologist and one of America's leading researchers in the field of cross-training.

The trick to optimising your training programme, he explains, is to pick the approach that best fits your current training goals in both running and fitness.

To make your decision easier, we've designed cross-training programmes for five different types of runner. Simply find the category that best describes you over the page and follow the suggested advice.

BEGINNER

This is for runners who do 5-15 miles per week. **THE BASICS** If you're running to get into shape, the first thing you need to do is build up your cardiovascular system. A strong heart and lungs will supply more fuel to your working leg muscles and allow you to run without constantly feeling out of breath.

If you're switching to running from another sport, you're probably fit enough to run a few miles without much problem, but don't overdo it. Running involves

Pedal your way
to faster feet

A STRONG HEART AND LUNGS WILL SUPPLY MORE FUEL TO YOUR LEG MUSCLES

more pounding than most other sports, and it takes time for the muscles, tendons and ligaments to adapt.

THE PROGRAMME The best cross-training programme for beginners is one that mixes running and cross-training in equal amounts. If you're running twice a week, try cross-training twice a week as well. This will allow you to build your cardio system and muscle strength without undue risk of injury. If you can't handle more than one hard run a week, split your workouts between running and cross-training.

THE EXERCISES As a beginner, almost any aerobic activity will help to increase your cardiovascular strength. The best exercises are those that also strengthen as many of your running muscles as possible. These exercises will improve the co-ordination of your running muscles and teach them to process and store fuel more effectively.

INTERMEDIATE

This is for runners who do 15-40 miles per week.

THE BASICS You have developed a strong cardio system through your running so easy cross-training workouts won't improve your running performance. You need to choose cross-training activities that either provide a very high-intensity cardiovascular workout or specifically target your running muscles.

THE PROGRAMME Run two to three times as much as you are cross-training. Run for two or three days, and then do cross-training. If you are doing two hard runs a week, select cross-training workouts that allow you to exercise at a moderate pace. You should be using these workouts just to give your running muscles some extra training without extra pounding. If your body can really handle only one hard run a week, then one of your cross-training workouts should be hard also.

THE EXERCISES Cross-training exercises that provide high-intensity cardio workouts are cross-country skiing, stair climbing and high-cadence stationary cycling. Grinding away in a high gear on a bike will slow your turnover, but using a high cadence (over 90rpm) will keep you quick and allow you to get your heart rate up.

ADVANCED

This is for those who run more than 40 miles per week.

THE BASICS You have probably maximised your cardiovascular conditioning, as well as the strength of your leg muscles, so cross-training won't directly do you much good. To improve your running performance, you need more quality in your runs. Running coaches and exercise physiologists generally recommend at least two hard runs a week – a shorter interval session on the track and a longer tempo run.

THE PROGRAMME Since both hard running and high mileage can increase your injury risk, your best bet may be complete rest rather

Make a splash with your training routine

than cross-training. This will allow your muscles to recover completely for your next run. If you don't want to take days off, you can consider low-intensity cross-training with a sport that doesn't tax your running muscles. This will burn calories, and variety will keep you mentally fresh.

If you choose to cross-train, replace one or two of your easy runs – preferably the ones that come a day after a hard run – with a cross-training activity.

THE EXERCISES Cycling, pool running, swimming and rowing will all give your running muscles a break and let them recover for your next hard run.

INJURY-PRONE

This is for runners who experience two or more running injuries in any given year.

THE BASICS Surveys show two out of three runners will be injured in the course of a year. Cross-training can help in two ways. Firstly, it can keep you healthy by allowing you to stay fit without the constant pounding of running. Secondly, cross-training can help forestall the performance losses that come when an injury keeps you from running. Studies have shown that runners can maintain their running times for up to six weeks by cross-training alone if it is done at the proper intensity.

THE PROGRAMME The best cross-training programme for injury-prone runners involves doing two to four runs per week (depending on how much your body can tolerate) and two cross-training workouts. Both of your cross-training workouts should target running-specific muscles in order to help to increase their strength and efficiency without subjecting them to more pavement pounding.

The extra training of these muscles through cross-training rarely produces injuries because high impact is the main injury cause, but if you're unsure, ask your doctor. And to reduce the risk, don't do more than one high-intensity workout per week.

THE EXERCISES So, injury-prone runners should keep their cross-training workouts as specific to training as possible. In-line skating, stair climbing, rowing and cross-country skiing are good choices. Unfortunately, some injuries – stress fractures in particular – don't allow many cross-training options. In these cases, cross-training in the pool by swimming or deep-water running is the best alternative. These are non-weight-bearing activities that don't hurt the legs.

GENERAL

This is for low- to mid-mileage runners more concerned with overall fitness than racing.

THE BASICS Look at any elite runner, and you'll notice that running doesn't do much for the upper body. It also neglects quadriceps in favour of the calves, hamstrings and buttocks. Furthermore, after the age of 30, all the muscles in bodies begin to lose strength. Fortunately, exercise can cut the rate almost in half.

THE PROGRAMME For total-body fitness, run twice a week and do a complementary exercise on one or two other days of the week. In addition, 20 minutes of circuit weight training twice a week will help you condition any muscles that you may have missed.

THE EXERCISES General-fitness runners need exercises that target the upper body and quads. Try rowing, swimming or using an elliptical trainer to ensure you work your upper body, too.

CENTRE OF ATTENTION

Forget crunches. If you want to get faster, fitter and stronger, you need to train your core like a runner

In the past you'd have been hard-pressed to find elite runners paying attention to their abdominal muscles. Today, it's almost mandatory. "It's so important. The stronger the core, the more likely you are to hold your form and less likely to get injured," explains marathon world record holder Paula Radcliffe. You simply can't run your personal best without a strong core: the muscles in your abdominals, lower back and glutes. They provide the stability, power and endurance that runners need for powering up hills, sprinting to the finish and maintaining form mile after mile. "When

your core is strong, everything else will follow," says running coach Greg McMillan, who has worked with scores of elite and recreational runners. "It's the foundation for all of your movement, no matter what level of running you're doing."

The key is to train your core like a specialist would. Quality core work is by no means easy, but it doesn't require that much of your time, says running coach Nick Anderson. "You don't need to put in any more than 15 minutes just a few times a week." It's an investment that will pay dividends when you are out on the road.

⊕ KNOW YOUR CORE
A close look at the muscle groups that make up your core

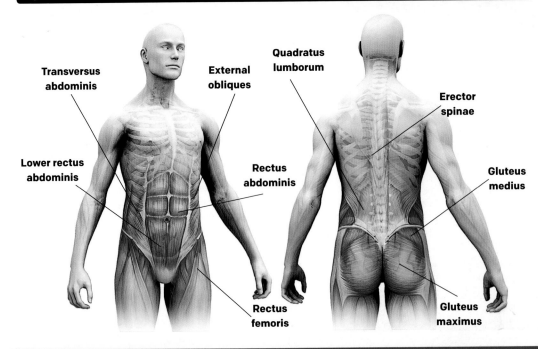

Transversus abdominis

External obliques

Quadratus lumborum

Erector spinae

Lower rectus abdominis

Rectus abdominis

Gluteus medius

Gluteus maximus

Rectus femoris

PHOTOGRAPHY: SARAH A FRIEDMAN. ILLUSTRATIONS: SUPERCORN, JOHN McNEIL

A healthy core equals a healthy body

Put your best
foot forward with
these stretches

CORE VALUES

Here's how a strong midsection will help avoid injury and finish races faster

SPEED

As you extend your
stride or quicken the
rate of your leg and
foot turnover when
you're trying to pick
up the pace, the lower
abs and lower back
are called into action.
The stronger and more
stable these muscles
are, the more force you
can generate as you
push off the ground.

UPHILLS

If your core is strong,
your legs will have
a stable plane to
push from, for a more
powerful ascent. When
you swing your leg
forward, the hip-flexor
muscles, such as the
rectus femoris, pull on
the pelvis. As you push
off the ground, the
glutes and hamstrings
are engaged.

DOWNHILLS

You need strong
gluteal muscles
to help absorb the
impact and counter
the momentum of
the forward motion.
Without core strength,
your quads and knee
joints bear the extra
pounding of your body
weight, which can lead
to fatigue, pain and
serious injury.

ENDURANCE

As you near the end
of a race, a solid core
helps you maintain
proper form and
run efficiently, even
through fatigue. With
strong lower abs and
lower-back muscles,
it's easier to stay
upright. A weak core
can put too much
stress on your hips,
knees and shins.

LATERAL MOVEMENT

Whenever you have
to suddenly move to
the side the obliques
provide stability and
help keep you upright.
If your core is weak,
then you may end
up leaning into the
movement, which can
put excess weight and
strain on the joints in
your legs and feet.

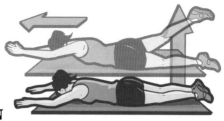

SUPERMAN

WHAT IT HITS Transversus abdominis (deep abs) and erector spinae (lower back).

HOW Start face down on the floor, with your arms and legs extended out in front. Raise your head, your left arm, and right leg five inches off the floor. Hold for three counts, then lower. Repeat with your right arm and left leg. Do up to 10 reps each side.

GET IT RIGHT Don't raise your shoulders too much.

MAKE IT HARDER Lift both arms and legs off the ground at the same time.

BRIDGE

WHAT IT HITS Glutes and hamstrings.

HOW Lie face up on the floor, with your knees bent 90 degrees, your feet on the floor. Lift your hips and back off the floor until your body forms a straight line from your shoulders to your knees. Hold for five to 10 seconds. Lower to the floor and repeat 10 to 12 times.

GET IT RIGHT Squeeze your glutes at the top of the movement, and don't let your spine sag.

MAKE IT HARDER Straighten one leg and point it out once your hips are lifted.

METRONOME

WHAT IT HITS Obliques.

HOW Lie face up with your knees bent and raised over your hips, your feet lifted, and your arms out. Rotate your legs to the left, bringing your knees as close to the floor as possible without touching.

Return to the centre, then rotate your knees to the right. Do 10 to 12 reps on each side.

GET IT RIGHT Don't swing your hips or use momentum

MAKE IT HARDER Keep your legs straight.

BEYOND CRUNCHES
A 15-minute workout for runners

Fortunately, quality core strength work doesn't require a great deal of time or equipment – just 15 minutes three times a week, a few feet of floor space and some key moves done correctly and consistently. This workout is designed by Greg McMillan, a running coach and exercise scientist, who has worked with recreational runners and world-class athletes. The workout is devised to strengthen specific muscles runners need for bounding up hills, sprinting to the finish, enduring long distances and preventing running injuries. Try doing two sets of these moves right before or after your run, three times a week.

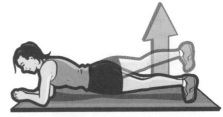

SIDE PLANK

WHAT IT HITS Obliques, transversus abdominis, lower back, hips and glutes.

HOW Lie on your right side, supporting your upper body on your right forearm, with your left arm at your side. Lift your hips and, keeping your body weight supported on the forearm and the side of the right foot, extend your left arm above your shoulder. Hold for 10 to 30 seconds. Switch sides and then repeat.

GET IT RIGHT Keep your hips up; don't let them sag.

MAKE IT HARDER Support your upper body with your right hand, not your forearm.

PLANK LIFT

WHAT IT HITS Transversus abdominis and lower back.

HOW Begin face down on the floor, propped up on your forearms, with knees and feet together. With your elbows under your shoulders, lift your torso, legs and hips in a straight line. Hold for 10 seconds. Raise your right leg a few inches, keeping the rest of the body still. Lower and repeat with your left leg.

GET IT RIGHT Pull in your belly and don't let your hips sag down towards the floor.

MAKE IT HARDER Extend the time of the exercise each time it becomes too easy.

ALL THE RIGHT MOVES

A few quick fixes to your training will pay off on the run

➡ **THE MISTAKE**

You're doing the wrong exercises

"The biggest mistake that runners tend to make is to take strength-training moves, such as crunches, straight from the fitness industry," says running coach Greg McMillan. For most runners, standard crunches aren't helpful because they don't work the deep core muscles that provide the stability to run mile after mile.

➡ **THE FIX**

Do workouts that hit the muscles and movements that runners need. Try exercises like the side plank or plank lift (above) that strengthen the obliques, on the sides of the trunk, and the transverse abs; core muscles that wrap around the trunk like a corset.

➡ **THE MISTAKE**

You're a creature of habit

Even if you've moved beyond crunches, you may find you have slipped into a non-beneficial routine. "You need to constantly challenge your muscles to get the best results," says running coach Sam Murphy.

➡ **THE FIX**

You need to mix up from your old training routine. Fine-tune your workout to make it more difficult than your previous sessions. Try balancing on one leg or changing your arm position. At the gym, use devices like a stability ball – an unstable platform that forces your core muscles to work harder to keep you steady. And as a rule, McMillan says, you should try to change your routine around every six weeks or so.

➡ **THE MISTAKE**

You whip through your workouts

If you're flying through the moves in your workout, you're using momentum, not muscles.

➡ **THE FIX**

Slow it down. Exercises like the plank, which require holding one position for 10 to 60 seconds, force you to work your muscles continuously. Even in exercises that involve repetitions, make steady – not rapid-fire – movements. "It takes intention," says Paula Coates, running coach, physiotherapist and author of *Running Repairs: A Runner's Guide to Keeping Injury Free* (A&C Black Publishers Ltd). "You must not rush your exercises or you can't be sure you're doing them properly."

➡ **THE MISTAKE**

You ignore what you don't see

Runners often have weak backs because they just forget about them, out of sight, out of mind, says running coach Nick Anderson. "But when you're running, especially if you're running for a long time, those muscles in the lower back are crucial for providing you with much needed stability and good support."

➡ **THE FIX**

Include at least one – but ideally more than one – exercise that targets the lower back area and glutes in each workout. Moves like the bridge and superman (previous page), help build muscles that will support and protect the spine, maintaining a healthy back.

CORE MELTDOWN

Maintain it correctly or suffer the consequences

Your core is like a power plant. If it's not working efficiently, you'll waste energy, says Tim Hilden, a physical therapist, coach and physiologist who specialises in running. "You'll see too much unwanted movement, which decreases performance or sets you up for injury." Here are three areas that can be injured as a result of a weak core.

LOWER BACK As your legs pound the pavement, your vertebrae absorb much of the force. That shock worsens if your core is weak, which will produce lower-back pain. Build those muscles with moves like the superman (previous page).

HAMSTRINGS When your core isn't stable, your hamstrings often have to work extra hard, says running coach and physiotherapist Paula Coates. The added work can leave them shorter, tighter, and more vulnerable to injury. To strengthen them, as well as your glutes, try exercises like bridges, lunges and squats.

KNEES Without a stable core, you can't control the movement of your torso as well, and you risk putting excess force on your joints each time your foot lands. This can lead to pain under the knee (known as 'runner's knee'), patellar tendinitis (a sharp pain in the bottom of the knee), and iliotibial-band tendinitis. The plank (opposite) strengthens the transversus abdominis, which help steady the core and prevent injury.

CROSS TRAINING

You can do it if you put your back into it

STRIKE A POSE

Try these approaches to ensure you have a long and satisfying running life

YOGA

Yoga has been credited with everything from helping people to reach a enlightenment to creating Madonna's muscles (nothing to do with running and resistance work, then?) Runners are divided about how much difference it will make to your performance. But yoga does offer mental space and a good stretch – which can't do any harm.

"Yoga teaches you to be in an intense situation and to bring awareness to your form and your breathing to make the situation manageable," says coach Sage Rountree. "This skill is invaluable at mile 18 of a marathon. You'll learn ways to cope that benefit you as an athlete and in life."

There are dozens of types of yoga out there. Treat the intense classes (Ashtanga or power yoga) as hard sessions and fit them into

your training accordingly. Classes in Hatha yoga are very popular and should offer a more gentle stretch. If you've not tried it before it's best to start with an instructor, but Rountree recommends developing a home-based practice that you can adjust to your running schedule: poses that stretch your muscles post-run; others that strengthen your core three times a week; and a longer routine that will work your whole body on a rest day.

ALL THE RIGHT MOVES

PYRAMID

Why? Promotes stability, stretches hamstrings.
How? Stand with your right leg in front of you. Hinge forward from the hips, tilting the pelvis forwards and keeping the back straight, with your knee bent. Lock your fingers behind your back and stretch them up and away from you.

REVERSE TABLE

Why? Strengthens your abdominals and back.
How? Sit with your knees bent, feet flat on the floor, hands directly under your shoulders with your fingers spread apart. Push up through your hands and feet until your torso and thighs are parallel with the floor.

LUNGE AND TWIST

Why? Stretches the hips.
How? Start by standing with your feet roughly shoulder width apart. Step your left foot back behind you and then slowly lower yourself down so that your knee and toes rest on the ground. Your right thigh should be just beyond a right-angle with your shin. Put your palms together in front of your chest and keep your shoulders down.

Now twist from the waist slowly until your left tricep is resting on your right quad. Look over your shoulder and up towards the ceiling. Hold this position for 10-15 seconds, working up to a minute as you become more experienced.

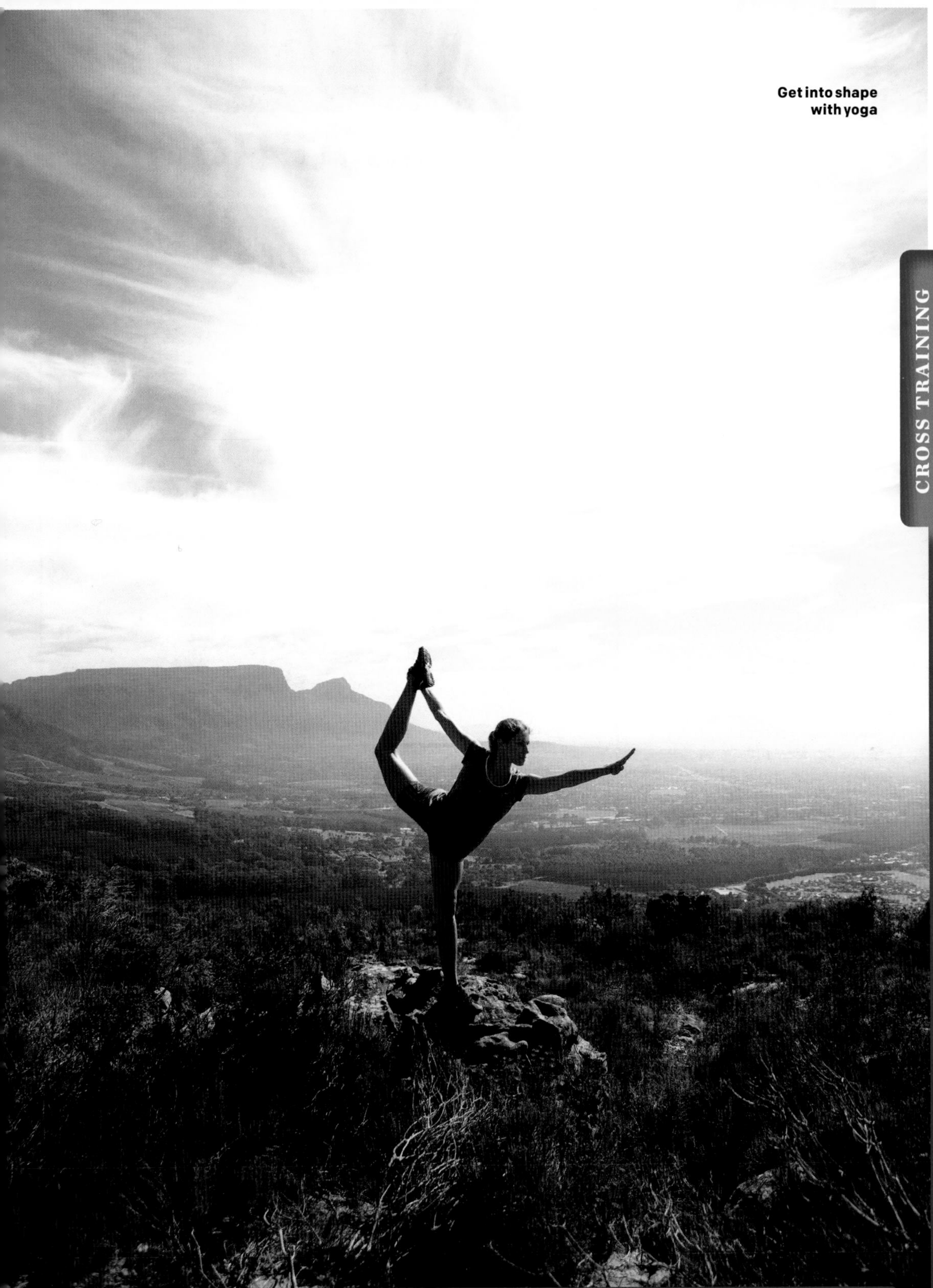

Get into shape
with yoga

PILATES

Core strength is a very popular term these days – you've probably seen it in the papers being celebrated by celebrities – but the actual idea of strengthening your back, abdominal and pelvic muscles to be beneficial to your whole body isn't in any way new. Creator of the technique, Joseph Pilates called the core the 'powerhouse'. Pilates was a German-born sportsman and fitness trainer, and began developing his method a long time ago while training other inmates in a prisoner-of-war camp during the First World War. Afterwards, he moved to New York where, with the help of his wife, he set up his first studio, then teaching 'Contrology', the system we know today by its more common name, Pilates.

Runners are often advised to take up Pilates as part of their training routine to aid in preventing various injuries, but anyone attempting it will require a lot of patience because Pilates is ideally meant to be performed slowly, in a controlled manner.

There are many different approaches to Pilates, but all of them can be beneficial to runners for a number of different reasons. This particular training technique can be performed using special equipment – such as the big inflatable ball that Pilates has become synonymous with – or on a mat. The one you use for yoga would be fine.

Your pelvic floor should be contracted throughout, but not strongly. Breathe "laterally" into the sides of your chest (use a mirror to watch your chest expanding and contracting, or have a partner check with their hands on your rib cage), so you can hold your tummy in through the exercises. The key is to perform movements on your exhalation.

TRY THIS AT HOME

BASIC PLANK AND INVERTED V

Why? Works core, stretches calves, hamstrings and back
How? Start in a plank – face down in a push-up position, supported by your forearms and toes. Your back should be straight, tummy in and pelvic floor lightly contracted.

Push your hips and bottom up into the air and let your heels drop so you're in an inverted V position. Return to the plank. Repeat 10 times, slowly, without resting.

REVERSE STOMACH CRUNCH AND V

Why? Works core and back
How? Start on your back with your arms by your side and use your stomach muscles to pull your hips up and legs over your head. Take your legs apart, then together.

Roll down and up into a V position. Bring your arms up and lightly hold the outside of your legs to help you balance. In the V position, take your legs apart and together again, roll back down again and Repeat.

SIDE KICKS AND FIGURE OF EIGHT

Why? Works the core, glutes and outer thigh muscles
How? Lie on your side, contract your abs and lift both legs. Move one leg forward and one leg back, then switch.

When you've completed 10, keep your legs off the floor and raise your upper leg slightly. Point your toes and draw a sideways figure of eight, keeping your upper body still. Build up to 10. Repeat on the other side.

ALEXANDER TECHNIQUE

You may have heard from other runners, coaches and various experts that it's always best to "run tall", but few of us seem to know what it actually means. You can force it, but you'll probably end up sticking your chest too far out. Consulting a trained teacher in the Alexander Technique can help you find the perfect position that will free up your legs and arms

Frederick Alexander was an Australian performer who specialised in monologues, but he noticed that he suffered a lot from hoarseness. He realised that he tensed up his whole body when he was performing, and set about letting go of the bad habits that were affecting his vocal chords. The result, now known as the Alexander Technique (AT), can be used to help everyone from musicians to sportspeople. AT teacher and sportsman Malcolm Balk has applied it to running, working to describe an approach to the sport that uses elements of both the Pose and Chi running methods but centres on the principles of AT, including the principal relationship between the head, neck and spine.

You will need a lot of patience and hands-on guidance to follow this approach so you should forget about run times while you're first learning the technique. One of the main principles is avoiding 'end-gaining'– you may be tempted to think, "I'm going to run 5K in 20 minutes for sure and if I don't I will feel terrible." Which is rubbish – don't set yourself up for failure."

When changing your running gait with the Alexander Technique you need to take a step back and set yourself realistic and achievable targets with the aid of a qualified AT expert.

⊕ THE ART OF RUNNING

Malcolm
Balk's running
workshop

Bad running techniques are picked up over years, so you might wonder how much you can learn about running well in three hours with Malcolm Balk and Liz Dodgson. The answer is: a lot. If you spend your days slouched over a desk you may carry your bad habits with you on every run. Balk and Dodgson's video analysis and workshop helps you relearn how to run by helping your gait.

Balk explains one common problem is that a lot of runners tend to use an up-and-down,

heel-striking gait. The problems with this: striking in front of the body causes braking, while the exaggerated push off the ground wastes energy.

Their workshop will pair up runners to support each other's necks, to give an awareness of walking with a long spine and balanced head. They then run through some drills designed to encourage a more efficient running action: swinging each leg to engage the hamstrings and glutes; lightly pawing the ground to learn the

'wheel- like' action of the correct gait; and lightly bouncing then jogging on the spot on the midfoot. Then it is time to put this together into a new, momentum-aided run.

Few may get it right first time. "If it doesn't feel weird, something's wrong," said Balk. "That would mean you're slipping back into your old habits."

No-one comes away with a set, super-efficient stride, but a second video analysis will show your improvements.

X FACTOR

Forget Simon Cowell – outdoor circuits will help you run faster, stronger and longer so you hit the right note come race day

Need a performance booster to slap on running-specific muscle and kick you into race shape? Try outdoor circuits of resistance training with minimal equipment. These sessions from Andrew Stemler of Crossfit London will help you clock faster times. Perform a few sessions a week. Treat each as a quality workout, so bookend with a day of easy running.

2 PRESS-UPS (X100)

A) Lie face down on the ground. Support your body with the balls of your feet and position your hands slightly wider than shoulder-width apart. Keep your arms straight.
B) With a straight back, lower yourself to the floor. Push back up. To make it easier, keep knees on the ground – this reduces the lifting load by about half.

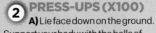

3 BODYWEIGHT SQUATS (X200)

A) Standing with your feet shoulder-width apart, keeping your back straight and looking forward, bend your hips and knees to lower yourself until the bottoms of your thighs touch your calves. Keep your knees in line with your feet.
B) Rise to the start position and imagine you're pulling the ground apart with your feet to involve your glutes.

1 Run 2km at whatever pace you feel comfortable with.

A BOOST ENDURANCE

"Perform the circuit once, as fast as you can," says Stemler. "Take as many rest periods between the exercises as you need to. You tire out all your muscles and keep running – this teaches your body to push through fatigue and builds incredible stamina."

5 Run 3km at whatever pace you feel comfortable with.

4 PULL-UPS (X20)

A) Grab a pull-up bar with an overhand grip that's shoulder-width apart. Hang at arm's length so your elbows are completely extended.
B) Bend your elbows to pull yourself up until your chin crosses the plane of the bar. Pause, then slowly lower yourself to the starting position without allowing your body to sway.

B BUILD POWER

"Perform this circuit as many times as you can in 25 minutes and you'll get legs that'll carry you anywhere," says Stemler. "It builds lower-body strength to power you up hills."

1 Run 400 metres at whatever pace you feel comfortable with.

2 WALL BALL SHOTS (X30)

A) Positioned 4ft away from a tall wall, with your feet shoulder-width apart and a medicine ball (or football) in both hands in front of your chest, sink into the deepest squat you can.

B) Explode upwards. Straighten your arms, letting the ball fly to a target on the wall about 10ft up. Catch it, then return to the start position and repeat.

3 BOX JUMPS (X30)

A) With your feet shoulder-width apart in front of a 24-inch box or park bench, bend your knees until the bottom of your thighs are parallel to the floor.

B) Jump up onto the box, landing with both feet together. Fling your arms above your head to generate momentum. Step back down and then repeat.

1 Run 400 metres at your fastest pace.

C IMPROVE PACE

"Perform the circuit five times," says Stemler. Scribble down the time it takes you to complete, then try to beat it next time. "In time you'll be able to run faster with less effort."

2 OVERHEAD SQUATS (X15)

A) Stand with your feet shoulder-width apart and hold a medicine ball above your head. Your arms should be directly above your shoulders.

B) Keep your back straight, squat until your thighs touch your calves. Stand up, imagining you're pulling the ground apart with your feet.

3 BODYWEIGHT LUNGES (10 ON EACH LEG)

A) Take a giant step forwards with your left foot and bend your left knee until your left thigh is parallel to the ground. Keep your back straight.

B) Reverse the motion, stepping back into the starting position. Repeat with your right leg.

PHOTOGRPAHY. JOHANNA
PARKIN, STYLING: MAUD EDEN

Chapter
4

NUTRITION

Find all the advice you need on healthy eating plans
that will help you on the road to victory

98 | **WHAT TO RUN ON**
Result-specific shopping lists

102 | **PERFECT TIMING**
Choose the right times of day to refuel

108 | **POWER OF WATER**
How much H_2O is too much?

114 | **40 TASTY TIPS**
Use these food hints to boost your body

120 | **FUELLING YOUR FIRE**
What to eat and drink while on the run

126 | **SAFER EATING**
Healthy versions of your favourite dishes

WHAT TO RUN ON

Build your weekly shopping list based on the improvements you want to make to your body

HOW TO USE THESE PAGES

1 Firstly use the category headings to help you to identify the body benefits that you're after.

2 Narrow it down by selecting the various foods from within that category that best suit your needs.

3 Add the selected foods together to assemble your weekly shopping list, knowing that you'll be supplying your body with potent sources of the nutrients needed to make you a better runner.

 PREVENT INJURY

RED PEPPER
This has more vitamin C – crucial for repairing connective tissue – than any citrus fruit, says performance nutritionist Drew Price.
Per week: 3 peppers

EDAMAME
These beans contain soy protein, which is rich in anti-inflammatory isoflavonoids. Oklahoma State University, found eating it daily for three months lessened knee pain.
Per week: 100g x3

OLIVE OIL MARGARINE
A great source of bone-building vitamin D, says sports dietitian Karen Reid – especially important as more than three-quarters of adults are D-deficient.
Per week: on toast x3

BLUEBERRIES
Packed with polyphenols that help to improve bone strength, according to research in the *Journal of Bone and Mineral Research.*
Per week: handful x3

HONEY
The amino acids in the sticky sweet stuff help your body absorb bone-boosting calcium effectively, say US scientists at Purdue University.
Per week: 1 tbsp x3

PUMPKIN SEEDS
These are packed full of magnesium, which fights the ageing of cells that create collagen in your tendons and ligaments, found research in the *Proceedings of the National Academies of Sciences.*
Per week: 20g x3

SMOKED MACKEREL
The fish's omega-3 fatty acids significantly reduce joint pain and shorten the duration of morning joint-stiffness – so say researchers at Harvard Medical School in the US.
Per week: fillet x2

The tastier way to become a better runner

CHAMPAGNE

Raise a glass to your heart, say Reading University scientists. Their studies found the polyphenols in bubbly reduce the loss of nitric oxide from the blood, improving circulation.
Per week: 3 glasses

MARMITE

Try to love it for your heart's sake: Bristol University found its benfotiamine has a beneficial effect on your cardiovascular function.
Per week: on toast x3

TOFU

Bean curd is a source of unsaturated fats. A study in the *Journal of the American College of Cardiology* found that eating these fats post-exercise boosts blood flow by up to 45 per cent.
Per week: 150g x2

STEAK

Each footstrike damages red blood cells, lowering your levels of iron – key to getting oxygen to the working muscles. Heme iron in steak is easily absorbed, says Reid.
Per week: 150g fillet x2

APPLE

It's crunch time. The quercetin found in apples improves lung capacity and protects against pollution, say scientists at the St George's Hospital, London.
Per week: 5

AVOCADO

The sodium, potassium and magnesium in these improve lung volume and oxygen flow, says a study in the *American Journal of Epidemiology*.
Per week: 2

Chapter 4

A PRE-RUN CHOCOLATE MILK BOOSTS MUSCLE REPAIR FOR THREE HOURS

Chuck them in your basket (try not to make a mess)

➕ MAINTAIN MUSCLE

CHOCOLATE MILK

Drinking fat-free chocolate milk before a run promotes muscle repair for up to three hours afterwards, according to the University of Connecticut.
Per week: 330ml x2

SPINACH

The nitric oxide in Popeye's favourite reduces the oxygen needed to power muscles by five per cent, according to the Karolinska Institute in Sweden.
Per week: 300g x2

EGGS

Egg protein is the most balanced food protein after human breast milk, which means it contains all the crucial amino acids your muscles need for recovery, says Price. One egg will deliver 10 per cent of your daily protein needs.
Per week: 3

PORK FILLET

A tasty way to get lean, mean, high-quality protein, says Price. It also contains thiamine, which is key to efficient metabolism of carbohydrate into energy, and to the repair of your muscle fibres.
Per week: 150g x2

POMEGRANATE JUICE

Ellagitannin, a phytonutrient found in pomegranates, reduces inflammation and post-workout soreness, according to research by physiologists at the University of Texas.
Per week: 200ml x3

SWEET POTATO

It's low GI for slow, sustained energy release, and has trace minerals manganese and copper – both crucial for healthy muscle function. Many runners fail to get enough, says Price.
Per week: 3

ALMONDS

These nuts are one of the best sources of alpha-tocopherol vitamin E, which can help prevent the free-radical damage found in muscles after hard efforts.
Per week: handful x7

⊕ GET LEAN

GREEN TEA

EGCG – a compound found in most green teas – speeds up your metabolism so that you burn more calories, says Price. Jasmine tea has the same properties, he adds.
Per week: 4 cups

CAYENNE PEPPER

The capsaicin in chilli peppers can help manage appetite and burn more calories after your meal, say researchers at Purdue University, in the US.
Per week: ½ tsp x 3

LAMB

Have that Sunday roast. Lamb packs carnitine – a mix of amino acids that shuttles fat into the mitochondria (the cells' power-producers), where it's metabolised, explains Price.
Per week: 150g x 2

PINE NUTS

Korean researchers found eating pine kernels prompts your body's release of cholecystokinin – a hormone that suppresses your appetite.
Per week: 3 x 20g

GRAPEFRUIT

Eating grapefruit before meals helped dieters lose up to 4.5kg in 12 weeks in research at Scripps Clinic, San Diego. A compound in the fruit lowers insulin, controlling hunger.
Per week: half x 9

COCONUT OIL

A study in the *Journal of Nutrition* found regular consumption resulted in a rise in metabolism, a higher rate of calorie-burning.
Per week: 1 tbsp x 3

⊕ RUN FASTER

COFFEE

Caffeine before an eight-miler improves times by 24 seconds or more, says the *Journal of Sports Science*.
Per week: 6 cups

WATERMELON

Citrulline in this fruit buffers muscle fatigue, so you can push harder, says a study the University of Córdoba.
Per week: 300g x 3

BEETROOT

St Louis University found you can run five per cent faster after eating beetroot. Nitrates boost blood flow.
Per week: 3

BRAN FLAKES

Betaine in bran helps with hydration, found The College of New Jersey. So you can train harder, for longer.
Per week: 30g x 3

⊕ STAY HEALTHY

MUSHROOMS

The humble button protects your immune system from invaders, say Arizona State University researchers.
Per week: 100g x 3

KALE

The prebiotics in this green are a type of beneficial fibre that helps feed 'good' probiotic gut bacteria, says Reid.
Per week: 150g x 2

CAPERS

US scientists from Appalachian State University found daily doses of quercetin, present in capers, reduced viral infections.
Per week: handful x 2

WALNUTS

Omega-3s in walnuts help reduce cholesterol, found a study in the *Journal of the American College of Nutrition*.
Per week: handful x 3

NUTRITION

PERFECT TIMING

Eating at the right time is almost as important as eating the right thing. So to produce your best running follow this guide to matching your meals to your training

Runners are not average citizens. We are different to the sedentary folk for whom dietary recommendations were created. We need more calories and protein. More carbohydrates. We need more nutrients in general. And runners covet foods that never figure in government recommendations — like carbohydrate and protein drinks and energy gels.

That's why we've designed this food plan, aimed specifically at runners, that, as well as being tasty, will help keep you on the move.

HOW TO GET YOUR TIMINGS RIGHT

Many runners know exactly what they should eat and when they should eat it. It's the practical application of this theory that messes them up. You are either ravenous when you don't want to be (during training) or not hungry when you should be (immediately after training). The problem is when you are planning your run around a busy work schedule, your brain, leg muscles and stomach aren't always in sync.

An early morning run, for example, can leave you feeling fatigued during your working day. A midday training session may become no more than an afterthought if hunger overrides your motivation. And an after-work jaunt may press your dinnertime perilously close to your bedtime.

If you are looking for ways to get back into sync, read on. The following advice will help coordinate your meals with your training schedule, based on the time of day you run.

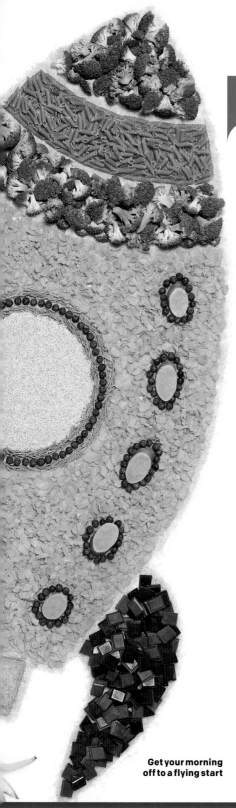

Get your morning off to a flying start

DAWN PATROLLING

To eat, or not to eat? That is the eternal question of those who like to run as the sun is coming up over the horizon. The answer is, if you can, you should fuel up before you set out on your morning run. This performs two important functions. Firstly, your muscles receive an energy supply to help you power through the run. Second, your entire body, especially your brain, receives the fuel and nutrients it needs for optimal functioning.

It shouldn't be a surprise that studies support this and that eating before a run boosts endurance compared with fasting for 12 hours. People who eat before working out rate the exercise as being better yet less rigorous compared with those of non-eaters.

That said, not everyone can eat before a morning run. If you're the type of person who sleeps until the minute before you head out the door, you might not be able to fit in a meal. Also, eating too close to your run may spoil it by causing nausea or cramps. On the other hand, if you're a true early bird, you may eat breakfast, read the paper and wash up before you head out.

Here are some refuelling tips and strategies for all types of morning exercisers:

EARLY RISERS

Choose high-carb foods that are low in fat and moderate in protein. Aim for about 400-800 calories, which will fuel your training without making you feel sluggish. Drink about half a pint of water two hours before your run to offset sweat loss. Try one of these 400-800 calorie pre-run breakfasts:

➡ Two slices of toast, a yoghurt and a piece of fruit.

➡ Cereal with skimmed or semi-skimmed milk and fresh fruit.

➡ A toasted sesame-seed bagel topped with low-fat cheese and a sliced tomato.

LATE SLEEPERS

Most runners will fall into this category: they don't have time to eat and digest a full meal before heading out. If you fall into this camp, experiment to see what you

FUEL UP THE NIGHT BEFORE WITH A BIG DINNER

can stomach before you train. But you could start off by trying:

➡ Have half a pint of any carbohydrate drink.

➡ An energy gel washed down with water.

THE THIRD WAY

If neither of these options sits well with you just before a run, then try fuelling up the night before with a large dinner. As long as you are not planning a long or intense run in the morning, a high-carbohydrate evening meal should still power you right through your pre-breakfast session. Try one of these classics

➡ Macaroni cheese

➡ Bangers and mash

➡ Spaghetti carbonara

➕ RECOVER RIGHT

Whether you're an early bird catching the worm or a late riser rushing out the door, your body needs calories from carbohydrate,

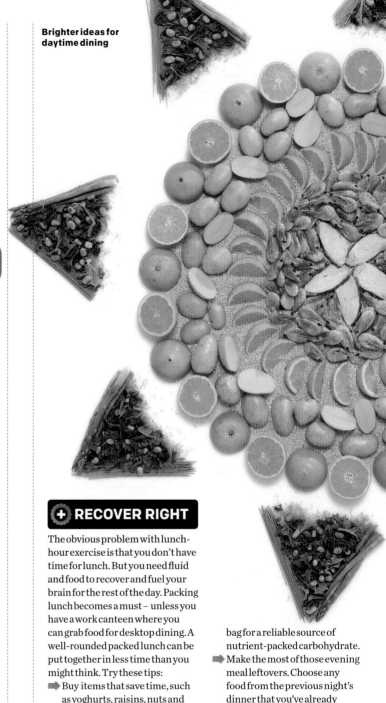

protein and other nutrients after you have finished running. A recovery meal will help fuel your morning at work, preventing post-run fatigue. Eat within an hour of your training and be sure to include both carbs and protein. Some options include:

➡ A fruit smoothie made with a tablespoon of protein powder.
➡ Eggs on whole-wheat toast, juice or fresh fruit.
➡ Leftovers from dinner – pasta, soup, chilli or even vegetarian pizza are proven winners.

THE LUNCHTIME CROWD

People who run during their lunch hours sometimes find hunger gets the better of them. That's because if you ate breakfast at 6am, you've gone about six hours without any food at all. By noon, your fuel from breakfast is long gone and your blood sugar may start to dip, causing tiredness and even dizziness. Rather than increasing the size of your breakfast (which may just leave you feeling sluggish), you should bring a light, pre-run snack to eat while at work.

Eat one to four hours before your run to allow enough time for food to leave your stomach, and consume 100-400 calories, depending upon your body size and how much you had for breakfast. Select foods that are rich in carbohydrate, low in fat and moderately high in nutrients. Try these mid-morning snacks to help keep you on the go:

➡ A breakfast or energy bar with five grams of fat or less.
➡ One slice of wholemeal toast topped with fruit spread.
➡ A 75g serving of dried fruit with a glass of vegetable juice.
➡ One packet of instant porridge made with skimmed or semi-skimmed milk.

Brighter ideas for daytime dining

⊕ RECOVER RIGHT

The obvious problem with lunch-hour exercise is that you don't have time for lunch. But you need fluid and food to recover and fuel your brain for the rest of the day. Packing lunch becomes a must – unless you have a work canteen where you can grab food for desktop dining. A well-rounded packed lunch can be put together in less time than you might think. Try these tips:

➡ Buy items that save time, such as yoghurts, raisins, nuts and health bars.
➡ Always add fruit. Toss one or two pieces of fruit in your lunch bag for a reliable source of nutrient-packed carbohydrate.
➡ Make the most of those evening meal leftovers. Choose any food from the previous night's dinner that you've already packed in a sealed container ready for you to transport and reheat whenever you like.

YOU NEED FLUID AND FOOD TO HELP RECOVER AND FUEL YOUR BRAIN

+ SERVING SENSE

When we recommend 8-15 daily servings of high-carbohydrate food and at least one portion of all the other foods listed here. You don't have to gorge yourself: a serving in each of the food groups isn't as hefty as most people think (or hope). Here are a few examples:

+ Complex carbs 100g of cooked pasta, beans, couscous or other grains (about the size of a computer mouse); one slice of bread; 25g of healthy cereal.

+ Vegetables 200g of raw leafy vegetables (about the size of a cricket ball).

+ Fruit One medium piece of fruit (about the size of a tennis ball); 250ml of juice; 100g of chopped or mixed fruit.

+ Calcium One pint of milk; 200g of yoghurt; two slices of cheese.

+ Protein 200g of soybeans; 50-75g of fish or lean meat (about the size of a deck of cards); two medium eggs.

+ Healthy foods 25g of nuts (about 20 almonds); an eighth of an avocado; two teaspoons of olive oil.

BETTER LATE THAN NEVER

After a stressful day at the office, there's nothing quite like a run to burn off some of the tension. The problem is you don't always feel like heading out the door if you're hungry or just exhausted. If you do manage to run, sometimes you will return home feeling so ravenous that you end up gorging yourself on anything in sight as you make your evening meal. Then you might eat your dinner as late as 9pm and end up going to bed with a full stomach.

The main rule to stick to if you are going for an evening run is to eat healthily during the day to avoid any intestinal upset that might thwart your training plans. Also eat often and enough that you're adequately fuelled for your session to avoid the "I'm too hungry" excuse..

Evening exercisers may also want to keep the following in mind:

➡ Never skip breakfast. Try to eat at least 500 calories for your morning meal. For example, throw together a fruit smoothie made with yoghurt, fruit and juice while you are preparing your toast. Or try cereal topped with nuts, skimmed milk and a piece of fruit.

➡ Make lunch your main meal of the day. Focus on high-quality protein, such as fish, tofu, lean beef or lamb, chicken or bread with cooked grain, along with fresh fruit. A smoothie, juice or natural yoghurt drink are also great, healthy lunch foods.

➡ Always eat a mid-afternoon snack. Around three hours before your run, have some fruit or an energy bar together with half a pint of water.

+ RECOVER RIGHT

Eating the right stuff after an evening run can be tricky. You need to replace lost sugars, but you don't want to overload on carbs so much that they get turned to fat while you sleep. Follow these tips to make your supper super:

➡ Eat moderately at dinner. Some people worry about eating too close to bedtime because they

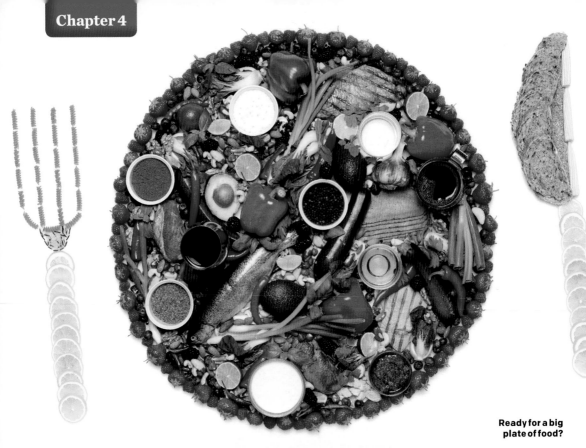

Ready for a big plate of food?

fear the calories will go straight to their fat cells. That's simply not true. Your body will actually use those calories to stockpile fuel in your muscles. On the other hand, if you eat more calories than your body burns off – no matter what time of day or night – your body will store the excess as fat. The key is not to eat more calories than you've used in your workout.

➡ Drink more fluids when possible. Grab a drink as soon as you step back through the door after your run. And keep drinking as you prepare your meal (no, not red wine). This helps replace sweat loss and may prevent you trying to eat all the contents of your kitchen cupboards in one big go.

➡ Don't eat anything an hour before bed to avoid indigestion that can interfere with sleep.

✚ IN SUMMARY...

The golden rules of tailoring your nutrition to your workout plan

✚ If you run in the morning, try to eat at least an hour before you begin. If you don't have time experiment with carb drinks and energy gels. Or eat a large meal the night before.

✚ If you run at lunch, have a mid-morning snack and pack your own lunch to eat afterwards at your desk.

✚ If you run in the evening, eat well during the day to prevent post-work slothing. Make lunch your main meal and eat healthy snacks.

✚ Eating junk food occasionally is not the end of the world. If it's not out of control, don't beat yourself up. Enjoy the rare indulgence

REFUELLING ON THE GO

Sometimes you need more than just food beforehand. If your runs last longer than an hour use energy bars, gels or drinks to refuel during your run. Because these foods contain easily digestible carbs, they make great

pre- and post-run snacks as well. Consume about 30-60g of carbs during each hour of running (most bars contain 30g or more of carbs; most gels contain about 25g). Simple foods such as jelly babies, fig rolls, dried fruit and honey can also supply fast, easily digestible carbohydrate while also being a motivational sweet treat.

PHOTOGRAPHY JOHANNA PARKIN

running as it should be

bournemouth marath$_2$on festival

5/6 october 2013

guaranteed places
www.run-bmf.com

a brand new running festival

full marathon
half marathon
supersonic 10k
speed of light 5k
junior 3k and 1.5k

THE POWER OF WATER

Staying hydrated is crucial to your performance. Here we take a look at how to do that... and also at how to sometimes you can get too much of a good thing

As he passed his family on Tower Bridge during the 2007 London Marathon, 22-year-old David Rogers did a star jump. "He saw us and waved, and then leapt in the air," said his father, Chris. "He was doing what he wanted to do."

Tragically, just hours after completing the race, David died in a London hospital, having collapsed once he'd crossed the finish line. What was the cause? Hyponatraemia, following kidney failure due to sodium deficiency, which is caused by excess fluid consumption.

We live in a water-obsessed society. Water bottles have replaced orange segments as the half-time refreshment at football and rugby matches; water coolers are as pervasive as tea bags in office kitchens, and schools increasingly encourage you to send your child to school with their own drink bottle. Why? At least in part because every fitness article in every newspaper and magazine insists you absolutely, positively must drink eight big glasses, or two litres, of water a day.

But where's the proof? Amazingly, there isn't any. Even in marathons, the available evidence indicates overhydrating is as potentially dangerous as underhydrating, with David Rogers' story serving as an unfortunate exclamation mark. Yes, we runners need to drink generously – no one questions that – but we need to drink with a fuller understanding of the facts, the medical science and the potential risks.

WATER, WATER EVERYWHERE

Water is by far the largest constituent of the human body, making up about 60 per cent of total body weight. This large pool of water performs many crucial functions, including nourishing the cells, carrying food throughout the body, eliminating waste, regulating body temperature, cushioning and lubricating the joints, and maintaining blood volume and blood pressure. Inadequate levels of fluid consumption have been associated with kidney stones and higher rates of urinary tract infections, bladder and colorectal cancers, and even heart disease.

Given this information, all experts agree that an adequate water supply is crucial to the body's optimal functioning. But how much is "adequate"?

THE TWO-LITRE MYTH

Most adults – at least those who read the health pages of magazines or newspapers – have come to believe that they should drink two litres of water a day, but there's little to no evidence supporting this particular rule.

Heinz Valtin, the Professor Emeritus of Physiology at Dartmouth Medical School, USA, committed himself to searching out medical-scientific verification for this theory. He couldn't locate any. "I have found no scientific proof that we must drink two litres of water a day," concluded Valtin. "The published data strongly suggest that we probably are drinking enough, and possibly even more than enough."

Ron Maughan, Visiting External Professor of Loughborough University and the foremost researcher on hydration in the UK, agrees. "You hear this advice from magazines, but where is it actually coming from? Not the Department of Health."

Tim Lawson, director of Science In Sport, a UK-based sports nutrition company, believes the two-litre rule might only apply if "you were eating dehydrated food". He says the figure is misquoted because it fails to take into account the moisture content from food (especially fruit and vegetables) and the fluid intake from other drinks.

Of course, Valtin was researching the hydration habits of non-exercising people. Runners sweat heavily and need to drink more than non-exercisers, and the heavier and more muscular you

OUR DAILY DRINKING REQUIREMENT

The old rule – everyone needs two litres of water – is out. It's been replaced by formulas based on gender and bodyweight. Here are they are (assuming moderate activity):

Male Daily Drinking Requirement
Bodyweight (lbs) x 10.36
Female Daily Drinking Requirement
Bodyweight (lbs) x 9.176

Example A 132lb women needs to drink 1,211ml of water a day: 132 x 9.176 = 1,211. She'll get the rest of her daily water supply from food and metabolic processes. Runners need to drink extra to cover daily sweat losses.

are, the hotter the weather and the faster you run, the more you sweat.

THE TRUTH ABOUT CAFFEINE

Meanwhile, a survey of 2,818 adults by the American-based International Bottled Water Association (IBWA) revealed an average adult drinks 4.5 litres of fluid a day. The IBWA argues that 1.5 litres of this amount is alcohol and caffeine drinks (both considered diuretics, meaning they increase urine production), and should be subtracted from the total intake.

However, subsequent research has reversed the age-old wisdom that caffeinated beverages are diuretics. Actually, to be more precise, the research confirmed that caffeinated beverages are diuretics but only to the same degree as plain water. If you drink a lot of water, you need to go to the toilet. It's the same with caffeinated beverages – no more, and no less.

"The research indicates caffeine stimulates a mild diuresis similar to water," says heat and hydration expert Larry Armstrong. Maughan who also reviewed the literature to find a diuretic effect occurred only when high caffeine doses of over 300mg were given to research subjects whose caffeine intake had been restricted for a few days prior to the test. He also noted the same myths surround alcohol – especially beer – which isn't, he claims, that much of a diuretic.

BEATING A PATH TO THE BATHROOM

If anything, truth be told, we're overhydrated. This isn't necessarily a bad thing. It's probably just adding to your daily mileage and calorie burn, with all those trips to the bathroom, but there's little evidence for dehydration ills – fatigue,

THE OLD FORMULA – EVERYONE NEEDS TWO LITRES OF WATER A DAY – IS OUT

headache, dry skin, lack of concentration and so on – put forth by some.

"Without any convincing data, I remain sceptical of all these so-called dehydration problems," says researcher Barbara Rolls, author of Thirst, and a leading expert on hydration. "It's a myth that's being perpetuated. The thirst mechanism is exquisitely tuned to keep us in fluid balance."

Maughan confirms the view that thirst is a useful mechanism, maintaining that it is simply a learned behaviour. Unlike children, who demand a drink as soon as they feel like it, but then only have a sip and are unable to finish the drink, adults learn to restrain the immediate impulse to take a drink.

A MATTER OF SEX

When it comes to sweat rates and fluid-replacement needs, men and women come from different planets. Because men are, on average, significantly heavier than women and have more muscle mass, they sweat more than women and need to drink more.

Women, meanwhile, have a smaller blood plasma "tank" than men, which is easier to overfill. Many women who are new to marathons are happy to finish in five hours or more. They reach the

16 THE THREE QUARTER RULE

Three-quarters of your dish should really only contain fresh produce and grains, with the last quarter saved for either fish, meat or chicken. This combination will supply longer-lasting energy and fuel for many hours.

17 KICK OUT THE JAM

Fruit is always very good for you, so the best yoghurt must surely be the kind with a big dollop of fruit hiding in the bottom or in its own compartment ready to mix in, right? Not necessarily. For the most nutritious yoghurt, skip the "fruit on the bottom" varieties. The fruit will be mostly jam, which packs the equivalent of eight or nine teaspoons of sugar per pot – nearly as much as a can of fizzy drink does. Instead, choose plain low-fat yoghurt and add your own berries. Fresh berries also provide a healthy dose of fibre.

18 MAKE IT AN ORANGE

Any fruit is good, but oranges are the king. They offer a massive dose of immune-system boosting vitamin C – over 130 per cent of the RDA. They also contain a good helping of potassium, folic acid and pectin, a fibre that helps balance blood sugar levels and keep hunger at bay. If that's not enough, there's a big bunch of cancer- and heart-disease-risk-reducing flavanoids.

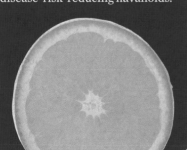

19 SHAKE IT, DON'T BAKE IT

To cut back on salt, don't add it to food during cooking. Instead shake it on when the plate reaches the table. Research shows people given totally unsalted food – but a free hand with the shaker – put in one fifth of the amount originally called for in the recipe.

20 BUY THE BERRY BEST

Before you buy strawberries or raspberries, turn the carton over. You're looking for nature's expiry date: juice stains. If you've already bought berries that are going soft, place a single layer of them on a baking sheet and freeze for 20 minutes before you scoff them down.

21 GET SOME LUCKY DIPS

Instead of buying those fatty no good for you sour cream-based dips to drag your salty nibbles through, think black-bean dip or go Middle Eastern and buy some hummus. It's made from chickpeas, which are naturally high in fibre, and it goes great with many a raw vegetables like celery and carrots.

22 MAKE COURGETTE CHIPS

Do you fancy a portion of chips with your meal or on their own? Then ditch the fatty potato variety and try the courgette variety instead. Simply slice two courgettes, sauté in half a teaspoon of oil in a large pan over a medium to high heat until they are lightly browned. Sprinkle with basil to taste. Try not to drown in salt and vinegar

23 BECOME A BREADWINNER

While in the bread aisle, you may be tempted to grab a loaf of something brown – it must be higher in fibre than the white stuff, right? Well, no – that dark complexion may be courtesy of food dyes. Look for "100 per cent whole wheat or whole grain."

24 TAKE POT LUCK

A pot of low-fat yoghurt provides half the recommended daily allowance of calcium, and as studies have shown the dietary calcium intakes of athletes with bone injuries such as stress fractures are abnormally low, you should eat more yoghurt. You don't have to just spoon it from the pot, though. Why not add it to your favourite low-sugar cereal; or use plain yoghurt instead of sour cream on top of that big baked potatoes.

25 RAISIN THE BAR

Sprinkle raisins into yoghurt, on your cereal or just snack on them throughout the day, as they are a fantastic energy snack. Four tablespoons of raisins contain 79g of carbohydrates, 302 calories, as well as potassium, iron and phytochemicals. And they're virtually fat-free, too.

NUTRITION

26 ENJOY YOUR CHOCOLATE

Obviously, scoffing 10 Mars Bars every day might lead to weight gain, but every now and then a chunk of chocolate is quite a healthy treat. Chocolate, especially the darkest varieties, contains the same phytochemicals found in red wine that have been shown to fight heart disease.

27 GO BETA BY MILES

It's long been known that the beta-carotene found in carrots protects against diseases such as cancer and can protect against muscle damage and soreness, but this antioxidant can also make you faster. In one US study, 5K runners were given the equivalent of five carrots' worth of beta-carotene a day. At the end of the 30 days, the runners ran on average 30 seconds quicker than before. If you don't fancy becoming Bugs Bunny, other good sources of beta-carotene include peaches, apricots, and red and yellow peppers.

28 HALVE YOUR BEEF AND EAT IT

Here's a way to make meaty dishes with a good deal less fat: start with extra-lean minced beef. Crumble your meat and brown it in a frying pan. Next, dump the browned beef on to a dish covered with a double thickness of kitchen paper. Place another paper towel over the meat and blot up the grease. To remove even more fat, put the beef into a strainer and rinse it with hot water. Squeeze out the water and add the meat to your sauce. Blotting and rinsing cuts 50 per cent of the fat from your beef.

29 GET THE MISSING ZINC

Another way to keep your bones healthy is to load up with zinc. This mineral helps manufacture healthy bone and cartilage cells. We need about 15mg a day and the easiest places to get it are from red meat and zinc supplements. Or you could be really fancy and start necking oysters. As well as – allegedly – doing wonders for your love life, these little shellfish are mega zinc-givers – down five and you'll consume 41mg of the mineral for a healthy boost.

30 SAY HI TO HONEY

You'd think something that tasted as good as honey would have to be bad for you. Nope. Honey is a mixture of glucose and fructose, so it's great for a quick energy boost. Pure honey also contains a huge range of vitamins such as B6, thiamine, riboflavin and patothenic acid, as well as calcium, copper, manganese, phosphorous potassium, sodium and zinc. It also containst amino acids and antioxidants.

31 CRUNCH BUNCH

Between meals snack on crunchy foods to wake up your mouth and your mind. Fresh vegetables such as radishes, broccoli and cauliflower dunked in a spicy dip – such as chilli, lime and low-fat yoghurt – will stop you flagging at your desk mid-morning.

32 CHEERS FOR TEARS

Chopping those onions at dinner time might make you cry like a baby, but they'll also stop your nose from weeping as well. Along with other vegetables from the allium family (such as garlic or leeks), onions contain quercetin, an antioxidant that smothers invading bacteria. So if you want to avoid the sniffles and aid recovery when you catch a cold, add onions to everything that you can think of.

33 PUT A LID ON IT

An easy cooking tip to give a helping hand to your health; reduce the amount of oil that you may need to pan-fry your foods by simply keeping the lid on the wok. The lid will catch and returns the moisture back to your food, preventing the need for more oil in your meal.

34 PACK TWO LUNCHES

We tend to feel hungry every four hours, but most of us don't eat to that timetable. Instead, we scrimp with breakfast and go easy on lunch before stuffing our faces in the evening. Instead, eat two 600-calorie "lunches" a day. Have one at 12pm and then 4pm and you'll boost your energy and "ruin" your appetite so that you don't stuff yourself with an unnecessarily large meal later on in the evening.

Beer: your perfect training partner?

37 MAKE YOURS A PINT

Don't get carried away with this one, but drinking one beer a day has been associated with a 40 per cent lower risk of developing kidney stones. One explanation put forward is that the hops contained within beer help prevent calcium leaching out of your bones and moving to your kidneys. Just make sure to stick only to a pint and not a yard of ale.

38 DO SOME PORRIDGE

A true wonder to have at breakfast, not only is porridge a great source of carbohydrates – it's also a great weapon in the battle of the bulge. It contains a high amount of water-soluble fibre so it keeps you full for longer – hence the old saying "it sticks to your ribs". Oats also help lower blood cholesterol.

39 TAKE YOUR TIME

After a run, it's easy to stuff food down without it touching the sides. By not rushing your meals, though, you'll actually lose weight. US researchers found people who extended their meal times by four minutes, simply by chewing more slowly and enjoying the taste of their food, burnt more body fat than those who wolf it straight down.

40 MELLOW YELLOW

Bananas are chock full of vitamin B6, which helps boost your body's production of the feel-good chemical serotonin. This helps elevate mood, giving you a calm, positive feeling. Slice a banana over your morning bowl of cereal or eat one as a mid-morning snack

35 GUZZLE GRAPE JUICE

The best health drink for people with heart trouble is a glass of purple grape juice – stay away from the white stuff because of its higher sugar content – after a daily aspirin. The aspirin protects your heart by preventing bloodclots, but this effect can be blocked by the adrenalin that exercise and stress produce. The flavonoids found in grape juice may stymie that response.

36 TEA'S UP

There is always time for a brew during the day and making yourself a cuppa doesn't just provide you with those vital fluids, it also helps protect against a number of age-related ailments. Tea, especially the healthier black and green varieties, contains catechins and flavanols, phytochemicals that fight the free radicals that can lead to illnesses such as cancer, Parkinson's disease and osteoporosis.

FUELLING YOUR FIRE

Run out of gas during a long run and you will crash to the Tarmac. The perfect nutrition strategy of personal mobile pit stops will have you clocking faster times and feeling stronger

You've been running for months. You've spent more early mornings in trainers than you have tucked up in bed; you've done short runs, long runs, quick ones and slow ones, all of them at paces ranging from "race" to "rather not actually, thanks". You've burnt through three pairs of shoes and set new personal bests along the way. You may be planning to enter a race, or simply to run faster for your own entertainment.

But despite all the hours of hard work, you won't reach that finish line or see the time you were hoping for on your watch if you're not prepared to provide your body with the fuel it needs along the way. A good nutrition strategy is as important to your success as registering for a race on time or doing up your laces. The time to start forming your mid-run habits is a long time before you're limbering up on the start line. It should start a few weeks into your schedule of marathon preparation — and should become a habit for all long runs.

WALL TO FALL

Regardless of whether it's a gel, a drink, a bar or even just sweets that you're knocking back on the move, you're doing it for one very visceral reason — the wall. The wall is what distance runners hit, traditionally somewhere after 18 miles. They feel light-headed and utterly without energy. In short, they would much prefer to just potter off home for a lie down than carry on going.

Is this you? And, if so, what happened? How could collapsing into a sofa or a bath become a viable alternative to strong running? When your body senses that

The right bar can give you a bolt of energy

A GOOD NUTRITIONAL STRATEGY IS AS IMPORTANT AS REGISTERING FOR A RACE ON TIME OR DOING UP YOUR LACES

your easily accessible reserves of carbohydrate energy have fallen to 40 or 50 per cent, it starts to use its fat as a source of fuel. It simply cannot let your blood sugar reserves empty completely, because your brain relies on them.

The trouble is that fat can't be turned into energy nearly as fast as blood sugar can, so your body becomes forced to either slow down or increase its effort dramatically to maintain the same speed. In both cases, you'll find yourself breathing more heavily, because fat conversion requires more oxygen.

"When running you burn through your main source of stored

energy — glycogen — very quickly, and the faster you go the more quickly you burn it," says coach Nick Anderson. "With shorter distances, 5-10km say, you need to remain hydrated for optimal performance, but you haven't got to worry about depleting your carbohydrate stores completely.

"However, once you're out there for longer than 90 minutes you can expect to see a depletion of those glycogen stores. You will slow down dramatically and hit what is known as the wall."

So, very simply put, if your body runs out of glycogen, it has no fuel left and to keep running it has to resort to its only other fuel source — stored fats. Processing stored fats requires a lot more oxygen, so you slow down to a jog or even a walk so that less of the oxygen you breathe in goes to your muscles and more is available to break down the energy. From the wall onwards it's a mental battle to the end of your run.

You don't want to hit the wall. It's not a clever name — walls hurt and this one will, too. Fortunately, with the right nutrition you don't have to experience the full horror of the face-brick interface. In fact,

Defuse the fat time bomb in your favourite foods

MACARONI CHEESE

1 GETTING STARTED

Runners have long relied on pasta's carbs to replenish glycogen stores – but, made from refined white wheat flour, white pasta has had its fibre and much of the nutrient-packed original grain removed. So use **wholewheat pasta**, which is loaded with fibre, B vitamins for energy metabolism, and disease-fighting phytochemicals.

2 PREPARE

Slash the fat and saturated fat content of the sauce by using **semi-skimmed milk** and **reduced fat cheddar**. Adding **fat-free Greek yoghurt** and deliver a calcium boost for your bones. Heat on the hob until it thickens, adding a tablespoon and a half of flour plus a spoonful of dijon mustard for extra flavour.

3 FINISH WITH

Combine the cooked pasta and sauce, and toss in a few handfuls of cooked **broccoli** and **red peppers** for a hefty dose of antioxidants, including vitamin C which assists in the creation of collagen to fortify bones, tendons and ligaments. Pour the lot into a heatproof dish. Cut fat and add extra flavour and texture by topping with a mix of **breadcrumbs** and **parmesan** instead of more cheddar. Place the dish under a grill until the top is browned.

BANGERS & MASH

1 GETTING STARTED

"Grill your bangers but swap the traditional pork for lean and highly flavoursome **venison sausages**," says nutritionist Rachel Love (bodyoptimum.co.uk). "Game meats contain omega-3 fatty acids, which diminish the production of prostaglandins – hormone-like substances associated with inflammation in the body."

2 PREPARE

Boil up some **cauliflower** and diced **sweet potato**. Both provide slow-releasing carbs for sustained energy, and are good sources of potassium – an essential electrolyte for muscle recovery. They also provide a potent blend of antioxidants, says Love. The cauliflower is rich in vitamin C, which aids the absorption of the fatigue-fighting iron found in sweet potato. Mash the veg up with a tablespoon of extra virgin olive oil, which contains oleocanthal, a natural anti-inflammatory that helps ease muscle soreness.

3 FINISH WITH

Slice up a few **leeks** and fry them in half a tablespoon of olive oil until golden brown. These green nutritional giants provide allicin, an antibiotic that may help reduce your cholesterolm level. Use these to top your upgraded bangers and mash.

CHILLI CON CARNE

1 GETTING STARTED

"Use **brown rice** as it retains many of the vitamins, minerals and proteins stripped from white rice," says Love. It's rich in magnesium and iron — needed to keep energy levels high — and Harvard scientists also found that two servings of brown rice a week cuts your risk of type 2 diabetes by 10 per cent.

2 PREPARE

Boost the performance-enhancing qualities of this favourite by switching beef for **turkey mince**, says Love. Turkey contains more muscle-building protein than beef – and less unhealthy saturated fat. 'It's also a good source of tryptophan – the precursor to melatonin, the hormone responsible for a healthy sleep-wake cycle, promoting recovery,' says Love. Brown in a pan with onions and garlic – a potent anti-inflammatory and antioxidant combo, says Love. Drain off excess fat.

3 FINISH WITH

"Add a **tin of chopped tomatoes**, plus **peppers** and **kidney beans**," says Love. "This ensures a broad spectrum of vitamins and minerals." Add mixed herbs, a teaspoon of **chilli powder**, half a teaspoon of **cumin**, and half a teaspoon of **turmeric**. Season and cook for 20 minutes, gently stirring occasionally.

PIZZA

① GETTING STARTED
"Using a halved **pitta bread** as a pizza base controls the portion size of your meal," says nutritionist Kim Pearson (kim-pearson.co.uk). Opt for wholemeal rather than white, she adds. "This lowers the glycaemic index [GI] of your meal to provide you with sustained energy release, keeping you fuelled for longer"

② PREPARE
"'Combine low-sugar tomato sauce with **green, yellow and red peppers** to provide a boost of antioxidants that can help combat post-exercise free radical damage,' says Pearson. Adding some sliced onions will notch up extra fibre and some immune-boosting allicin. Then throw on some mushrooms: in a US study at Johns Hopkins University participants who swapped beef for the fungi consumed 400kcal less, and felt just as sated as when they ate meaty meals.

③ FINISH WITH
Satisfy that cheese craving by adding strips of fresh **mozzarella**, which is lower in fat than hard cheeses. Finally throw on some sliced chicken breast to deliver more muscle-building protein. Research has shown that runners require 50-75 per cent more protein than non-runners to help rebuild muscles. Bake for 10 minutes at 200°C.

FISH & CHIPS

① GETTING STARTED
For maximum nutritional benefits, swap cod for pan-seared **salmon**, says Pearson. "It's packed with high-quality protein and one omega-3 fats to help muscle recovery." Crisp up your fillets in a pan with **olive oil** and **oregano**, which has up to 20 times more antioxidants than other herbs.

② PREPARE
Ditch traditional fatty fried chips in favour of **sweet potato wedges**, oven cooked in a splash of olive oil, advises Pearson. Sweet potatoes have a lower GI and are a great source of beta carotene – which a study published in *Medicine & Science in Sport & Exercise* linked to improved performance in runners. Sweet potatoes also contain minerals crucial for healthy muscle function, which many runners may be deficient in.

③ FINISH WITH
Instead of sugar-loaded mushy peas, cook up some **petit pois** and crush them with a dash of olive oil. For more flavour and an added health kick, throw in some roughly chopped mint. The compounds released by it 'stimulate biliary secretions, aiding your body's digestion of fats', says Pearson. Considerably better than your usual Saturday-evening trip to The Codfather...

FRUIT CRUMBLE

① GETTING STARTED
Start with **blueberries**, **blackberries** and **raspberries**, which are packed with muscle-repairing anthocyanins. Add dried apricots, peaches and figs to boost iron, calcium and fibre. "Add a couple of tablespoons of **pure fruit juice** to sweeten up the mix," says Porter. Pour into a oven dish.

② PREPARE
"For a low GI topping, blend equal quantities of oats and wholemeal flour,' says Porter. Mix in crushed **hazelnuts** for fibre, vitamin E, plus potassium, calcium and magnesium, all of which can help lower blood pressure. Studies at Loma Linda University, US, have shown that eating nuts a few times a week lowers artery-clogging LDL cholesterol by 7.4 per cent, cutting your heart-disease risk. Top the fruit with the crumble and bake.

③ FINISH WITH
Making custard puts you in nutritional control, says Porter. "Heat up **skimmed milk** with a splash of **vanilla essence**. For a smooth texture, add some **low-fat yoghurt**. It's a good source of protein and calcium, and the healthy bacteria your digestive tract needs to function optimally." Heat, stirring until you get a custardy consistency, pour over the crumble. Enjoy.

Chapter

5

WEIGHT LOSS

Here are the fastest, scientifically proven ways
to burn calories and reduce your waistline

132 | **49 GREATEST WEIGHT-LOSS TIPS**
Quick ways to supercharge your fat burning

138 | **LOSE 10LB IN A MONTH**
A complete diet and exercise plan

142 | **RUN IT OFF**
Slim down by speeding up

144 | **PSYCH OUT FAT**
Expand your mind to reduce your waist

PHOTOGRAPHY MITCH MANDEL

49 TOP FAT-BURNING TIPS

Need to shift a few pounds? It's not all about doing mega mileage.
Make these easy changes to your diet – and watch the fat fall off

1 SWAP YOUR REGULAR CHEESE FOR GOAT'S CHEESE

It's 40 per cent lower in calories than the stuff made from cow's milk.

2 SPRINKLE ON SOME CINNAMON

Try it on your coffee in the morning. The spice is a powerful metabolism raiser; half a teaspoon a day is enough to burn an extra kilo a month.

3 SIP GREEN TEA

It contains a compound that reacts with caffeine to boost both fat oxidisation and resting metabolic rate by 20 per cent.

4 EAT BEANS

Try the cannellini, haricot or kidney varieties. People who add them to each meal are 22 per cent less likely to become obese.

5 IF IT DIDN'T GROW, WALK OR SWIM, DON'T EAT IT

Processed foods are loaded with harmful trans-fats and artificial sweeteners that play havoc with your metabolic system.

6 PUT SOME TOMATOES IN YOUR SANDWICH

They keep you feeling fuller for longer, and will make you less likely to gorge on mid afternoon snacks. The fruit suppresses the hunger hormone ghrelin, which is responsible for hunger pangs.

7 GRAB A HANDFUL OF PEANUTS A DAY

These will provide you with heart-healthy folates and fibre, plus a higher satiety level than other foods to stop you grazing.

8 SLICE YOUR FOOD

You'll eat 20 per cent fewer calories. People rate sliced servings as 27 per cent larger than

9 DRINK MILK

Calcium prevents the storage of fat at a cellular level.

10 ADD CHILLI SAUCE TO YOUR MEALS

The fiery pepper will add a big kick to the dish, rev up your metabolism and help to process fats more efficiently.

11 EAT THREE 250KCAL PROTEIN-RICH SNACKS A DAY

Those who followed this simple tip were 30 per cent more likely to lose weight than those who didn't.

12 DRINK SOME GRAPEFRUIT JUICE

One study showed that if you have this for breakfast every day you'll lose four and a half pounds in 12 weeks thanks to its insulin-lowering enzymes.

13 ADD LENTILS TO EACH MEAL

You'll lose over 15lb in 10 weeks. These pulses are packed with the fat-burning amino acid leucine.

14 EAT SOME POMEGRANATES

Their seed oil reduces the body's ability to store fat and they're so sweet they'll curb your desire for sugary snacks.

15 EAT MORE BERRIES

When aiming to eat more fruit it's worth being clever about what you pick. Most berries make a great choice. Other fruits contain lots of fructose, which can combine with carbohydrates to add body fat.

16 EAT HIGH-FIBRE, LOW-STARCH CARBOHYDRATES

Try raw nuts, quinoa, barley and oats. These will regulate your insulin levels and reduce hunger pangs throughout the day.

17 EAT SOME CHILLI CON CARNE

An enzyme in kidney beans tells the body to break down stored fat instead of carbs for energy, while the minced beef helps to boost your metabolism.

18 ADD SOME CHOPPED SPRING ONIONS TO YOUR POST-RUN MEAL

They help you metabolise carbs for fuel, plus they're full of fibre and calcium, which aids weight loss.

19 LEAVE A MAXIMUM OF THREE HOURS BETWEEN MEALS

This will ensure your metabolic rate doesn't fluctuate.

20 EAT BREAKFAST EVERY DAY

Those who fail to kick-start their metabolism with a meal in the morning eat 100 more calories during the course of the day.

21 EAT GOOD FATS TO BURN FAT

Eggs, avocado, olive oil and the dark meat of chicken are all good for your body and have also been shown to help cut your the risk of heart disease.

22 SCOFF EGGS FOR BREAKFAST

They contain low-calorie protein, which is perfect for weight-loss, plus they will keep you feeling full all morning.

23 DON'T OVERDO SPORTS DRINKS

These can contain high-GI carbs, which can increase body fat. For runs of less than one hour, drink water instead.

26 DRINK SOME OOLONG TEA

Scientists at the University of Tokushima, Japan, discovered this will increase your fat burning by as much as 12 per cent.

27 EAT PINEAPPLE

Not only is it a great snack to spark your metabolism, but it also contains the enzyme bromelain, which helps to break down protein, essential for muscle recovery.

28 DRINK JUICE THAT HAS BITS IN IT

The fibre is processed at a slower rate, staving off hunger.

29 HAVE A DAILY GLASS OF WINE

The red kind in particular can stop you putting on weight around your belly. The antioxidant resveratrol, found in the grapes, inhibits the development of fat cells around your waistline.

30 ADD PAPRIKA TO YOUR MEALS

The mild ground red peppers have been found to contain nearly six times the vitamin C found in tomatoes, which is crucial for enabling your body to convert fat into energy.

31 SIT DOWN AT THE TABLE TO EAT

Studies have shonw that you will consume a third less than when you're munching on the move.

32 SPLASH ON LOW-SALT SOY SAUCE

Research shows that soy proteins interact with the receptors in our brains that tell us we're full. The low-salt variety means you can sidestep any health downsides.

33 MAKE A SMOOTHIE FOR BREAKFAST

If you can't face much to eat when you first wake up try this recipe. Blend 200g strawberries, 125ml soya milk and two teaspoons of vanilla extract for a belly-banishing drink.

34 DRIZZLE OLIVE OIL ON SALADS

Its packed full of good fatty acids that trigger the release of a hormone that tells the body it's full.

35 WAIT BEFORE HAVING SECONDS

Diving in for a second portion because you still feel hungry is a mistake. It takes 20 minutes for your stomach to send the message to your brain that it's full.

24 EAT POPCORN

The cinema favourite will help to lower your blood glucose levels, which in turn switches your body into fat-burning mode fat. Just make sure it's plain, air-popped, not sweet or buttered.

25 DRINK A GLASS OF CARROT JUICE

Just one a day will help you lose four pounds in 12 weeks compared with non-juice drinkers. It's high in fibre and nutrients that help burn the blubber.

WEIGHT LOSS

36 EAT AN APPLE

Eat it 15 minutes before a meal and you'll consume around 180 fewer calories in total.

37 EAT THE PERFECT PROTEIN RATIO

To get your ideal body fat percentage eat three grams of protein per five pounds of body weight every day; only 20-30 per cent of your total calorie intake should come from fat.

38 GO FOR VINEGAR-BASED DRESSINGS

These contain acetic acid, which has been shown to speed up the rate at which your body burns fat. Add a few glugs to all your salads and sauces.

39 DILUTE THE MILK IN YOUR CEREAL

A splash of water will help to reduce the absorption of sugar and decrease fat intake.

40 EAT RED PEPPERS

They contain capsaicin, the chemical that gives them their taste and which boosts your resting metabolic rate by up to 25 per cent.

41 MAKE A BLACK BEAN SALAD

Add to the beans peppers, tomatoes, onion and sweet corn with an olive oil and lemon dressing for an ideal weight loss meal. The combination of fibre, hunger suppressants and fat-burning chemicals will shed pounds.

42 EAT A PORTION OF DAIRY EVERY DAY

Research has found that doubling calcium intake increases fat metabolism by 50 per cent.

43 INVEST IN A GRAVY SEPARATOR

It removes fat from homemade gravy, so you can pour a skimmed version over your Sunday roast.

Fire up your fat burning

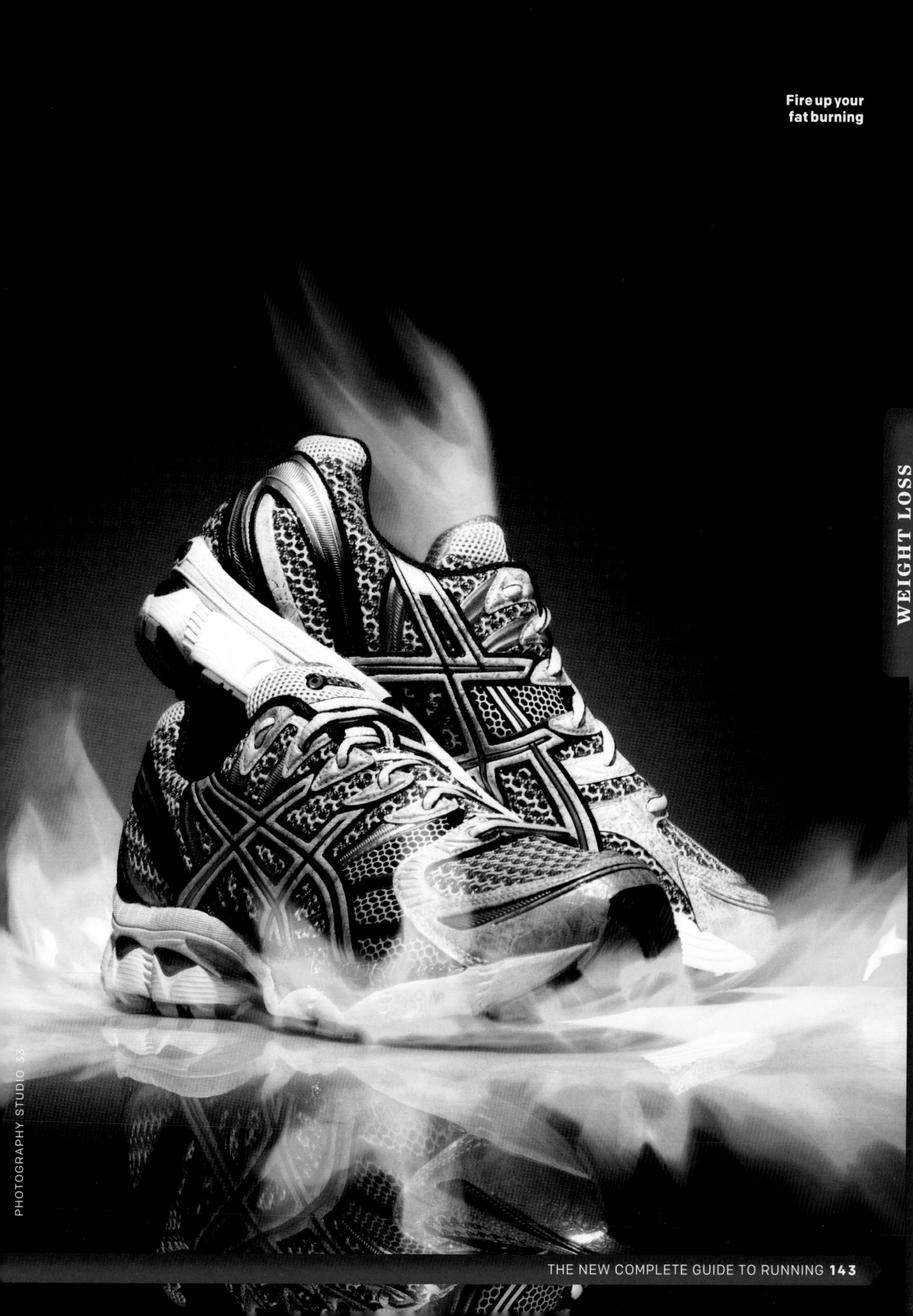

WEIGHT LOSS

PHOTOGRAPHY STUDIO 33

PSYCH OUT FAT

If losing weight is one of your primary reasons for taking up running, you'll want to brush up on the latest scientific breakthroughs for burning fat fast

THINK THIN

Why? Several studies have shown that visualising the results that you want can actually help you achieve them. In research at Harvard University, US, housekeeping staff at a hotel were told that their daily work counted as all the exercise they needed to be healthy. They made no changes to their lifestyle and, after only four weeks, had lost an average of two pounds and lowered their systolic blood pressure by 10 points. It might sound wacky, but is it really any wackier than people feeling physically better after having taken placebo pills that they think will make them feel better?

In another study, Canadian researchers compared two groups – one where participants exercised three times a week and one where they listened to CDs that guided them to imagine they were doing the same workout as the exercisers. The exercisers improved their muscle strength by an impressive 28 per cent, but amazingly the non-exercisers improved theirs by almost the same – 24 per cent.

How? Janet Thomson, author of *Think More, Eat Less* (£12.99, Hay House) suggests a visualisation exercise you can try every day. "Think about how you will look and feel a month after you have achieved your weight-loss goal – slim and healthy," she says. "Now, visualise yourself three months later and six months after that. Commit to spending one minute just before you go to sleep each night and one minute when you wake each morning visualising yourself like this." Also picture the healthy food choices you will make and the exercise that will help build the new you. "Creating powerful positive emotions helps generate faith in your ability to succeed," says Thomson.

You can further reinforce this by tracking your progress, on a weekly basis, by writing down whatever it is you're trying to improve – your weight, your waistline or how long your regular running route takes. After a month you should see real differences.

CLENCH YOUR FIST

Why? Trying to resist that Dairy Milk? Try clenching your fist or tensing your abs. A report published in the *Journal of Consumer Research* showed that firming your muscles can help strengthen your willpower which, in turn, increases your ability to overcome food temptation. In one experiment, volunteers who tensed their hand muscles on their way to buy snacks bought less junk food than those who didn't.

This research is part of a larger area of science, known as embodied cognition. It looks at the way in which our physical and mental behaviours are inextricably linked in a way that is not yet fully understood,

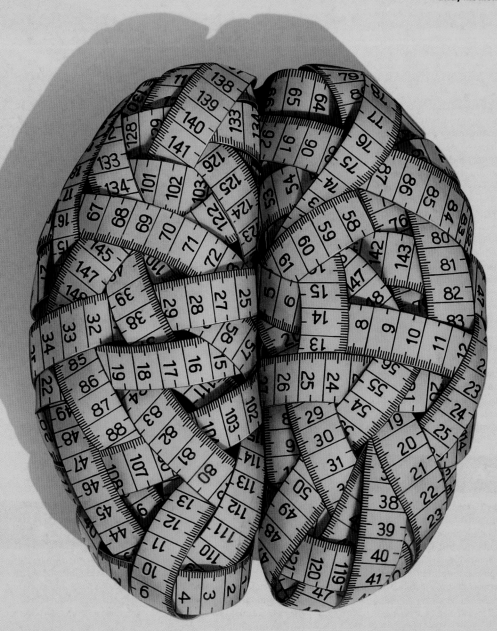

but suggests that the way we physically feel can affect our mental perception. For example, in research at Yale University, US, participants holding warm cups of coffee were more likely to judge someone as trustworthy – literally warm to them – than those holding cold cups of coffee.

The same idea is at play here – by steeling yourself physically, you can also steel yourself mentally. "Simply engaging in these bodily actions, which often result from an exertion of willpower, can serve as a non-conscious source to recruit willpower and facilitate self-control," says Iris Hung, one of the authors of the Yale study. And, if all else fails, at least your abs will look good as you try to turn down that extra pint or glass of wine.

How? Do exactly as those involved in the study did – when confronted by temptation, or when you're trying to make a conscious decision to choose something that's healthier, clench your fist or consciously tense another muscle group. But make sure you time your move right – researchers found that it only worked when employed at the exact moment of temptation, and not when used beforehand.

EAT SLOWLY

Why? It takes the stomach about 20 minutes to register satiety, so bolting a huge pizza in 10 minutes flat usually means you go from being starving to feeling unpleasantly full. But you won't just feel fuller, you'll probably have taken on unnecessary calories, and feel less satisfied.

In a study at the University of Rhode Island, US, researchers found that when subjects ate as fast as they could, they consumed, on average, 646kcal in just nine minutes. When presented with the same plate of food and told to put their cutlery down in between bites, they ate an average of 579kcal in 29 minutes. Plus, an hour after they finished they felt hungrier after bolting their meal than when they had taken their time. By eating more slowly, we engage all our senses, which helps us to enjoy the food more and feel fuller. The Rhode Island researchers also found that eating slowly was associated with a greater consumption of water, which they believe might account, in part, for the diminished calorie consumption.

How? Do exactly the same as the subjects did in the study. Ensure that you have a large glass of water with each meal, and put down your cutlery in between each bite, or use chopsticks when eating a stir fry, giving yourself time to properly chew your food, rather than just shovelling it in.

OUTSMART CRAVINGS

Why? "Your mind's main job is to do what it thinks you want it to do," says psychotherapist and hypnotherapist Marisa Peer (marisapeer.com). "So if you eat sweets when you're down and tell yourself that they're a naughty treat to cheer you up, then next time you are low your mind will fill your head with the idea of sweets, believing that's what you want to

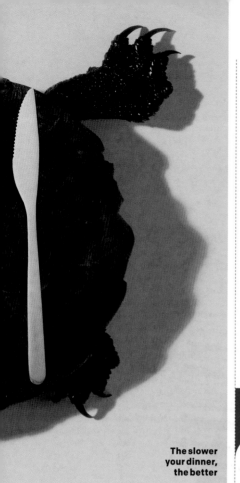

The slower your dinner, the better

BY EATING MORE SLOWLY WE ENGAGE ALL OUR SENSES, WHICH HELPS US TO ENJOY THE FOOD MORE AND FEEL FULLER

increases." As is so often the case when something is forbidden. It's important to vocalise these thoughts because speaking a thought out loud exercises more areas of the brain than simply thinking it, making it a more effective way of communicating with your subconscious. Bonus: talking to yourself ensures you will always get a table to yourself even in the most crowded Starbucks.

FOCUS ON YOUR FOOD

Why? Studies have found that when you're distracted by the TV, games or your phone, you eat more. Clinical hypnotherapist, chronobiologist and behavioural therapist Angela McKrill (angelamckrill.com) says that's because when we're distracted we rely solely on our stomachs to tell us when we're full, whereas all our senses should be involved.

"As hunter-gatherers, we wouldn't just grab a sandwich and eat it out of the packet, or shovel in pasta with our eyes on a screen. We had to rely on our eyes and our noses to differentiate between the good berries and the poisonous berries."

McKrill believes that by robbing ourselves of this more engaged way of consuming food, our digestion is not geared up to digest it properly – because it hasn't been prepped with visual and olfactory (smelling) cues – which means we don't get the best of the nutrients from it. What's

more, we don't get the full pleasure that we might from food, meaning we eat more than we should in an effort to feel sated, because our other senses haven't been satisfied. **How?** To force yourself to concentrate on your food, try switching the hands you usually use for your cutlery. A study published in *Personality and Social Psychology Bulletin* showed that people using their non-dominant hand to eat popcorn ate around 30 per cent less, and were more focused on taste and how hungry/full they were.

GET SNAP HAPPY

Why? US researchers at the University of Wisconsin-Madison have found that taking photos of your food can be a very effective way of subconsciously encouraging you to make healthy eating choices.

They asked dieters to keep written and photo diaries of what they ate in a week. The researchers found that the photo diaries were a far more accurate record of daily calories and a far more powerful disincentive to overeat.

"Rather than just eating mindlessly, taking a photograph of your plate before you eat helps you actually look at what you're eating," says McKrill. "Over time, this sort of approach can help people subconsciously adjust not only how much they're eating, but

feel better." Of course it's up to you how you think and Peer says that rather than programming your mind to think you want something but that you shouldn't have it, you're far better off making it clear to yourself – and to your subconscious – that this is an informed decision you have made. **How?** "If you're making a decision not to have a piece of cake because you know you're not really hungry, you just fancy it, try saying out loud, 'I have chosen not to eat this because I am not hungry,'" says Peer. "Using words like this informs your subconscious that you are making the right choice and feel good about it. It's when you say, 'I can't have that, I'm on a diet' that desire for that thing actually

also what they're eating. We're programmed to want to see a good balance of colour in our meals and simply by improving the aesthetics of our plate – something that's instinctive – we improve the nutritional content." That's assuming you don't eat a colourful pizza with a side of jelly beans every night.

How? "Before you eat or drink anything, whip out your phone and take a snap," says McKrill. "Seeing your food like this should help you subconsciously adjust what – and how much – you're eating."

If you want to make more of an effort, take a moment to look at everything you've consumed at the end of each day. Then, at the end of the week, upload all the pictures to your computer. Because your camera will have recorded the time you took each picture, you should

Does your crockery measure up?

be able to see patterns in poor food choices – maybe you're most likely to grab a chocolate bar from the machine when your energy dips in the afternoon. You can then start to develop strategies to address this, such as ensuring you have some nuts or fruit in your desk drawer.

PICK YOUR PLATES

Why? We've all hidden chocolate in the back of the cupboard from time to time in a bid to keep it out of sight and out of mind. But don't dismiss this trick as cliché: you are in fact around 70 per cent more likely to eat chocolate if you can actually see it

Dr Brian Wansink, author of *Mindless Eating* (£6.95, Hay House), carried out various experiments leaving chocolates in clear or opaque containers, either on the desks of office workers or on a filing cabinet six feet from their desks. In every instance, the more people could see the chocolates, the more likely they were to eat more of them.

"We eat more of these visible foods because we think about them more," says Wansink. "Every time we see the sweet jar, we have to decide whether we want a chocolate or whether we don't. Every time we see it we have to say no to something that is tasty and tempting." Ultimately, the more times you have to say no, the more likely you are to slip and say yes. **How?** Ideally you wouldn't have any unhealthy food in the house at all. But, if that's not realistically possible, hide your snacks in an opaque container and put the box in the back of the cupboard, or somewhere equally difficult for you to get to.

HIDE THE JUNK

Why? You probably think that it's only the food on your plate that counts, but the plate matters, too. Several studies have shown that the crockery you use can make a huge difference to how you perceive the taste of food, and how much of it you eat. US researchers from Cornell University served an identical brownie to three different groups of people: one group had it served on a china plate, the second on a paper plate and the third on a napkin. The better the presentation, the better people thought the brownie tasted.

The size of the plate is also important, as another Cornell study demonstrated. When a fixed portion of food was presented on a large plate, diners felt they had been given a smaller-than-average portion, so ate more. The same portion served on a smaller dish appeared more substantial, so they ate less. Similarly, a study published in the *British Medical Journal* discovered that people poured 20-30 per cent more alcohol into short, wide glasses than they did when they used taller, thinner ones.

Finally, further Cornell research has shown that you're likely to eat less if the food on your plate is a different colour from the plate, and if the tablecloth matches the plate. Probably best to write that all down before you head to John Lewis's homeware department. **How?** If you're trying to eat healthier foods that don't necessarily appeal, make the effort to serve them on good crockery. Bin the huge trendy platters and serve up your dinner on a side plate instead. So, to sum up, serve your pre-dinner G&T in a highball, pick a white tablecloth, serve your spaghetti bolognese on a small white plate and a salad on a large green plate. OK? Tuck in...

WEIGHT LOSS

⊕ QUICK BYTES

Here's our pick of the best weight-loss apps for your smartphone

80 BITES
(Apple, 69p; Android, 61p)
Not exactly the sort of app we can imagine using in public, but the idea is that this 'pedometer for the mouth' counts how many bites of food you take. The aim is both to eat more slowly and cut down your portion size.

VIRTUAL GASTRIC BAND HYPNOSIS
(Apple, £4.99)
Fans rave about how easy they've found it to change their eating habits after using this app, which contains three sessions of hypnotherapy as well as food photo diary functions and weight-loss tips.

MY FITNESS PAL
(myfitnesspal.com; Android, Apple, BlackBerry, Windows, free)
Essentially this website/app is a very clever diary in which you log food and exercise, and find out if you're getting a balanced diet and burning as many calories as you're consuming.

40.30.30
(Apple, free)
If you're following a diet that suggests a carbs:protein:fat ratio – say 40:30:30, but you can pick the right one for you – you'll like this app. The nutrition labels on food display this info in grams so you just tap the numbers in, and it does the maths for you

why, if you stop too suddenly, you can cause blood to pool in the legs, leaving you feeling dizzy or shaky. Coming to a more gradual stop helps prevent this, but there's no evidence that it will reduce muscle soreness afterwards. In one South African study, subjects were assigned a workout to instigate sore leg muscles. Some did a cool-down (walking slowly for 10 minutes) while others simply stopped. There was no difference in levels of reported muscle soreness. That said, a cool-down marks the transition between running and getting back to your day. A study from Atlanta found that cooling-down enhanced the overall exercise experience by allowing time to take stock of and reflect upon your achievements.

RECOVERY STRATEGY

If you've been running at a faster pace or for a prolonged period, take a few minutes to slow down gradually, allowing your heart rate and breathing frequency to return to normal.

COMPRESSION GEAR
Use compression tights post-run to reduce aches and pains

The fact that a recent study by Indiana University, US, concluded that compression clothing had no significant effect on athletic performance hasn't stopped many a runner donning full-length tights or knee-high socks. And the good news is that science is proving to be a little more promising on the benefits of the big squeeze on recovery. In other words, donning compression gear after exercise rather than during it. Research published in the *Journal of Sports Science and Medicine* found that graduated compression tights (where the compression is greatest at the ankle and diminishes further up the leg) hastened recovery after a period of downhill walking by allowing faster cell repair.

Vanessa Davies, the physiologist who conducted the study, found reduced levels of creatine kinase (an enzyme that indicates muscle damage), 24 and 48 hours after subjects performed repeated jumps from a height, when they recovered in compression tights.

In other research from Ball State University, US, use of compression gear following maximal exercise prevented loss of range of motion, reduced swelling and promoted the recovery of force production. Davies' study subjects, in common with those from the Ball State University study, reported that they felt that putting on compression tights helped reduce muscle soreness. "The psychological element could be as strong a factor as the physical," says Davies.

RECOVERY STRATEGY

After a shower and stretch, slip (OK, squeeze) on a pair of compression tights or socks. You can even put them on under your jeans thanks to the tight fit, and no one will be any the wiser. Some athletes even sleep in them.

Have you got your recovery mix right?

INJURY CLINIC

If you suffer any of these five common injuries, our doctors are in – and can fix you

CONTENTS

A ITB SYNDROME

B RUNNER'S KNEE

C SHIN SPLINTS

D ACHILLES HEEL

E PLANTAR FASCIITIS

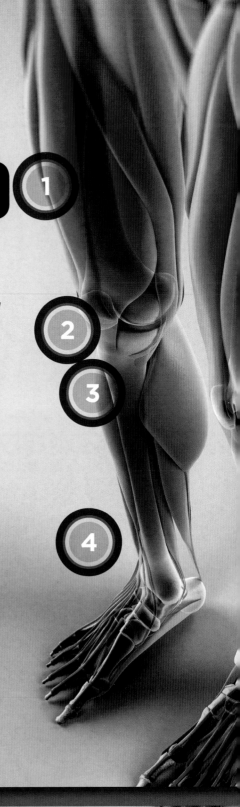

A ILIOTIBIAL BAND SYNDROME

PAIN, EXPLAINED

Leading sports performance specialist Dr Carlyle Jenkins explains why your knee feels like it's got a stake driven through it

❶ ILIOTIBIAL BAND

Your iliotibial band (ITB) is a ligament-like structure that starts at your pelvis and runs along the outside of your thigh to the outside of the top of your shinbone (tibia). When you run, your ITB rubs back and forth over a bony outcrop on your knee, which helps to stabilise it.

❷ LATERAL EPICONDYLE

If you have poor running mechanics, muscle imbalance, increase your body weight or add hill running to your training, then your ITB can track out of line, slipping out of the groove created by this bony outcrop.

❸ SWELLING

As it tracks out of its natural alignment it rubs against other structures in your leg, creating friction on the band. This results in inflammation and a click when you bend your knee.

❹ HOLD UP

The scarring thickens and tightens the ITB, and limits the blood flow to it. If you continue to run, you'll feel a stinging sensation. This can result in you limping as soon after you have finished a run.

CAUSE & EFFECT

Why it happens and how you are able to spot it

WHAT CAUSES IT?

According to research in the *Clinical Journal of Sports Medicine*, these are the roots of the problem:

➡ Inadequate warm-up
➡ Increasing distance, speed or excessive downhill running
➡ High or low arches in your feet that cause your feet to overpronate
➡ Uneven leg length
➡ Bow legs
➡ Excessive wear on the outside heel edge of a running shoe
➡ Weak hip abductors
➡ Running on a banked surface, such as the shoulder of a road or track

SPOT IT!

According to Dr Jenkins, you're a likely ITB sufferer if you experience one of the following signs:

➡ A sharp or burning pain on the outside of the knee. The symptoms may subside shortly after a run is over, but will return with the next run.
➡ You feel tenderness on the outside of your knee if you apply pressure, especially when bending.
➡ You may have problems standing on one leg on the affected side, usually due to a weak gluteus medius.

HOW TO REHABILITATE IT

Decrease your training load by 50 per cent and apply the principles of RICE (rest, ice, compression and elevation), then use these tips

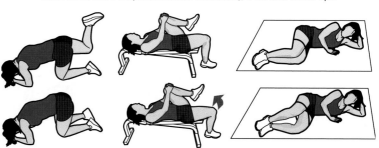

DONKEY KICKS

➡ On all fours, rest your bodyweight on your knees and flatten your elbows on the floor into a position similar to that of The Sphinx.

➡ Keep your head down and your right knee bent as you slowly lift your right leg up behind you so your foot rises up towards the ceiling.

➡ Hold that position for one second, then slowly return to the start. Perform four sets of 12 repetitions on each leg.

WHY?

This move strengthens your gluteus maximus and medius. Research in the journal Physical Therapy in Sport has found that these muscles are vital for keeping your ITB strong.

LYING ITB STRETCH

➡ Sit on the edge of a bench or firm bed. Lay your torso back and pull the unaffected leg to your chest to flatten your lower back.

➡ With your affected leg flat to the bench, maintain a 90-degree bend in its knee. Shift that knee as far inwards to the side as possible.

➡ Hold this position for 30 seconds and repeat four times on each leg. Increase time if it feels too easy.

WHY?

"The ITB is difficult to elongate, as it doesn't have nerves that allow you to feel if you're actually stretching it. You might not feel this move in the ITB, but it does isolate the band," says Jenkins.

SIDE-CLAMSHELL

➡ Lie on a mat on your side bending knees and hips to a 90 degree angle. Wrap a resistance band around both of your thighs.

➡ With the resistance band in place lift your top knee up towards the ceiling, making sure that the insides of both feet stay together.

➡ Perform 10 to 15 reps, or continue until you get a burn in the outside of your hip indicating you should stop.

WHY?

This move works your gluteus medius (on the outer surface of the pelvis). This muscle prevents your thigh from buckling inwards when you run, which is the root of ITB aches and pains.

HOW LONG UNTIL YOU'RE RECOVERED?

According to Jenkins, these are the recovery rates of iliotibial band syndrome depending on the severity of your injury

➡ MILD INJURY	100% AFTER 2-4 WEEKS
➡ AVERAGE INJURY	100% AFTER 7-8 WEEKS
➡ SEVERE INJURY	100% AFTER 9-24 WEEKS

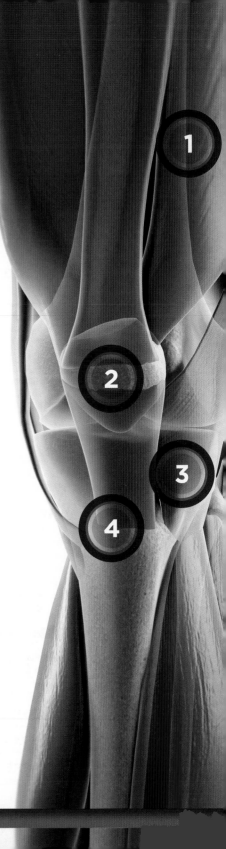

RUNNER'S KNEE

PAIN, EXPLAINED

Dr Ross Sherman, senior exercise physiologist and sports science consultant at Kingston University, London, explains what causes it

❶ QUADS

The thigh muscles above the knee hold your kneecap in place. When you run, your kneecap moves up and down your thighbone (femur) without touching it.

❷ KNEECAP

If your quads are weak or you have poor foot mechanics, your kneecap will move left and right, creating pressure, friction and irritation. As you clock up the miles and stride out your misaligned steps, your kneecap rubs against the end of your thighbone.

❸ CARTILAGE

This wobbling and rubbing grinds down the cartilage underneath your kneecap so that it becomes rough, like sandpaper. This makes your kneecap unable to bend smoothly and efficiently.

❹ FRONT KNEE PAIN

When this happens, you will experience a dull, aching pain under or around the front of your kneecap. The pinch will be the worst when running down a hill, walking down stairs, squatting down or sitting with a bent knee.

CAUSE & EFFECT

Why it happens and how you are able to spot it

WHAT CAUSES IT?

According to research in the *Journal of Sports Medicine*, these are the main culprits:
➡ Weak quadriceps
➡ Over-use or a sudden increase in mileage
➡ Knock knees
➡ Tight hamstrings or calves
➡ Overpronation or supination
➡ Running on uneven surfaces
➡ A previous injury, such as a dislocation of the kneecap

SPOT IT!

Your doctor will give you the Clarke's Test, but you can do it yourself. Here's how:
➡ Sit on a chair and rest your stretched-out leg on another chair in front of you. Tense your quadricep.
➡ Gently squeeze above the offending knee with your right hand and push on the outside of the kneecap with your left hand.
➡ If you feel a scorching twinge then you've got runner's knee.
➡ "If a pain radiates into your back, hips and feet when you do this then see a physiotherapist, who can examine you correctly and determine the route of the problem," says Richard Scrivener, a running and injury lecturer at Premier Training.

HOW TO REHABILITATE IT

After applying the rules of RICE, rest from all sports for one to two weeks. Then do these moves from Sherman two to three times a week

LYING LEG LIFTS

➡ Lie flat on your back. Bend your left knee at 90 degrees, keeping your foot flat on floor.

➡ Keep your right leg perfectly straight and lift it to the height of the left knee.

➡ Hold for five to 10 seconds and repeat five to 10 times on both legs.

WHY?

"When out running on the road, your bodyweight lands on a near-straightened knee," says Sherman. "This move strengthens your quads – the muscle that absorbs the blow – in the position they receive the impact. This stabilises the injured knee."

BALL HALF SQUATS

➡ Put a Swiss ball between you – on your lower back – and a stable wall.

➡ Lower yourself towards the floor. Stop when your knees are bent at 90 degrees.

➡ Straighten your legs to rise to the top without locking your knees.

WHY?

"You should do four to five sets these with 12 repetitions to strengthen your quads, lower back, glutes and core area. These muscle groups all work together to teach your knees to start bending correctly through their natural range of movement," advises Sherman.

FOOT TURNS

➡ Stretch both legs out straight in front of you, feet pointed straight up.

➡ Turn both feet out as far as possible. Hold for 12 seconds while tensing your quads.

➡ Turn them inwards for 12 seconds. That's one set; do six sets.

WHY?

"The idea of this is to strengthen both your outer and inner quadricep muscles. This will then in turn strengthen and develop the cartilage that surrounds either side of the knee cap, which will stop it from tracking out of line in the future," says Sherman.

HOW LONG UNTIL YOU'RE RECOVERED?

According to Dr Sherman, these are the recovery rates depending on the severity of your injury. If your injury is only mild you can be recovered in six weeks, as long as you take his advice to rest up for the first two weeks and do his rehabilitation exercises to help overcome the injury. If the injury is particularly severe, it could take up to six months to recover

➡ **MILD INJURY**

40-50% BETTER AFTER 1-2 WEEKS
60-75% BETTER AFTER A MONTH
100% BETTER AFTER 6-8 WEEKS

➡ **SEVERE INJURY**

30-40% BETTER AFTER 2-3 WEEKS
50-60 BETTER AFTER 2 MONTHS
100% BETTER AFTER 4-6 MONTHS

SHIN SPLINTS

PAIN, EXPLAINED

Dr Carlyle Jenkins, a leading sports rehabilitation specialist, explains the reasons for that persistent ache in your shins

❶ TIBIALIS ANTERIOR

Shin splints are an overuse injury. The muscle most affected by this is the tibialis anterior, stretching from your knee down to your ankle. A new or excessive stress from running can irritate it.

❷ TIBIA

By resting and applying our rehab tips when you feel mild tenderness in your shin bone (tibia), you'll eliminate further damage. But if you soldier on with more miles, then you'll create micro-tears.

❸ OUTER SHIN PAIN

This is when you'll feel a razor sharp pain on the outer edges of the mid region of your lower leg, next to the shin bone. The aching area can measure 10 to 15 centimetres, and the pain often subsides after warming up and returns after the workout is finished.

❹ REST UP

Worst-case scenario is that the swelling in the muscle and sheath continues unabated, increasing the pressure in the sheath to intolerable levels. This can lead to 'Compartment Syndrome', a condition that can require surgery.

CAUSE & EFFECT

Why it happens and how you are able to spot it

WHAT CAUSES IT?

The Mayo Clinic in the USA found that shin splints are caused by an overload on the shin bone and connective tissues, which attach your muscles to the bone. This overload is often caused by:

➡ Running downhill
➡ Running on a slanted or tilted surface, such as crowned roads
➡ Running in worn-out footwear
➡ Doing sports with frequent starts and stops, such as tennis
➡ Shin splints can also be caused by training too hard, too fast or for too long
➡ Overpronation; the tibia is forced to twist in the opposite direction. Too much twisting can lead to shin splints
➡ A return to exercise after a long layoff period

SPOT IT!

The Mayo Clinic found that there are several tell-tale signs of shin splints, which are:

➡ Tenderness, soreness or pain running along the outer part of your lower leg.
➡ Mild swelling of the muscles around your shin bone.
➡ At first, the pain may end when you've finished your warm-up. Eventually, however, the pain may be continuous.

 # HOW TO REHABILITATE IT

Decrease your training load by 90 to 95 per cent and use RICE then do these rehabilitation moves from Dr Carlyle Jenkins once a day

KNEELING STRETCH

➡ Get into a kneeling position with your toes tucked under, sitting on the back of your ankles.

➡ Lean forward towards the floor, spread out your fingers and rest them on the ground in front of you.

➡ Gently sit back onto your heels so that your ankles almost flatten against the floor. Hold for 30 seconds and repeat as needed.

WHY?

"This move will stretch out the muscles and connective tissue that is in the front of your legs and will alleviate some of the pressure in the painful part of your shin," says Jenkins.

SEATED STRETCH

➡ Sit on a chair with your feet roughly hip-width apart on the floor and place your hands on your knees.

➡ Bend your right leg behind you underneath the chair and rest the top part of your foot on the floor.

➡ Push your foot into the floor and press down on your right knee with your right hand. Hold for 30 seconds, switch legs and repeat.

WHY?

"This move is very efficient at isolating and loosening your shin muscles," says Jenkins. "This move can also be easily done several times during the day while you are sat at your desk doing work,"

STANDING STRETCH

➡ Stand with your feet roughly hip-width apart while being at arm's length away from a wall.

➡ Lean forward and place your hands on the wall while keep both your feet and knees straight.

➡ Lean as far forward as possible while keeping your feet flat. Stop leaning when you feel an intense stretch and hold for 30 seconds.

WHY?

This move gives the muscles at the back of your calves a comprehensive stretch and also resets the muscles in your lower leg into the correct position to enable healing to commence effectively.

 ## HOW LONG UNTIL YOU'RE RECOVERED?

An online poll on the fitness website attackpoint.org found that these were the expected recovery rates for shin splints

➡ **MILD INJURY** | 100% AFTER 1-2 WEEKS

➡ **AVERAGE INJURY** | 100% AFTER 7-8 WEEKS

➡ **SEVERE INJURY** | 100% AFTER 9-24 WEEKS

HOW TO REHABILITATE IT

Apply the principles of RICE and take a break from sport for at least two weeks. Then do these strengthening moves once a day

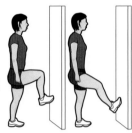

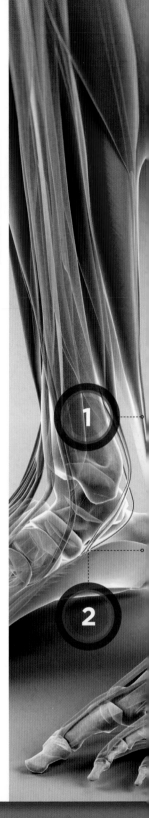

STRAIGHT-LEG CALF LOWERING

➡ Stand with the balls of your feet on the edge of a step. Hold on to a support if necessary.

➡ Rise up onto your toes then remove the unaffected leg from the step so you're holding the tiptoe position.

➡ Take five seconds to lower your affected heel as far down as is comfortable. Do three sets of 15 twice a day.

WHY?
A study at the University Hospital of Northern Sweden found that 12 weeks of this and the next exercise combined could eradicate Achilles pain.

BENT-LEG CALF LOWERING

➡ Sit on a chair, place a weight on top of your thighs and rest the balls of your feet on a ledge or step.

➡ Rise up onto your toes then remove the unaffected leg from the step so you're on tiptoes on the sore leg.

➡ Lower your affected heel as far downwards as is comfortable. Do three sets of 15 twice a day.

WHY?
Doing this exercise with a bent leg forces your deep calf muscle to work, which strengthens the major calf muscles needed to heal Achilles tendonitis.

STANDING WALL STRETCH

➡ Stand with both feet parallel to each other roughly hip width apart, facing a wall at about arm's length away.

➡ Put the affected foot on the wall at knee height and try to press its heel against the wall as flat as you can.

➡ Lift your chest until you are standing straight. Hold this position for three minutes on each leg.

WHY?
A study in the journal *Foot & Ankle International* found that holding an Achilles tendon stretch for this exact period of time helped to reduce pain.

HOW LONG UNTIL YOU'RE RECOVERED?

According to Dr Carlyle Jenkins, these are the recovery rates of Achilles tendonitis depending on the severity of your injury

➡ **MILD INJURY** | 100% AFTER 2-10 DAYS

➡ **AVERAGE INJURY** | 100% AFTER 7-8 WEEKS

➡ **SEVERE INJURY** | 100% AFTER 3-6 MONTHS

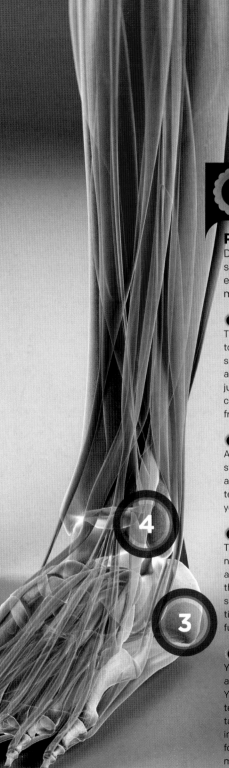

PAIN, EXPLAINED

Dr Carlyle Jenkins, a leading sports performance specialist, explains why your Achilles heel may be aching

① ACHILLES TENDON

This connects the calf muscles to the heel bone. It's the thick, springy tissue just above the heel and is used when you walk, run, jump or push up on your toes. Injury can occur if you up your training frequency or intensity.

② FEEL THE BURN

Achilles tendonitis is a "chronic stress" injury where small stresses accumulate and damage the tendon. This strain is increased if you're inflexible or you overpronate.

③ HEEL

The inflammation is often at the narrow point of the tendon just above the heel area. This is because that area has the smallest blood supply, which slows the healing time considerably. Rest to avoid further pain.

④ ANKLE

You'll feel an ache at the back of your ankle and a burning or piercing pain. You'll experience redness on the tendon and/or severe pain when you take your first few steps out of bed in the morning or after sitting down for a while. This will subside as you move around.

CAUSE & EFFECT

Why it happens and how you are able to spot it

WHAT CAUSES IT?

The American Academy of Orthopaedic Surgeons say these can trigger Achilles tendonitis:

➡ Rapidly increasing your running mileage or speed
➡ Adding hill running or stair climbing to your training routine
➡ Starting up too quickly after a layoff from exercise
➡ Trauma caused by sudden and/ or hard contraction of your calf muscles when putting out extra effort, such as in a final sprint
➡ Overuse resulting from a lack of flexibility in your calf muscles
➡ Flattening of the arch of your foot can place stress on your Achilles

SPOT IT!

Research at the Mayo Clinic, USA, found that it's likely you have Achilles tendonitis if you suffer with one or more of these symptoms:

➡ Dull ache or pain on the tendon when pushing off your foot during walking or when rising onto your toes.
➡ Tenderness of your Achilles tendon.
➡ Stiffness that lessens as your tendon warms up.
➡ A 'bump' on your tendon.
➡ A crackling or creaking sound when you touch or move your Achilles tendon.

PLANTAR FASCIITIS

PAIN, EXPLAINED

Dr Ross Sherman, senior exercise physiologist and sports science consultant at Kingston University, London, explains why your heel hurts

❶ FEELING PAIN?

This is an overuse injury so you won't remember any particular incident where you've damaged your heel while running. You'll sow the seeds if you've increased your training frequency or intensity or started running hill sprints

❷ PLANTAR FASCIA

It's a thick broad band of tissue that runs along the bottom of your foot. It supports your foot's arch and acts like a shock-absorbing bow-string. When an abnormally high load is forced on it you get a small split in this tissue.

❸ WAKE UP!

At the time, this rip will only create mild discomfort, which you probably won't even notice. But when you sleep, your body starts the repair process – making the plantar fascia stiff. Upon waking, it will be inflexible. When you take your first strides you'll stretch too far and tear it slightly.

❹ HEEL

The tear can lead to additional micro-tearing, which results in the stinging pain at the base of your heel pad, which can last all day if you're on your feet.

CAUSE & EFFECT

Why it happens and how you are able to spot it

WHAT CAUSES IT?

The American Academy of Orthopaedic Surgeons cites these as the root of plantar fasciitis:

➡ A job that requires you to stand for long periods
➡ Poor foot mechanics, flat feet or high arches
➡ Being overweight – this places additional pressure on your plantar fascia
➡ Tight calves that limit the amount you can flex your ankles
➡ An aggressive increase in training load or exertion
➡ Arthritis can cause inflammation in the tendons at the bottom of your foot
➡ Diabetes increases your risk, as diabetics have less blood going to their feet
➡ Poor or worn-out shoes

SPOT IT!

Research at the Mayo Clinic, USA, found it's likely you have plantar fasciitis if you experience one or more of the following symptoms:

➡ A sharp pain in the inside of the bottom of your heel that may spread under your foot.
➡ Heel pain when you wake, stand or climb stairs.
➡ Heel pain after long periods of standing or after getting up.
➡ Mild swelling in the heel.

3

AQUA RUNNING ALLOWS ATHLETES TO TRAIN WITHOUT RISKING INJURY

can attain the same positive mood state as they do when they run out on the road.

Killgore adds that running in water produces physiological changes in your body that assist the body in tissue healing, accelerating recovery from training sessions and injuries. It is a philosophy that the Ulster rugby team applies after games when they take to the pool for an aqua running session. "It takes the soreness out and reduces the lactic acid," says Paul McAllister, an aqua jog instructor at Queen's University in Belfast, where the team trains.

Once beginners have mastered the technique (see box out, left) they can start to reap maximum benefits from a session, tailoring it to their own fitness levels, injury restrictions and goals.

It can take time to attain the perfect form – and even seasoned aqua runner Pavey says she experiences a period of adjustment when she has been out of the pool for a while. "When I start aqua jogging again I can really feel the resistance of the water and I can't work as hard in it. But as you adapt you get stronger at moving through the water, and therefore you achieve greater benefits."

MIXING IT UP

Pavey does hour-long sessions including a warm-up and cool-down, typically comprising 10 three-minute intervals, or five sessions of five minutes each, both with a minute's recovery

in between each one. Recovery time is thought to be faster in the water because of reduced stress on the body, and Pavey emphasises the importance of keeping the intensity high and recoveries short. "You can play around with the exact length of your intervals, but you must make sure you really push yourself."

Mixing up your sessions also can reduce the monotony of running in the same place all the time, says Pavey. "Mentally, I can find it harder to do a continual aqua run compared with a track run, but structuring the session really helps to keep me focused and motivated." Some aqua running classes are designed to do this, breaking down sessions according to speed and changing the emphasis on different body parts. Some classes available will also incorporate games, such as 'tag' to bring in a much needed element of fun to the training.

McAllister says that while aqua running may look easy to an outsider considering it, many are surprised by the intensity of the workout – particularly the men. "They assume it's like aqua aerobics and aren't keen to try it, but once they do they realise it is a really powerful training session for your whole body."

AQUA SESSIONS

WORKOUT 1 ▶ BASE BUILDING
10 minutes easy jog; 2 minutes straight leg kicks, driving from the hip with toes pointed down; 10 minutes steady-state run; 2 minutes straight leg kicks; 10 minutes steady-state run; 2 minutes straight leg kick; 10 minutes easy jog.

46 MINS

WORKOUT 2 ▶ INTERVALS
10 minutes easy jog, running with normal motion; 5x20 second intervals hard running alternated with 5x40 second intervals easy jog; 5x90 second intervals hard running with 5x3 minute intervals easy jog; 10 minutes easy jog.

47 MINS

WORKOUT 3 ▶ PYRAMID
10 minutes easy jog; 1 minute hard running then 1 minute easy jog; 2 minutes hard running then 2 minutes easy jog; 3 minutes hard running then 3 minutes easy jog; 4 minutes hard running then 4 minutes easy jog; 5 minutes hard running; 10 minutes easy jog.

45 MINS

WORKOUT 4 ▶ DRILLS
10 minutes easy jog; 30 seconds at high turnover – quick, short strides; 3 minutes easy; 30 seconds backward-kicks, with quick flexion of knee; 3 minutes easy; 30 seconds high-knees; 3 minutes easy; 30 seconds straight-leg kicks; 10 minutes easy jog.

31 MINS

MINIMALISM & FORM

Could ditching your trainers and changing your stride really make you a better runner? Here's the latest science

182 | **PIMP MY STRIDE**
How to run faster for longer with less effort

190 | **THE NAKED TRUTH**
Getting back to nature with bare feet

PIMP MY STRIDE

If you want to improve your times, cut down on injury and run more efficiently, then you need to focus on tweaking your form. *Runner's World's* Kerry McCarthy enrolled at The Running School to find out how

L eft foot. Right foot. Repeat. Job done, right? Not according to a growing school of thought that says incorrect form could be not only hindering your performance, but also setting you up for injury misery. In search of the perfect form, we sent RW's senior writer back to running school. His first report? Unsatisfactory. Happily, he discovered that with hard work, determination and a well-padded ego, efficient running is something anyone can achieve

LESSON ONE

THINK YOU CAN RUN? THINK AGAIN...

"Are the cameras running?" says Mike. "OK, hop on the treadmill and we'll see what's wrong." As I embark on my tale of injury woe, Mike holds up a hand. "I don't want to hear it, I want to see it." He hits the 'on' button. Twenty seconds

later he hits 'off'. "I know what the problem is."

"But I've only been running for..." I start to argue.

"You've got a problem in your left hamstring, which causes it to cramp regularly. You also get pain in your lower back and tightness in your glutes, and all this has been going on for, I'd say, more than two years?" I mumble something about a lucky guess, but follow Mike's crooked finger to a video replay of my 20-second stint.

Over the next five minutes, using freeze frames and some fancy software that lets him draw on the screen, Mike Antoniades, founder of The Running School, mercilessly breaks down my action: my heel lift is too low (weak hamstrings); my right foot is encroaching on the left foot's territory as it hits the floor (lazy form); my hips collapse downwards on footstrike (poor core strength); my knees roll

inwards (weak glutes); my feet splay outwards (overloaded quads); my arms rotate across my body (core strength again), and my pelvis – the foundation stone of the runner's body – is too weak to stop any of this. Steve Prefontaine I ain't – that much is clear. But before you shake your head in a perfect condescending arc, take a look in the mirror by the treadmill. Mike, says all runners have at least two of these issues – including elite athletes, more on that later. And the over-two-years thing? "You were doing all that so naturally you've obviously been overcompensating for a while," says Mike. "But don't worry, we'll fix you."

Which is exactly why I signed up to have my self-esteem politely shredded to pieces over 12 weekly one-hour sessions. The Running School claims that it can make a thoroughbred out of any old ass, and I was ready to trade Blackpool beach for Ascot. My running career

Tread carefully and
your form can be
improved

started eight years ago when a colleague claimed I couldn't put down my Cornish pasty long enough to train for a marathon. Fuelled by umbrage, I ran seven miles that night and increased the mileage arbitrarily as the weeks progressed, with no clue about nutrition, recovery or cross-training. I finished the marathon 16 weeks later with supports on both knees and one ankle, plus a torn hamstring. After several similar experiences I arrived at *Runner's World* unable to run more than 10K without a walk break to loosen everything up – a state of affairs which, to my shame, had more or less continued until now.

Admittedly, I'm a fairly extreme case. But even if none of that story sounds familiar, a growing swathe of opinion holds that form-focused philosophy could help you, too. In most sports, it's well established that technique and performance are closely linked. Golfers derive power from their hips, for example, so hip engagement and rotation are pretty well correlated with how far

WHICH RUNNER ARE YOU?

Find out which of Mike Antoniades' running types you are, and learn how to put things right. Either watch yourself running in a mirror at the gym, or get someone to film you to discover what you need to work on

THE THUMPER

SPOT YOURSELF You hit the ground hard – and spend too long there, putting pressure on ankles, knees and hips.

INJURY RISK Overuse injuries: shin splints, knee pain, iliotibial (IT) band syndrome, achilles tendinitis, hamstring tears...you name it.

FIX YOURSELF Be lighter on your feet. Run on a treadmill on a gradient over five per cent to force yourself to pick your feet. Do 30 second incline intervals.

THE TWISTER

SPOT YOURSELF Your arms move side to side, crossing the centre line of your torso. Your feet also start crossing.

INJURY RISK Lower back pain and hip flexor strain.

FIX YOURSELF Imagine your arms are on rails. Facing a mirror. Bend your arms 90 degrees at the elbow, forearms horizontal to the ground, hands cupped. Pump them back with your shoulder blades, not your elbows. Keep the 90-degree angle.

THE OCTOPUS

SPOT YOURSELF Arms and legs move differently (think Phoebe from *Friends*). Common in new runners, especially at the end of races.

INJURY RISK IT band syndrome, lower back pain and abdominal muscle pulls.

FIX YOURSELF Strengthen your core with crunches, planks, and Superman curls (runnersworld.co.uk/core has more moves). Also use your arms properly (see The Twister) and stretch regularly.

WEEKEND WARRIOR

SPOT YOURSELF You can only run at weekends. So you work too hard in too short a time or always do the same thing – both cause tightness in your chest, and your arms get stuck in the 'T-Rex' position.

INJURY RISK Hamstring strains, groin pulls, trapped nerves around the neck.

FIX YOURSELF Flexibility and variety are key. Yoga, Pilates, stretching, core stability moves and mixing up your training all help.

THE NAKED TRUTH

The barefoot movement is gathering pace, promising closer connection to the terrain. But is the key to better running really what you wear – or don't wear – on your feet? Sam Murphy investigates

As we buy into the seductive promise of the 'barefoot revolution', the shoe manufacturers who sold – and still sell – cushioning and motion-control footwear are jumping fully on board. This seemingly uneasy alliance has created a barefoot/ minimalist industry worth £1.1 billion, but the question remains: does the secret to better running really lie inside a shoebox?

Stepping on to a New York ferry, I breathe in the crisp, fresh autumn air. I'm heading out to the island where my race begins – but it's not the race you're thinking of. A far cry from the 45,000-strong field of the NYC Marathon, this event – the

New York City Barefoot Run – is on a rather smaller scale. But the fact that it's happening at all, attracting over 400 runners in its second year, is testament to the recent revolution in our sport; a revolution that has seen many – myself included – swap their cushioned or motion-control shoes for barely-there minimalist footwear or shun shoes altogether.

I'm in good company. Among those boarding the ferry are Daniel Lieberman, professor of human evolutionary biology at Harvard University and co-author of a landmark paper, published in the journal Nature, outlining the evidence that shows humans were

'born to run'. Talking of Born to Run (£8.99, Profile Books), the author, Chris McDougall, is also with me, chatting to Barefoot Ted, who stars in the book, and legendary barefoot running coach Lee Saxby, who McDougall credits for ridding him of injuries.

It's a Who's Who of today's barefoot scene's leading lights and, unsurprisingly, talk centres on barefoot running. How long it takes to adapt. How it's enabled someone perennially injured to run pain-free. The best surface to run on. Whether or not Nike Free really qualifies as a minimal shoe. Which gyms are sniffy about letting you run barefoot on the treadmill.

("Soon enough this argument will be over," opines McDougall. "They'll be falling over themselves to teach barefoot running, not banning it."). There's no 'Why?' or 'Should I?' being asked here today – it's all 'How do I?' and 'How long?' and 'How far?'

This is a refreshing change from the scepticism, bemusement or downright hostility that barefoot running can often elicit. But Lieberman believes scepticism should be encouraged. "People are

Lieberman. "The issue isn't whether you run barefoot or not, but how you run – your form."

BACK TO OUR ROOTS

There's a 20-minute walk to the start line when we land on Governors Island. Hundreds of soles pad silently along the asphalt road, gathering for the pre-event briefing under a huge banner brandishing the 'I love NY' logo – the heart replaced by a bare footprint. The Statue of Liberty

End your sole searching by going sans shoe

"START WITH JUST SMALL DISTANCES. JUST A QUARTER OF A MILE IS ENOUGH TO BEGIN WITH, THEN ADD ONE-EIGHTH OF A MILE EACH TIME. BE SURE TO TRANSITION SLOWLY"

Jason Robillard (barefoot runninguniversity.com)

suspicious about what the shoe companies have been saying, but they need to be suspicious about what both the barefooters and minimalist shoe manufacturers are saying, too," he says. "There are a lot of opinions and very few facts about most things in running, and barefoot running is no exception. More research is needed."

That may come as a surprise. It's easy to assume, given all the media hullabaloo, that dozens of papers have been published proving that barefoot running is 'better' in every way – the answer to a whole litany of injury problems and even the key to improved performance. But whatever the growing number of barefoot aficionados and minimalist shoe manufacturers would have you believe, that isn't the case.

"'Is barefoot better?' is the wrong question to ask," says

looms proudly across the glittering bay. "Welcome back," says John Durant loudly, event organiser and founder of the group Barefoot Runners NYC. "And I mean that, even if you were not running here last year. Welcome back to natural human movement."

The New York City Barefoot Run isn't a race, as such. There are no timing chips, no clocks and not even a set distance, but my pre-race butterflies are still all aflutter. My husband Jeff, a rather competitive runner, is bemused by the 'as many laps as you like' format. I know it's not just about winning, he says, but many people like to know how they performed and make comparisons. McDougall is more enthusiastic: "I think this will be the next wave," he says, between signing quite a few well-thumbed copies of his book and doling out temporary tattoos. "Look around you, everyone's

smiling. Competition makes people anxious and encourages them to do too much."

It's true that there's more emphasis on fun and freedom in barefoot running. As the race gets under way, I don't see many people setting their Garmins or elbowing their way to the front. Barefoot Ted isn't even going in the right direction, choosing instead to whisk people anticlockwise right around the course in a charming foot-powered rickshaw. "It's all about testing the limits of what's pleasurable to you, not what's possible," he says.

I can see the appeal of getting in touch with nature and making running more playful, but both as a

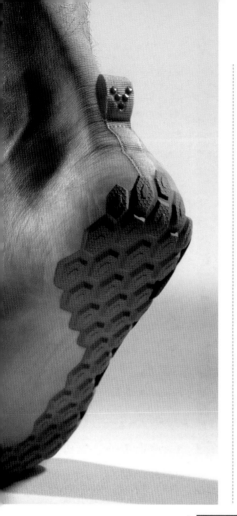

efforts to get rid of it, I tried almost everything – stretches, exercises, orthotics, injections, stability shoes – but when none of it worked, I resolved to rebuild my form from the ground up. And that meant going barefoot. There's nowhere to hide poor technique when your feet are bare, I figured.

It's a theory backed partially by Lieberman's research. In 2010, he published a study showing that habitually barefoot people run differently from those accustomed to wearing running shoes. For a start, they tend to land on their forefoot or midfoot rather than their heels (where 75 per cent of shod runners land). Secondly, they land more softly, generating smaller initial impact forces than heel strikers wearing shoes, in spite of the absence of cushioning. They also have greater springiness (or 'compliance') and less stiffness in their stride.

DO THE EVOLUTION

"We evolved to run barefoot and did so exclusively until recently, in evolutionary terms," Lieberman tells me and Jeff, as we make our first lap of the 2.1-mile course. "The

runner and a coach, what lured me in was the idea of running more efficiently and without injury.

My barefoot journey began back in 2007 when researching an article on whether or not it was possible to change the way you run. I tinkered with my own form, switching from a heel strike to a forefoot strike and, as I did so, I started to find my usual shoes cumbersome and heavy. I began to wear lighter, more pared-down shoes. My PBs over 10K, 10 miles and the half marathon all notably improved over the next couple of years (despite having already been running for 17 years) and my mileage soared. But then injury struck: plantar fasciitis. In my

"BE PRUDENT. BE SCEPTICAL. HAVE FUN"

Daniel Lieberman, Harvard University professor of human evolutionary biology

lower collision forces and greater compliance are what allow unshod people to run barefoot and for it to be safe and comfortable." He compliments Jeff on his form and trots ahead sporting a T-shirt that reads 'Evolved to Run'.

But for most of us, who have spent a lifetime with our gentle,

+ Q&A

Q CAN ANYONE RUN BAREFOOT?

A If you believe barefoot running is our evolutionary heritage, it certainly follows that anyone can. Or almost anyone. "Certain neuropathies, such as diabetes, makes it inadvisable," says Daniel Lieberman. If you're overweight or out of shape? You need to build up your conditioning and fitness slowly, just as you would if you were running in shoes.

Q HOW LONG WILL IT TAKE ME TO CHANGE MY FORM?

A "It can take around 10-12 weeks to change flexibility, and around six to eight weeks to increase strength - but proprioception could take a matter of days or weeks, it's very individual," says Jay Dicharry. "Most of changing your form is about 'software' – the nerve-to-muscle communication –rather than the 'hardware', or your musculoskeletal system." See On Good Form, page 197, for how to do it.

natural movement pattern that Lieberman describes, are likely to be somewhat rusty, to say the least. "Simply taking off your shoes and going for a run does not ensure good form," he concedes. "It's possible to run badly barefoot and very well in shoes. How you run is more important than what's on your feet."

The trouble is, in traditional built-up running shoes, that wad of cushioning between you and the ground makes it very difficult to know how you are running. "Proprioception is the foundation of skill," says Lee Saxby. "A cushioned running shoe damps down your awareness and takes away valuable feedback."

MINIMALISM & FORM

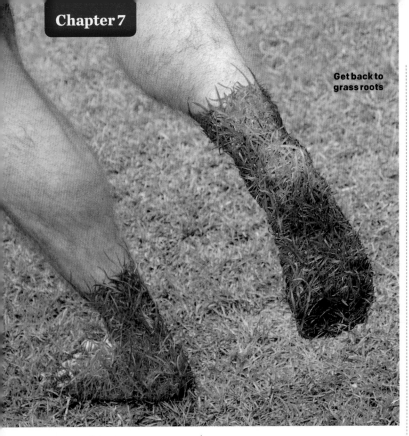

Get back to grass roots

This idea of being closer to and more 'in touch' with the ground is one of the biggest selling points of minimalist footwear. But not all minimalist shoes are created equal. In fact, with many major brands jumping on the bandwagon (while continuing to make and promote their conventional running shoes), natural running proponents are now beginning to distinguish between the terms 'barefoot' and 'minimalist', as if defending their territory from the invading army of lightweight running shoes.

SHOCK'N'SOLE

Purists are scathing about the brands paying lip service to minimalism. "It's about giving people what they want rather than what they need," says Saxby. But Nick Pearson, managing director of Sweatshop, the largest running shoe retailer in the UK, believes

"LIFT YOUR FEET, NOT YOUR BODY"

Barefoot Ken Bob, author of Barefoot Running Step by Step (£14.99, Fair Winds)

there is a genuine place for these more moderate products. "They won't change your gait, but they may help you get stronger and reduce your risk of injury," he says. And perhaps just as importantly, from a marketing point of view, they might make you feel as if you're part of what's new and exciting in running.

The idea of 'semi barefoot' footwear that can help runners transition from the traditional cushioned shoe is catching on among manufacturers. One British

brand, Inov-8, has a fittingly innovative solution: its minimalist range is rated using 'arrows' – the fewer arrows on the shoe, the more minimalist it is, allowing you to transition your way through the range over time, until you're in the featherweight, 150g Bare-X Lite.

"It seems logical that you gradually reduce the level of cushioning in your shoes, but it's based on the wrong premise," says Saxby. That premise being that it's the shoes that are at the heart of the matter and not how you run. "No shoe can protect you from the forces of running, so if you aren't going to change your form to be able to handle those forces more efficiently, then stick with more traditional padded trainers."

I see Saxby's point, but in my experience I think 'transitional' shoes definitely have their place in reacquainting runners with what's beneath their feet and facilitating a more natural running style.

Sweatshop offers a wide range of minimalist shoes across its stores. Two London branches stock the Vivobarefoot brand which, with no cushioning and a sole just 4mm thick, could be described as truly barefoot (the company has even sent staff from the stores on a barefoot coaching course to ensure they dispense the right advice). But if Sweatshop has bought into barefoot, then how can it justify the remaining 99 per cent of its stock being pairs of the traditional old-school trainer?

"The industry has been guilty of making too many outrageous claims about what a shoe can do for you that cannot be substantiated," says Pearson. "It's often presented as a black and white scenario: buy the right shoe and you won't get injured; get the wrong shoe and you will." But, he points out, that's just as much of a problem with barefoot and minimalist shoes as it has been historically with traditional shoes.

McDougall agrees. "My initial concern is that the barefoot trend is being led by products," he says. "The minimalist shoe industry is now worth $1.1 billion. You've got many of the major shoe companies making minimal shoes but not telling people how to run in them. The shoes don't change anything by themselves – it's your form that needs to change."

And therein lies the difficulty for companies such as Sweatshop. "Moving away from conventional footwear requires a period of adaptation," explains Pearson. "And while a customer might have read Born to Run and have been inspired and excited by it, in reality they may not have the time or commitment required to change their gait or gain the conditioning needed to adapt successfully."

And if they don't? "As a retailer, our role is to inform, educate and protect the consumer – they need to understand the choice they are making," says Pearson. "There's a

BAREFOOT RUNNING **V** MINIMAL RUNNING

VIVOBAREFOOT
• Zero heel-to-toe drop • No cushioning
• No midsole • Extremely flexible
• Lightweight (224g)

SAUCONY KINVARA
• Some cushioning • 4mm heel drop
• More flexible than a traditional shoe
• Midsole • Lightweight (219g)

quantum difference between something like a Vivobarefoot, with no cushioning or heel raise whatsoever, and a Saucony Kinvara, which is really more just tipping its hat to minimalism."

According to Spencer White, head of Saucony's Human Performance and Innovation Laboratory, the Kinvara is actually designed to allow you to heel strike if you need to. "When you're in the process of changing your gait, you will still heel strike occasionally,

say, when you're getting tired," he says. In fact, Saucony's Step into Minimalism brochure and guide recommends using minimal shoes for just short bouts to begin with, supplemented by runs in your 'normal' shoes.

This 'minimalism-lite' category of shoes, which tend to be lightweight, less cushioned and less structured, might sound like the perfect compromise for someone who wants to dip their toes into natural running. (The

---

✚ PREPARE TO BARE
"You need to take a few steps back from where you are now," says Lee Saxby. "As a baby has to learn to walk, so you need to acquire – or regain – new motor skills before you are ready to run barefoot." Here's how…

BAREFOOT WALKING

Why? You need to start somewhere and this will start to hone your proprioception and will begin to 'wake up' those dormant muscles in your feet that you will require later on. Backwards walking can also develop a good range of motion in the foot and ankle.

How? Spend as much time as you can – at home, at work and outdoors – unshod. Play around with a selection of different surfaces and incorporate backwards walking too.

BAREFOOT SQUATTING

Why? "If you can't do a barefoot squat, you shouldn't be barefoot running," says Saxby.

How? Squat down for 30 seconds a few times a day. Once you can keep your heels down, progress to squatting with a weighted bar (5kg is fine) balanced across your collarbone with your arms outstretched in front. The final step is to squat with perfect posture and the bar raised overhead.

BAREFOOT JUMPING

Why? Natural running requires higher cadence (the rate at which your feet hit the ground).

How? Mark a line on the floor. Jump on the spot, keeping the jumps quick and just a few centimetres high. After 10 jumps, check your position in relation to the line. If you've travelled forward or back, you need to adjust your posture. "When you're perfectly aligned, you will stay on the spot," says Saxby.

BARE ESSENTIALS

CADENCE
The number of steps you take per minute.

COLLISION FORCE
The initial force your body experiences when your foot hits the ground.

ELASTIC RECOIL
Energy stored in tendo-muscular structures - such as the achilles tendon and plantar fascia - which contributes to propelling you forwards.

HEEL-TO-TOE DIFFERENTIAL
The difference in height between the heel and the forefoot of the shoe. Traditional running shoes typically have a difference of 12-14mm, so the heel is effectively raised.

ZERO DROP
A zero drop shoe is one that has absolutely no difference between the height of the shoe measured at the heel and that at the forefoot.

OVERSTRIDING
This occurs when your forward landing foot touches down ahead of your body.

PROPRIOCEPTION
Your body's sense of its own position, balance and movement based on sensory feedback.

TOE SPRING
The way the front of a shoe curls upward, designed to assist the 'toe off' motion when running.

Kinvara has become Saucony's third most popular shoe.) But some experts see them as more of a red herring within the industry. "It's much easier to change your form in a non-cushioned running shoe," says Jay Dicharry, director of the Speed Performance Clinic at the University of Virginia and a leading researcher and lecturer on running biomechanics, injuries and footwear.

Saxby couldn't agree with this statement more. As we steadily fall into step on our second lap of the Governors Island course, both of us unshod, he proceeds to makes an observation. "A lot of these people have got rid of their shoes, or put on a pair of FiveFingers or whatever, but they're still running with crap technique," he says, with characteristic bluntness. "When I come across injuries in people who have been running barefoot or in their minimal shoes it's usually because they haven't changed their form at all. They need to learn the correct technique, and build up the proper conditioning first, to be able to back it up."

THINK OUTSIDE THE (SHOE) BOX

Saxby believes the overriding problem is people don't consider running to be a skill. "They'll take up tennis and readily book a series of lessons to acquire the skills to play well," he says. "They don't expect to buy a racket that instantly improves their game. And it should be the same thought that goes in to running."

So what exactly is good form – and how do you master it? When I cadged a lift in Barefoot Ted's rickshaw, he likened learning to correctly run barefoot to learning a language. A language is a concrete thing with set principles and rules – but how we master it might differ (we all have our own unique ways of learning and understanding). That made sense to me – but when I attended some of the clinics organised as part of the New York Barefoot Run, the day before the race, I was surprised to find the various coaches in attendance were definitely not all speaking the same language.

Among the advice I heard: always let the heel touch down/ don't let the heel touch down; Stand up straight/adopt a forward lean; snap your bellybutton back against your spine/belly-breathe; start on concrete/stick to soft surfaces. So now we're all clear on that now, yes?

This disparity in coaching advice, and the attendant notion that everyone has their 'own' way, exasperates Saxby's thoughts on the matter. "There is only one way to run," he says. "Like it or not, we are all subject to exactly the same biomechanical laws. Imagine an engineer building a bridge. He ignores all the laws of physics and decides he'll just 'feel' his way through the task. It's never going to work. The hierarchy of human movement is physics."

Erwan Le Corre, the much-heralded founder of MovNat (movnat.com), which promotes and teaches natural movement to

"LISTEN TO THE SOUND YOUR FEET MAKE. THE GOAL IS A QUIET, GENTLE LANDING"

Barefoot Ted, barefoot ultra runner (barefooted.com)

Avoid tripping over your laces by ditching them

us 'zoo humans', agrees. "There are lots of ways to run, but only one way to run efficiently, in a way that uses the body how it was designed to move," he says. Watch one of Le Corre's natural movement videos on his website and you'll see he's well qualified to comment.

Lieberman's research tells us that we're designed to land on the balls of our feet. But if you're thinking that simply switching from your customary heel strike to a forefoot landing will turn you into a proficient barefoot runner, you're well and truly mistaken. "Where your foot lands in relation to your body is every bit as important as what part of your foot touches the ground first," says Dicharry.

Lieberman concurs: "If you are landing on the forefoot but it's still out in front of you (overstriding), you simply put higher loading through the calf and achilles." In fact, research from his Harvard laboratory indicates that 'bad' barefoot technique causes loading rates that could be as detrimental as heel striking in shoes.

Good form demands three interrelated elements, says Saxby. His mantra is 'posture, rhythm, relaxation'. "An upright body posture, with the head above the hips and the feet beneath them, combined with the right rhythm or

✦ ON GOOD FORM

1 "You should feel as though your feet are landing underneath you," says Lee Saxby. "The footstrike should be quiet, without slapping down or scuffing."

2 When you land, your shoulders, hips and ankles should all be aligned.

3 Your trailing leg should bend swiftly. A long, lazy trailing leg can cause two very undesirable outcomes: either it will result in the upper body tilting forward or it allows the leading leg to travel too far forward, both of these increase the chances of a heel strike.

4 "Looking straight ahead of you – at the horizon – and you'll be less likely to 'bend' at the hip," says Saxby.

5 "Your arms should preferably match the rhythm of your feet, and a greater bend at the elbow joint is also desirable," explains Saxby.

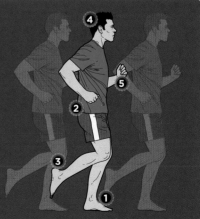

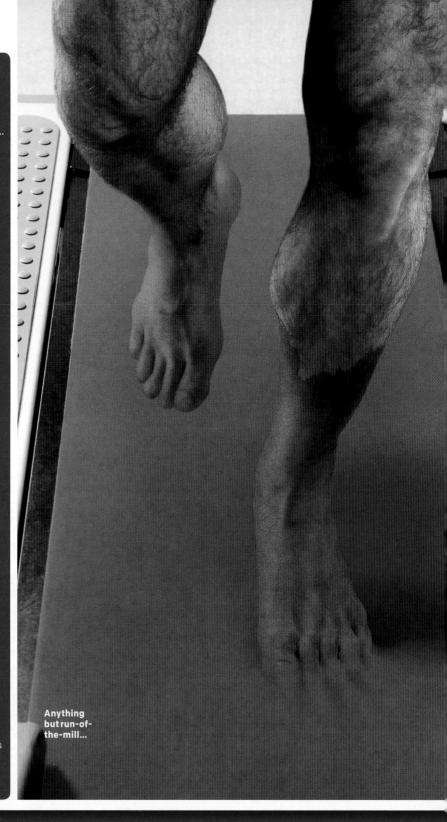

＋ DARE YOU BARE?

Will gyms let you run barefoot?

....

VIRGIN ACTIVE
(70+ UK branches)
"Appropriate clean exercise clothing and shoes must be worn while exercising."

DAVID LLOYD
(70+ UK branches)
"While you are at the club, you are expected to behave and dress appropriately." (No specific rule on footwear, but there have been several cases reported of runners being told to put footwear on.)

LA FITNESS
(79 UK branches)
"You must always wear appropriate clothes/ shoes in the club."

CANNONS
(50+ UK branches)
"If you mean literally barefoot, we can't accept this because of risk control measures. All members running on the treadmill should be wearing trainers."

FITNESS FIRST
(150+ UK branches)
"For health and safety reasons, all members are required to wear footwear while using equipment in the gym."

BANNATYNE'S HEALTH
Club (60+ UK branches):
"We have a policy that footwear must be worn when using the gym facilities. Those members wanting the benefits of barefoot training choose to use Vibram shoes."

Anything but run-of-the-mill...

'cadence' of 170-185 steps per minute stops you overstriding and enables you to land with the foot underneath you rather than extended in front," he explains. "Then you need to relax into it. Tension sabotages rhythm and relies on excessive muscle action." (See 'The Barefoot Form Guide' for more on improving your form).

Le Corre adds the point that running with correct form doesn't mean every stride should be identical. "Form should not be rigid," he says. "You may need to overstride for a few steps because of the terrain – the environment influences your form and part of being an efficient runner is your ability to adapt to it."

THE ROAD TO BEING A BETTER RUNNER

There wasn't much call at all for adaptability in the New York run. The course was pancake-flat and 100 per cent asphalt. After 4.2 miles, my bare soles were smarting and a large blood blister had formed on my toe. Besides, it seemed more people were now after-partying than running. As I joined the first-aid queue in search of a blister plaster, the paramedic glanced up at us all and quipped, "I have Nikes for sale."

For a moment I could picture the scene from his point of view – a bunch of crazies following this latest fad. With so much hype, even non-runners are aware of the 'barefoot' trend. But I worry that now the buzzword has become a misleading umbrella term, referring to everything from running literally barefoot or in FiveFingers to just a slightly-less-clunky trainer. It's important to understand the distinctions between these differing degrees of commitment, as well as their relative risks and rewards. If all you want to do is shave a few grams and millimetres off your heel lift, go

"FIRST GO FULLY BAREFOOT, RATHER THAN STRAIGHT INTO MINIMAL SHOES"

Michael Sandler, author of Barefoot Running (£10.85, Three Rivers Press)

ahead. But if you plan to go the whole hog, be prepared to put in the necessary work and accept that adapting will take time.

I went literally barefoot in New York to enter fully into the spirit, but in all honesty, I run barefoot infrequently at home. A mile or two here, a few drills or strides there – the remainder of the time I'm in shoes, albeit very minimal

ones. But I don't think that's an issue. For me, I know going 'barefoot', without the cushioning, guidance, stability and support of a traditional running shoe, has taught me how to run better. Instead of silencing the feedback and supporting my weaknesses I've listened to what my body's saying and addressed shortfalls in strength and mobility.

A few years ago, in the last week before the London Marathon was set to commence, my new puppy chewed up one of my orthotics. I nearly had a nervous breakdown and spent a fortune having a new one made in time for race day. Now I have the confidence, know-how and the new freedom of being able to run in anything – or nothing at all, well on my feet anyway. The lesson here is that the answers you may seek to good form and injury-free running do not simply lie inside a shoebox.

⊕ WHAT'S TOE MATTER?

In the 1930s, orthopaedic surgeon Dudley Morton identified a condition in which the second metatarsal head was longer than the first. "Morton's toe is a structural spanner in the works," explains Saxby.

HAVE YOU GOT MORTON'S TOE?

Hold your foot firmly, and bend at the metatarsals, looking at the 'knuckles' that will go white with the pressure. Is your second toe's knuckle closer to the tip of your toes than the first? If so, you have Morton's toe.

WHAT TO DO...

Barefoot walking, squatting and jumping will help establish correct loading patterns, but these exercises will also be useful.

➡ Practise driving the big toe downwards, as if pressing a drawing pin into the ground. Don't curl the toe over – keep it straight.

➡ Roll a golf ball under your sole to ease the plantar fascia, then from side to side under the metatarsal heads to mobilise the joint.

➡ Press the big toe into the floor and curl the other four toes under, keeping the foot as straight as possible (not tilting it inwards).

➡ Try a thin insole with a raised area under the first metatarsal head (Posture Control Insoles, £55, back2feet.net).

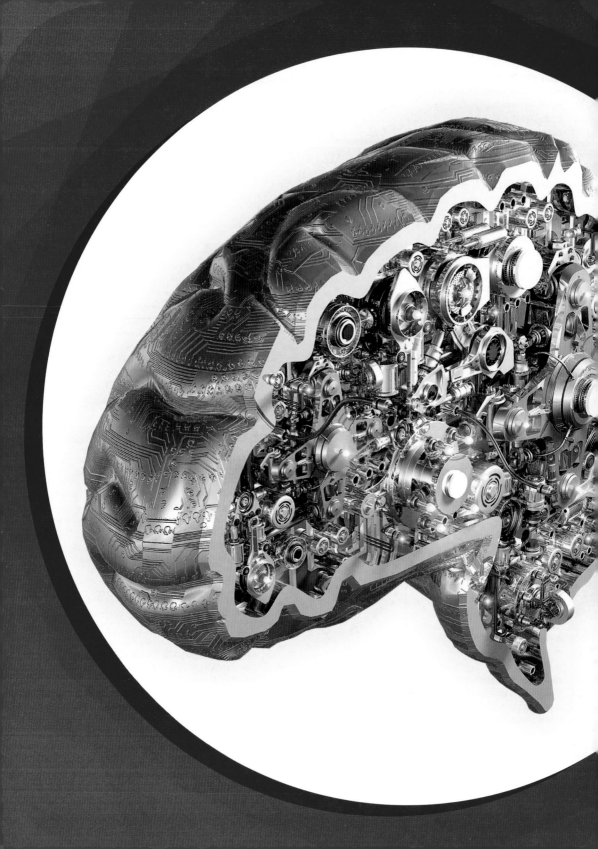

Chapter 8

MIND CONTROL

Your brain is one of your most powerful allies on any run.
Here's how to bend it to your will and run stronger

202 | **BREAK THE BARRIERS**
Smash through negativity

206 | **48 WAYS TO KEEP GOING**
Keep motivated with this list

212 | **QUICK THINKING**
Train your mind to help you run better

218 | **BRAIN BOOSTING SERUM**
How running will make you smarter

ILLUSTRATION OLIVER BURSTON

BREAK THE BARRIERS

A strong mind makes a strong runner, so it's time to smash through the negativity holding you back...

I t's an all too common story: runner sets achievable goals; runner puts in the necessary physical training to meet goals; runner falls short on race day. So, what's the problem? Could it be that you're spending too much time becoming a stronger runner on the road, and precious little on becoming a stronger runner in your mind? Big mistake. To achieve your true potential, it's essential to train mentally as well as physically.

"The athlete who ignores the mental element of training quite simply won't enjoy their running or achieve as much, and might even give up altogether," explains sports psychologist Jamie Edwards (trained-brain.com). "As a runner you really get to know yourself and what kind of mental toughness you have inside – once you've realised what you're capable of, and can block out the negative voices, you become not just a stronger runner, but a stronger person." With the help of the UK's premier sports psychologists, we've come up with solutions for the most common mental hurdles standing between you and the happier, stronger runner fighting to get out.

I CAN'T HANDLE THE PAIN BARRIER

➡ **WHAT'S HAPPENING?**
The brain always gives up before the body, according to Simone Lewis, sports psychologist at Bath University. "Unless you're used

to pushing yourself to the limit, the only possible credible option to improve the situation you're in appears to be stopping."

➡ **YOUR STRATEGY** "There are two essential strategies for handling the pain – dissociating to externalise it and distract yourself away from it, and associating to actually focus on the feeling," says Lewis. To associate, start from the head and work down, assessing each area or group of muscles. "Keep your pace in line with the information you will gain from your body monitoring, from heart rate to basic breathing, not being afraid to increase the pace if you feel good enough."

To dissociate, focus more on your surroundings – the sounds, sights and smells – and let them distract you temporarily. "The most successful runners switch between the two," says Lewis, "using association during the more crucial sections of a race and dissociation at times where you can give yourself a break from the tough mental demands – associating for long periods simply isn't possible, because the mind is going to wander."

PRE-RACE NERVES RUIN MY PERFORMANCES

➡ **WHAT'S HAPPENING?**
You've got textbook "what if" syndrome. "The reason you're nervous – burning precious

glycogen, as well as being away from the calm zone from where athletes are able to perform best – is that you're panicking about what might happen in the future, rather than dealing with what is happening presently," says sports psychologist Jamie Edwards.

➡ **YOUR STRATEGY** You should try Edwards' principle technique: structured belly breathing. Begin

AS A RUNNER YOU REALLY GET TO KNOW THE MENTAL TOUGHNESS THAT YOU HAVE INSIDE

by inhaling through your nose to a count of three, pause, then slowly exhale through your mouth for a count of four. How does this help? "Short, staccato breathing floods your respiratory system with carbon dioxide, which means your brain and muscles aren't getting the oxygen that they need to function properly," says Edwards. "Deep, long breaths will activate the parasympathetic nervous system, slowing down your heart rate and reducing anxiety."

ILLUSTRATIONS: OSCAR GIMENEZ

Demolish your
personal best

Stamp out those negative thoughts

break from running competitively and only lace-up for pure pleasure, says Bishop. "You'll know deep down inside when you're ready to come back."

NEGATIVE MEMORIES ABOUT OLD INJURIES WILL ALWAYS HOLD YOU BACK

MY LAST RACE WAS A SHOCKER – AND NOW I'VE LOST MY MOTIVATION

➡ WHAT'S HAPPENING?
That brick wall standing between you and the starting line is your pride. "Not long after you started running, being a runner probably became a part of your self-identity

– and pivotal to your identity in your peers' eyes," says Dr Dan Bishop, a sports psychologist at Brunel University, and sub-three-hour marathon runner. "You're 'The Runner' that your friends know, which is a very brittle concept – and one that is easily shattered in your own mind through one bad performance."
➡ YOUR STRATEGY "Without the disappointments, the successes simply wouldn't be as sweet," says Bishop, who advises first getting to the root cause of your poor performance – the weather, a poorly executed race plan – and venting your frustration about it. "Moan to as many people as will listen to get it out of your system." Now congratulate yourself for having the courage to take risks. "Accept and savour your mistakes as learning experiences." If that still doesn't help, take a

I ALWAYS CHOKE WHEN I SEEM TO BE PERFORMING WELL

➡ WHAT'S HAPPENING?
While many people leap ceiling-high at the sight of a spider, yours is a different kind of fear: success. "Many of us find something frightening about surpassing our own or others' expectations – and that can be enough to keep us from doing so," says Bishop. "For some it's lacking the confidence to challenge the status quo, while others fear that if they're successful they'll have to take the sport too seriously; that too much will be expected of them; or even that they'll be resented."
➡ YOUR STRATEGY
Acknowledge that your fear exists – then pump yourself up with positive affirmation. "See yourself accepting success," says Bishop. "While nobody likes a big-head, modesty in runners all too often leads to self-deprecation." Take your lead from athletes in post-race TV interviews, he suggests. "When someone says 'Nice race', reply with 'Thanks, I worked hard for it' – rather than 'I was lucky' or 'I should've done better'." Building self-belief without over-selling yourself will pay dividends, says Bishop. "It will empower you to take the lead in the next race."

I FEEL COMPLETELY BURNT OUT

➡ WHAT'S HAPPENING?
Quite simply, you're expecting too much of yourself physically, which means that mentally your main sail drops. "Too often runners get to this point and become dispirited," says Lewis. "The mind and body work as one, so your brain helps

you overcome hurdles when your running is on the up, but can turn on you if you continually push yourself to chase new PBs without much success."

➡ **YOUR STRATEGY** Know your limits. "Accept that consistent improvement simply isn't sustainable and that you'll have set-backs," explains Lewis. "Plan several scheduled time-outs a year – at least a week at a time – to rest, regenerate and develop that hunger for running again." Forget your times, unstrap your stopwatch and rekindle your running desire by throwing some variety into your training, advises Lewis. "Try shorter distances, take different routes, enter a race somewhere you've never been to before or just do your usual run back to front."

WORRYING ABOUT AN OLD INJURY IS HOLDING ME BACK

➡ **WHAT'S HAPPENING?** Your brain is behaving like an over-protective mum. "People develop a defensive memory function to help prevent them from re-injuring themselves," says Paul Russell, sports and exercise psychologist at the University of Bolton and private consultant (thefifthspace. com). "Until those negative memories are replaced with the confidence that your injury is fully healed, you'll always be holding back." You'll also potentially be risking fresh damage. "Anxiety leads to muscle tension, which can result in new injuries," he adds.

➡ **YOUR STRATEGY** You must take your know-how of the injury up a gear to gain mental control. "Develop specific visualisation of problem area(s) by becoming familiar with anatomical drawings of the muscles of the body," says Russell. "Being able to 'see' those muscles widening and lengthening as you run will encourage them to

relax, which in turn will ward off the tension that causes them to shorten, tighten and fatigue."

I LOSE ALL FOCUS IN RACES

➡ **WHAT'S HAPPENING?** En route to the finish line, the racing environment bombards us with information, and we have the necessary tools (ears, eyes etc) to pick up the lot. "Being stressed can cause our focus to narrow, cutting out important information, such as the position of a competitor," says sports psychologist Ian Maynard from Sheffield Hallam University. "Or we can be so relaxed (or determined to shut out the stressor) that we begin to

focus too much on things that are superfluous to our performance."

➡ **YOUR STRATEGY** Take your cue. Maynard recommends this tried-and-tested re-focusing technique: "I like the simple routine of 'breathe', 'talk' and 'race'," he explains. "'Breathe' is your cue to focus on the movement of your chest, which should instantly take you away from the distraction; the 'talk' element introduces an instructional cue word, such as 'relax', 'rhythm' or '100 per cent'. Lastly, focus on your 'race' – your splits, breathing, strategy. This process brings you back into the here and now, where your good concentration always will need to be."

Achieve all your running goals

MIND

48 WAYS TO KEEP GOING

There are reasons but no excuses for losing motivation to run. We can combat them all, with tips, inspiring stories and more

1 START A BLOG
Post your daily mileage, then give out the url to your friends and family. Do you really want Auntie Susan or Uncle Bob asking why you skipped your four-miler on Wednesday?

2 FORGET TIME
Running coach Shane Bogan advises leaving your watch at home once in a while. "It's liberating not to be worried about pace," he says. Just enjoy a run for its own sake.

3 TREAT YOURSELF
That new running watch you're hankering after? Go ahead and buy it – after timing 10 more speed sessions with your old one.

4 LOOK TO THE PAST
Emil Zatopek, who won four Olympic gold medals in his career, was a tough-as-nails athlete known for his intense training methods, such as running in work boots. Competing with a gland infection and against his doctor's orders, the Czech won three distance events, including the marathon, at the 1952 Helsinki Olympics in Finland.

5 THINK FAST
The runners coach Christy Coughlin works with always get a boost from this simple negative-splits workout: run for 20 minutes as slowly as you want, then turn around and run home faster. "The long warm-up helps you feel great and run faster on the way back," says Coughlin.

6 BLAZE A NEW PATH
"If you do the same runs all the time, it can beat you down," says Alan Culpepper, an Olympic marathon runner. Try a GPS system, or check out mapmyrun. com to find new routes.

7 SIGN UP FOR A WINTER RACE
Or for running holiday in a warm country. Every training mile you log takes you closer to that winter marathon in Bangkok (thailandmarathon. org), Las Vegas (las-vegas. competitor.com) or Sydney (sydneymarathon.org).

8 GET YOUR KIT ON
The simple act of throwing on the appropriate clothes will get you out the door. You can take them off again, after you've gone outside and sweated on them a bit.

Running in the cold is easy if you've got a hot race planned

ILLUSTRATION: ADAM MCCAULEY

⑨ ENTER A RELAY RACE

Either as part of a large running team, or do the run leg of a triathlon with a cycling and a swimming friend. You'll be less likely to skimp on your training as you won't want to let your teammates down.

⑩ DEVISE YOUR OWN LOYALTY SCHEME

Try one mile equals one point. Start collecting for yourself today and soon you could have saved up enough points for a new pair of running shoes, an afternoon at a health spa, a ticket to the big game or a small but guilt-free treat from a very expensive chocolate shop.

⑪ FEEL INSPIRED

In 1949, nine-year-old Wilma Rudolph learned to walk without leg braces after suffering from polio and spending most of her first years in bed. Rudolph went on to win three gold medals for the USA in the 1960 Olympics.

⑫ SET SOME DAILY GOALS

Scott Jurek, seven-time winner of the Western States 100-Mile Endurance Run in the USA, sets himself a variety of goals for big races and for training sessions. "Maybe it is a technique goal, maybe a pace goal, maybe a goal of running faster at the end," he says.

⑬ SPOIL YOURSELF

Book a massage for the day after your long run. It's very good for your muscles and can be considered as an appropriate treat after all that hard running.

⑭ RUN WHEN IT'S TIPPING DOWN

Trust us – with rain lashing down on you sideways and the wind whipping you across your face, you will feel wonderfully alive. Just

Turn your run into a money making machine

make sure that you have a spare kit and a dry pair of shoes for tomorrow's wet weather run.

15 FOR EMERGENCY USE ONLY

Consider taking a short break from running if you think you've got the beginning of an injury or you're truly fatigued. A couple of days rest may reinvigorate you. Call this one instant running motivation for three days from now.

16 YOU WANT TO LOOK GOOD ON THE BEACH

Don't you?

17 IT'S SUMMER!
Well, it may not be when you read this, but when it is, go outside and run. Read the rest of this later.

18 IT'S NEVER TOO LATE

Mary Peters was 33 and near the end of her career when she defeated local favourite Heide Rosendahl to take gold in the pentathlon at the 1972 Olympics in Munich. Her victory brought temporary calmness to Northern Ireland with rival factions celebrating together the country's greatest ever sporting success.

19 GET PAID
Set a price for attaining a certain mileage. When you hit it, pay up. Keep the money in a jar, and once it accumulates, buy that new running jacket.

20 IF YOU'RE REALLY IN THE MOOD...

...for a change, check out the list of clothing-optional races and other running events at british-naturism.org.uk/events.

21 WATCH THIS
Endurance – a 1999 docudrama which shows how Ethiopian Haile Gebrselassie became one of the best distance runners of all time.

22 EXERCISE MAKES SEX BETTER

According to thorough research. Enough said.

23 GET WET
If it gets too hot outside, coach Bruce Gross suggests logging your miles by running in the deep end of a pool while wearing a flotation vest. Gross tells his runners to break it up by going hard for five minutes, then resting for one minute. Build up to an hour.

24 RACE RESULTS STAY ON GOOGLE FOREVER

Well, until the end of either the internet or the world, anyway. Need any more motivation to clock the best time you can?

25 TURN THINGS AROUND

"A poor performance is a strong motivator for me," says elite marathon runner Clint Verran. "I can't wait to prove to myself that I'm a better runner than my last showing." Verran also says negative comments from his coaches fire him up. "For me, proving somebody else to be wrong is key."

26 RUN LOADS OF MARATHONS?

Maybe try an ultra. Or a mile.

27 BECOME A RUNNING MENTOR

Once you get a cohort hooked on your sport they'll be counting on your continued support, guidance – and company.

MIND

28 IF YOU ARE STAYING IN

The Four-Minute Mile is a 1988 UK film that tells the story of how Roger Bannister became the first man to run the mile in under four minutes, despite conventional wisdom of the time insisting that such an achievement was physiologically impossible.

29 DUST OFF YOUR TRACK SPIKES

Some athletics clubs organise Olympic-style summer games where you can compete in events like the mile or even the 400-metre hurdles.

30 REMEMBER THE SIMPLE TRUTH

That you almost always feel better after a run than you do before it.

31 MAKE A CONNECTION

Try logging on to dateactive.co.uk, a website that connects active people looking for love. Get in your run and go on a date at the same time.

32 DON'T EXPECT EVERY DAY TO BE BETTER THAN THE LAST

Some days will be slower than others, and some days might hurt a bit more than others. But as long as you're out there running, it's a good day.

33 FILL THE BATH...

...with hot water, then head out for a three-miler on a freezing morning. The sooner you get back, the hotter your bath is.

It's time to get your fill

34 JUST... START!

If the thought of running your full session is too much to bear, just go out to run around the block. Chances are, once you're outside, you'll start to feel better and put in at least a few miles.

35 FOCUS ON THE COMPETITION

Shawn Crawford, the 2004 Olympic 200-metre gold medalist, says his two chief competitors are himself and his stopwatch, and they keep him heading out every day. "I want to break records, and you can't break records sitting on the sofa at home."

36 FORGET ABOUT THE BIG PICTURE

every now and then. Put away your training manual and set aside your race calendar. Stop overthinking it all, and just run for today.

37 THINK ON... AND STRONG

Roger Bannister and John Landy (the only two men to have broken four minutes in the mile at the time) raced at the 1954 British Empire and Commonwealth Games in Vancouver in what was billed as 'The Miracle Mile.' Landy led for most of the race, but Bannister passed him on the final turn, proving the old saying 'it ain't over till it's over'.

38 BECOME A RACE DIRECTOR

If you live in a small town with no road races, start your own. Most towns have some sort of annual celebration in the summer, and you can tie the race to that. Work with local track and cross-country teams to help promote it.

39 STOP RUNNING IN CIRCLES

Andy Steinfeld, who coaches marathon runners, says group

ILLUSTRATION (PREVIOUS PAGE): PETER CROWTHER ASSOCIATES AT DEBUT ART. PHOTOGRAPHY DAVID WOOLLEY, STUDIO 33 point-to-point runs are a fun way to add a new twist to training. His runners head out for 12 to 20 miles, then refuel together at a local restaurant before hopping on the bus to travel back to the starting point.

40 LIVE IN THE NOW

Ultrarunner Scott Jurek focuses on the moment to get him through difficult patches on his long runs and races. "I tune in to my breath, my technique, and my current pace, and I stay away from what lies ahead," he says. This is an especially helpful technique when what lies ahead is another 99 miles.

41 GET SOME PERSPECTIVE

Meb Keflezighi, the Eritrean-born US runner and 2009 New York Marathon winner, listens to songs about his former country's struggle for independence from Ethiopia when he needs a boost. "The true heroes are the soldiers," he says. "Those are the real tough guys."

Medal with your motivation

MIND

42 BRING HOME SOME HARDWARE

Okay, so you're not going to win the London Marathon, but that doesn't mean you can't score a medal. Find a few sall races where you might be able to compete for the top spots in your age group.

43 BUY A FULL-LENGTH MIRROR

Make sure you look in it every day. If you're running regularly (and eating well) you will soon see changes to your body composition that make you want to carry on.

44 TRY A TRI

By doing a portion of your weekly miles swimming in the pool and pedaling on the bike for a triathlon can reinvigorate your mind, body and spirit. As well as your running.

45 INVEST IN SOME GOOD GEAR

For beginners, this may mean a good pair of running shoes to avoid injuries and technical clothes made of fabric that wicks away moisture and prevents chafing. For others, experimenting with the latest GPS unit or footpod can be a fun way to stay motivated.

46 BE CREATIVE

If the idea of going on your regular four-miler just sinks you further into the sofa, remember

that there are other ways to put in some miles – like a game of five-a-side football. A midfielder runs up to six miles in a 90-minute football game.

47 IGNORE THE DIRTY DISHES

They can wait until the sun goes down, your run can't. Okay?

48 LET US HELP

Visit runnersworld.co.uk for pages of ideas and inspiration from the experts.

QUICK THINKING

What if that heaviness in your legs that grinds you to a halt is your mind playing tricks on you? Here's how you can train it to make you go faster and longer

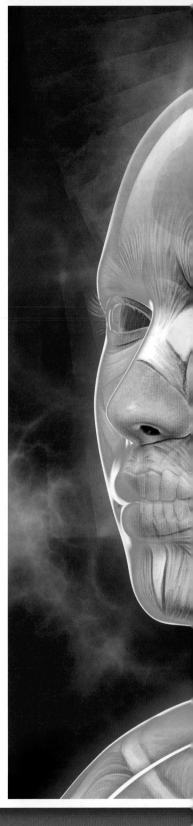

You know it all too well: that awful moment when your overworked lungs and leaden lower limbs combine to create an overbearing desire to S-L-O-W D-O-W-N. When the burden of placing one foot in front of the other grows intensely with every limping stride and you reach the end of your run – far earlier than intended – convinced that you just don't have another step in you. You are, to use the scientific parlance, absolutely knackered.

Given where these go-slow sensations manifest, it's unsurprising that most research into improving endurance has been based primarily around the theory that fatigue occurs as a result of the body – the muscles,

lungs and heart – letting your brain know that it has reached its limit. But what if that turns out to be a false assumption? What if it's the other way around?

Acknowledging the role your mind plays in reaching peak athletic performance is nothing new. Though somewhat intangible, elite athletes have long exalted the merits of mental power in eking out a physical edge that can mean the difference between a podium finish and also-ran. Sir Roger Bannister, a man who knows a thing or two about pushing the performance envelope, even hinted beyond the notion of willpower: "It is the brain, and not the heart or lungs, that is the critical organ."

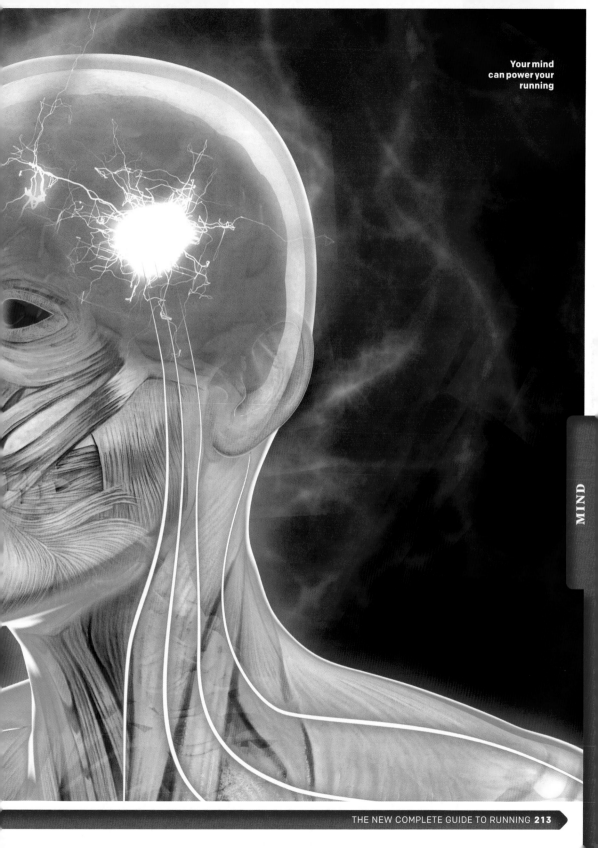

Your mind can power your running

GREY MATTERS

A growing number of scientists are now in agreement, and many have centered studies on the precise role of the brain when it comes to endurance performance and fatigue. Among the first was Tim Noakes, professor of exercise and sports at the University of Cape Town and author of *Lore of Running* (£20, Human Kinetics Europe). Based on his findings, he argues that it is the brain that limits our endurance efforts before the body gives out.

"But what about VO_2 max?" you may ask, quite possibly in snatched breaths, bent double by the side of a track. After all, scientists and coaches have been pushing us to our lung-bursting limits based on the theory that a lack of oxygen

When it comes to fatigue's red stop light, he says, your brain isn't merely receiving the information, it's in control. "Fatigue is just a sensation – it's your brain telling your body it's tired, not the other way round," says Noakes. And how does the brain pull rank on your brawn? "It inhibits force output by reducing drive to the muscles," says Noakes, which cuts the number of motor units that are activated during exercise. In other words, your brain tells your muscles to slow down, rather than your muscles telling your brain that it's time to rest.

If this alternative theory of muscle fatigue is correct, the significance is huge. But first things first, is the research there to back it up? Studying the levels of electrical

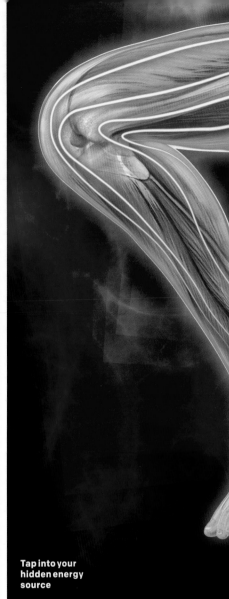

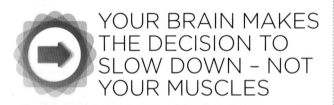

YOUR BRAIN MAKES THE DECISION TO SLOW DOWN – NOT YOUR MUSCLES

to the working muscles is what limits performance since Nobel Prize-winning British physiologist AV Hill presented the basis for that theory some 90 years ago. The idea that oxygen delivery is the whole story seems neat and logical. But it's wrong, contends Noakes, who first challenged Hill's model as far back as 1987. In research published in the journal *Medicine & Science in Sports & Exercise*, Noakes reanalysed Hill's data and discovered that Hill's studies hadn't actually *proven* that runners had run out of oxygen.

So what is happening? Noakes's own research-based theory on endurance performance is known as the 'central governor' model.

activity in working muscles does provide compelling evidence: theoretically, as muscle fibres tire, more should be recruited to pick up the slack. However, in a study that required experienced cyclists to perform 1,000m and 4,000m sprints over the course of a 100K time trial, Noakes noted that electrical activity in the muscles actually dropped as fatigue set in – even when the cyclists were pedalling as fast as they could. "They felt as though they'd reached their physical limits, but they were actually only using 30 per cent of their muscle fibres," says Noakes.

But Noakes isn't on his own here. A University of Birmingham study revealed even more about

Tap into your hidden energy source

the brain's tendency to ring-fence our energy supplies. Athletes were asked to rinse their mouths with (but not swallow) either a solution of water and a flavourless carbohydrate called maltodextrin, or a placebo. Those who had swished the carb-based solution improved their performance in intense bouts of exercise lasting an hour or so. It appears that the brain can sense carbohydrates in the mouth, even tasteless ones,

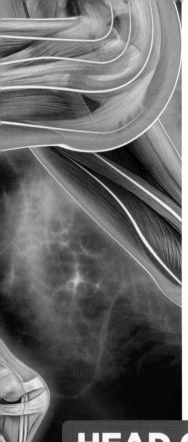

says Matt Bridge, a senior sports science lecturer at the university. "Your brain tells your body that carbohydrates are on the way. And with that message, muscles and nerves are prompted to work harder and longer." Remember, the carbs were not consumed, so there was no actual fuel boost. It was, as they say, all in the mind.

So why, exactly, is our grey matter so keen to slow us down that it pulls one over on us? According to Noakes's central governor model, our brains are constantly keeping an eye on the bigger picture – stopping us pushing past the point where we have the potential to do harm to muscles or other organs. To guard against an internal catastrophe, "a control system in a small area of the brain constantly monitors the signals sent from all over your body," says Noakes. If it interprets the information as a threat, your brain produces feelings of discomfort and reduces electrical output to the muscles to keep you safe."

That's when those fairly convincing 'I must stop right now' messages start bouncing around inside your head. You may feel them as coming express mail from your searing quads and stabbing calves, but they've actually never ventured to the business end of your running machinery. In fact, "those messages are sent from the sub-conscious brain to the conscious brain," says Noakes.

THE EXTRA YARDS IN YOUR HEAD

The central governor theory may explain the phenomenon of seemingly utterly exhausted marathoners somehow finding enough gas in their tanks to rally for the final mile. Noakes suggests

HEAD CANDY

Your greedy grey matter consumes 20 per cent of your body's energy, so fuel smartly to keep it primed for peak performance

YOUR PLAN B

Load up on choline. The most recently discovered member of the vitamin B family, this nutrient feeds your brain's neurotransmitters and has been proven to improve your reaction times, says Dr Qiang Li of Duke University in the US. "Neuro-transmitters are responsible for firing muscle cells, so any problem with these affects performance," says Drew Price, performance nutrition consultant (drewprice. co.uk). "Some B vitamins act as co-factors in the release of energy from foods, so a shortage will put a bottleneck in the system that releases energy." Eggs, tomatoes and potatoes are all high in choline.

LIQUID ASSETS

Your brain is over 70 per cent water. If this percentage dips when you become dehydrated, you'll feel listless. "Cells are bags of chemicals, and life – function and performance – is those chemicals reacting, which they do mostly in solution," says Price. "When the concentration of that solution goes out of the very narrow ideal band it changes your body chemistry – cells can't function as they're designed to and performance is the first thing to suffer." Stay energised by starting your morning off with a 300ml glass of H_2O. And keep a bottle handy, too: the British Dietetic Association recommends that you drink around two and a half litres a day.

SWEET IT OUT

Your brain needs a constant supply of glucose for optimum function, says Price. "But consuming lots of sugar or high-GI carbs such as white bread or pasta will leave you feeling more lethargic. It causes a large release of insulin which, after a time, drops your blood sugar below where it should be. Also, processed foods containing white starches and sugars supply few of the vitamin co-factors or minerals needed for enzymes to access energy easily." A few simple swaps will stabilise your energy. Go for sweet potato over white, porridge over cereals with added sugar, and basmati rice rather than short grain. All have a lower GI value.

that the subconscious brain senses the end of exercise is near, so it allows any extra energy to be released for use by your muscles. This regulation mechanism is there to ensure you always reach the finish line safely, says Noakes. "You always have a little reserve."

So far, so geeky. But there's an obvious practical question popping up here: if we know that there's rest and refuelling on the way, and we know that there's more in reserve than our subconscious brain wants us to get access to, can we short-circuit the subconscious safety catch and tap into that extra potential? The knowledge that there's more in the tank than our brains want to let on is pretty empowering in itself, but is there something we can do to trick our subconscious into halting the feelings of fatigue and removing the physiological shackles to let more muscle fibres get involved in moving us from A to B, ASAP?

The tantalising promise is that we can con our grey matter into giving us more oomph when we need it. But how do you get one over on your (central) guv'nor? A little trickery goes a long way, according to a Northumbria University study. Researchers put cyclists through a 4,000m time challenge; after several repeats, participants felt they understood their limits over the distance. Next, each of the cyclists was presented with two avatars on a screen in front of them. One moved at the rate of their own pedalling, while their virtual competitor, they were told, was programmed to move at the

---

MIND GAINS
Use these psychological tricks to fool your brain into boosting your performance

REDEFINE YOUR LIMITS
Show your brain what your body can *really* do

Think you consciously decided how fast you were going to run today? Think again. At the University of Cape Town, two groups of cyclists completed time trials in the hot and the cold. Those exercising in the heat clocked slower times – but they dropped pace well before their core temperatures rose significantly. This suggests pace is pre-emptively set by the brain. How can you counter this? There's no way to sugarcoat it: learn to deal with discomfort the hard way, says Noakes. Running at race pace and faster in 1,000m intervals is the best way to show your brain what your body can do.

FREE SOME HEADSPACE
Tough day? Time to reach for the remote...

Give yourself a performance boost with Robson Green's *Extreme Fishing*. Yes, you heard that right. Disengaging your brain for a little while could give you an edge on the track or field. In a Bangor University study, athletes were asked to perform high-intensity sessions after spending 90 minutes watching a documentary or completing a hard problem-solving task. While physiological responses barely differed between the groups, the more mentally fatigued athletes had higher levels of perceived exertion and gave up 15 per cent earlier than the TV-watchers.

STRENGTH IN NUMBERS
Take on a friend to tap into your fuel reserves

Portsmouth University researchers asked cyclists to race as fast as they could for 2,000m, as a figure representing them moved along a virtual course on a screen. Next, they were told a second figure would represent the efforts of a competitor. The cyclists stormed to victory over their 'rivals' with an average speed increase of one and a half per cent over the final stages. "Our results show that competition provides the motivation to tell the brain to eat into a greater part of the fuel reserve that athletes have left at the end of a race," says study author Dr Jo Corbett, a physiologist.

REST, ASSURED
Banish mental fatigue with proper recovery

Hard training sessions release cytokines – immune-system cells that aid the repair of exercise-related muscle damage. One of these (IL-6) enters the brain and alters our neurochemistry, causing exhaustion. Researchers at the Appalachian State University in the US discovered that high-intensity training, with insufficient rest afterwards, causes levels of IL-6 to stay elevated, which can leave you extremely fatigued. Always get your full quota of shut-eye (eight hours during heavy training periods) and find time for a healthy post-run meal – see Brain Food, on the page before.

MIND OVER MATTER
Meditate away your aches and pains

Taking time out to say "ommm" can relieve the ouch, according to US studies at Wake Forest Baptist Medical Centre. One hour 20 minutes of meditation was found to reduce 'pain intensity' by 40 per cent and 'pain unpleasantness' by 57 per cent. And brain scans demonstrated reduced pain-related activation. The trick is to let your mind run wild and acknowledge all your thoughts, says study author Fadel Zeidan, but without dwelling on them. Pay close attention to your breathing, says Zeidan. "Follow [the air] as it enters at your nose; notice any tingling – scan your body for sensations."

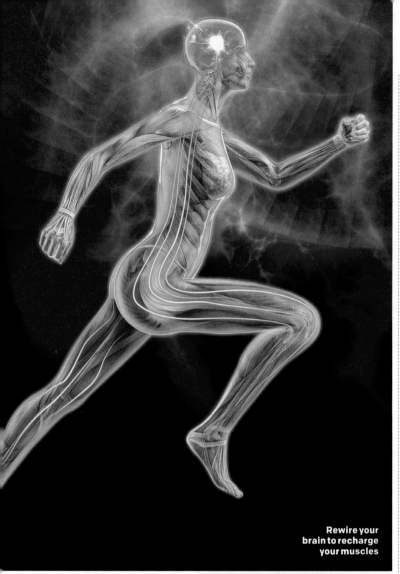

Rewire your brain to recharge your muscles

dip into are still limited, says Noakes. "Ultimately, physiological forces will always have the final say over the brain."

Using the same approach as before, Dr Thompson attempted to find out where that physiological line is drawn. Again two groups of cyclists competed against an avatar, but while the first group were told the second avatar would be racing either two or five per cent harder than their best efforts, the second group were kept in the dark about the increase in speed. The first group gave up the chase almost from the off, only matching their own best efforts. The second group, however, kept up with the avatars that were programmed to perform two per cent harder, but five per cent proved too much, with the cyclists giving up halfway through.

ACCESS YOUR EMERGENCY POWER

So, what does this mean for you? "Our findings demonstrate that a metabolic reserve exists which, if it can be accessed, can release a performance improvement of between two and five per cent," says Thompson. "At a competitive level, an average speed increase of just one per cent can make the difference between whether you're placed in a race or not."

The lesson is that if muscle fatigue does originate in the brain, then your efforts to prevent fatigue should target your mind as well as your muscles. And central to this, says Noakes, is convincing your brain of your actual ability. "Coaches have known this for a long time," he says. "They teach people to train harder so their brains learn what they're capable of." See Mind Gains *left* for more ways to release that performance reserve.

pace of their own best effort – but it was actually travelling one per cent faster. The cyclists ended up matching their speedier avatars on their virtual rides, achieving faster times over the distance than they had previously been able to.

"A small deception of the brain can enhance your performance," says Professor Kevin Thompson, head of sport and exercise sciences at Northumbria University. "Despite the internal feedback to the brain being heightened by the extra power output being produced, the study subjects still

A SMALL DECEPTION OF THE BRAIN CAN ENHANCE YOUR PERFORMANCE

believed that it was possible to beat their virtual opponent."

But it obviously only goes so far. No matter how cunning you become at out-manoeuvring your brain, the energy reserves it can

WORDS MATT GILBERT
ILLUSTRATIONS ROGER HARRIS

MIND

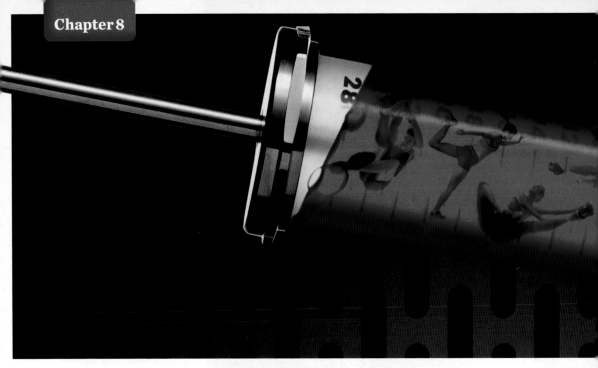

BRAIN-BOOSTING SERUM

It's true: clever people run. Here's how giving yourself an extra shot of exercise can help boost your mental performance

So, you already know that running will make your heart and lungs stronger. But if your enthusiasm has been pummeled by plateauing performances, there's more to help get you out of the door: new research shows a strong link between running and a 'younger', more nimble brain. Vigorous cardiovascular activity pumps more oxygen- and glucose-rich blood to your noggin and when you make running a frequent habit, the

rewards are long-term. All forms of exercise generate more energy for the brain, but research shows that the more aerobically challenging the exercise, the greater the payoff for your grey cells. Here's how your workout gets your brain in shape.

NEW THINKING

The bus-plus-crossword combo may give you a chance to flex your grey matter, but it can't compete with working up a sweat. Running sparks the growth of

fresh nerve cells – a process called neurogenesis – and new blood vessels, which is known as angiogenesis, says Dr J Carson Smith, an assistant professor at the University of Maryland, US, who studies the role exercise plays in brain function. "We know that neurogenesis and angiogenesis increase brain tissue volume, which otherwise shrinks as we age," he says. In a recent study reported in the *Proceedings of the National Academy of Sciences*

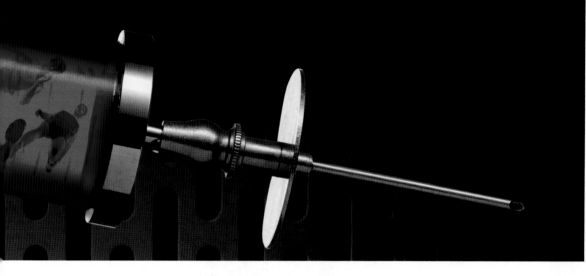

Running is a smart drug

(*PNAS*), older adults who exercised regularly increased the volume of their hippocampus – the region of our brains linked to learning and memory – by two per cent, compared to their inactive peers. That may not sound like much until you consider that this part of the brain isn't known for increasing at any point in adulthood. What's more, running appears to 'rescue' many brain cells that would otherwise die. Now, if you could just manage the crossword on the treadmill...

SWEAT THE DETAILS

Running improves your ability to store new information and memories, and can potentially stave off age-related dementia. The hippocampus, a seahorse-shaped structure tucked under the medial temporal lobe, is most affected by neurodegenerative diseases such as Alzheimer's. In another recent study, also published in *PNAS*, adult mice 'runners' grew new neurons that made them better at making fine distinctions between shapes and colours than sedentary

RESEARCH SHOWS A LINK BETWEEN RUNNING AND A NIMBLE BRAIN

rodents. Earlier studies on conducted on humans candidates came to similar conclusions. These types of cognitive skills, including improved focus, help keep dementia at bay.

POWER PLANNING

Lacing up may sharpen the executive functions that happen in your frontal cortex – decision-making, planning, organising and juggling mental tasks – according to Japanese research. So a daytime run could clear the cobwebs away and help ensure that your online supermarket order doesn't arrive at your sister's house for her birthday, while you're left looking at a cashmere scarf for dinner.

THINKING POSITIVE

Running may be as effective as – and sometimes better than antidepressants. The pills work by keeping neurotransmitters such as serotonin in the synapses longer, improving mood. It turns out that aerobic exercise does the same thing. And in studies, patients who were successfully treated with pills relapsed sooner than those who stayed physically active.

QUICK RECALL

Being active is key not just to making memories, but finding them when you want to. In a study of patients diagnosed with the early stages of Alzheimer's, those who exercised were better able to recall the names of famous people. Brain scans reveal activity in the caudate nucleus, an area involved in motor function and which also supports memory circuits. Running appears to boost the quality of the signals being transmitted through those circuits, which means you have better access to the zillions of details you've got stored there. It may even include the useful things.

MIND

Chapter 9

WOMEN'S RUNNING

It's true: some things are different for girls. Here's what every woman needs to know before hitting the road

222 | **WOMEN'S HEALTH**
Ailments that can affect female runners

224 | **21 TIPS FOR WOMEN RUNNERS**
Inspiration to attain peak fitness

228 | **BABY STEPS**
How to adapt to postpartum running

236 | **COME BACK STRONG**
An Olympic-standard workout

PHOTOGRAPHY: MARK CAMERON
MODEL: MICHELLE COWLEY

WOMEN'S HEALTH

When it comes to lacing up, women have a few extra things to think about. Here's all you need to know to ensure that hitting the road isn't a worry

Apart from the sort of injuries that can plague all runners – shin splints, black toenails, tendinitis – there are some health issues that are more prevalent in women runners, and some that are exclusively female.

MENSTRUAL PROBLEMS

Although some women complain of discomfort during their periods, it is generally accepted menstruation has limited impact on exercise performance. Women have run well, set records and won titles at all phases of the menstrual cycle.

nutrition are all very possible contributing factors.

One of the single most serious consequences of amenorrhoea is osteoporosis. This happens when the female hormones, which serve to protect your bone's calcium, are in short supply. An early onset of osteoporosis can lead to a risk of stress fractures and acute fractures, and since decreased bone density is not easily reversed, it might last for the rest of your life.

An additional concern is lack of ovulation. Because it is possible for women to menstruate even when

ovulation. To track this cycle, take your temperature first thing in the morning. If your conditions point towards any sort of irregularity, consult your doctor.

THE PILL

Researchers disagree about the impact of the pill on athletic performance. Though most studies have shown the pill has no effect on performance, some research indicates it may cause a slight reduction in aerobic capacity.

On the other hand, some runners feel the pill helps performance by reducing menstrual symptoms. These runners prefer taking the pill so they can control their cycle and don't have to race when they are having their period. Although it is safe to manipulate the timing of your period, experts generally agree this practice should be reserved for major competitions and done only a few times a year.

If you run recreationally, you probably don't have to worry about any athletic impact of the pill. But if you race and don't want to sacrifice aerobic capacity, consider another type of contraception.

THERE ARE SOME HEALTH ISSUES FAR MORE PREVALENT IN WOMEN RUNNERS

Studies have shown no change in heart-rate, strength or endurance during the cycle. Exercise can improve your feelings of well-being, so some doctors recommend exercise for women who suffer discomfort at this time of the month.

However, a potential problem for women who run strenuously is irregular or absent periods, which is known as "athletic amenorrhoea". Training stress, performance pressure, low body fat and poor

not ovulating, the presence of a period does not guarantee a healthy menstrual cycle. A lack of ovulation can signal insufficient levels of progesterone, which can lead to over-stimulation of the uterine lining, putting you at greater risk of endometrial cancer.

A woman's body temperature is generally lower at the beginning of her monthly cycle and higher for the last two weeks. The increase in temperature occurs at the time of

OSTEOPOROSIS

Exercise can help build and maintain bone density levels in women, but women who have abnormal menstrual cycles, may not gain these benefits.

Several studies have shown women who have disrupted

A fitter, healthier body will be yours

INCONTINENCE

Women are more prone to stress incontinence because of their anatomy. It's estimated that one in two women experience some level of urine leakage and it is annoying and disconcerting.

Although running does not cause incontinence, the activity can induce leakage in women who are already prone to it. Many women find that strengthening the muscles in the pelvic area with Kegel exercises helps. To do these, contract your pelvic muscles as if you are attempting to stop a flow of urine. Hold for a few seconds, and then release. There are also several devices that can be bought over the counter or with a prescription that help control leakage. Talk to your GP about what might work for you.

ACNE

Women runners can be plagued by skin breakouts on their face, hairline, upper back, chest, upper arms and buttocks. Sweat production combined with hair follicles or friction from rubbing clothes is a formula for acne. Increased temperature and humidity exacerbate the problem, as do products such as sun screen and make-up, which sweat off on to the skin and clog pores. To fend off acne, try the following:

➡ Minimise the use of make-up and hair products before running. Wash your face before you run, and again prior to re-applying make-up post-run.

➡ Use a sunscreen specifically formulated for the face on your face and neck. Choose a gel or lotion for the rest of your body.

➡ Cleanse acne-prone areas with a face wipe immediately after you finish running.

➡ Change out of sweaty exercise clothes straight after running, and shower as soon as possible.

➡ If you are prone to acne, consult a dermatologist.

menstrual cycles suffer more stress fractures than their counterparts with normal cycles. These women typically exhibit lower levels of bone mineral density. Although it's generally accepted that hormonal disruptions and premature loss of bone density are linked in female athletes, the cause and effect relationship is not clear. For example, some researchers think the kind of woman drawn to intense exercise are more likely to exhibit stress in all areas of life, which could affect hormone levels even without doing a high level of exercise.

Experts agree women must act to protect themselves from early onset osteoporosis. It's particularly important as once they are past the mid-thirties, a woman is no longer able to build bone mass, but only maintain her reserves. You should take every precaution to ensure you are not losing bone mass. That means eating a properly balanced diet – in addition to all the many important nutrients, and calcium in particular, you should make sure you are consuming the correct amount of fat and calories overall in your diet to sustain your level of exercise. Monitor your menstrual cycle, and if there you notice any irregularities you should then consult your doctor.

Chapter 8

21 TIPS FOR WOMEN RUNNERS

Use these tips to overcome any willpower wobbles and inspire your fitness. Remember, you're just a few steps away from a better body – inside and out

Knowledge is power, in running as in any other pursuit. The more you know about training, nutrition and health, the better you'll be at maximising your running, whether that means fitness, weight loss, great race performances or just plain fun. In this section, you'll find loads of information to help you reach your goals.

These tips cover health, psychology, weight loss, pregnancy and motherhood, training, racing and more, and address the specific needs of women to help you become the runner you want to be.

① ANAEROBIC RESULTS

For female runners, controlled anaerobic training – intervals, hills, fartlek training – may lead to gains in strength and speed similar to those produced by steroids, but without the noxious side effects. Why? High-intensity anaerobic running is one of the most potent stimulators of natural human growth hormones – those that contribute to stronger muscles and enhanced performance.

② BE AN EARLY BIRD

Running first thing in the morning means you can get the sweaty business out of the way before applying make-up and dressing for work. But perhaps more importantly, statistics show that women are more likely to be attacked later in the day. Don't be scared off, but do take precautions. More on that later...

③ RUNNING DURING PREGNANCY

Doctors agree that moderate exercise during a normal pregnancy is completely safe for your baby. Running should cause no problems in the first trimester and it should be fine for most people in the second trimester. Few women would run in their final three months, however. The most important precaution is to avoid becoming overheated; a core body temperature above 38°F could increase the risk of birth defects. So make sure you're staying cool enough, and if in doubt, take your temperature after a run. If it's over 101°F, you're probably overdoing it. Also, skip that post-run soak in a hot bath.

④ SHOE SELECTION

Women generally have narrower feet than men, so when buying running shoes, you're best off going for a pair designed specifically for women. That said, everyone's different, so if your feet are wide, you may feel more comfortable in shoes designed for men. The bottom line: buy the shoe that's best for you. A good place to start is at a specialist running shop where you can have your gait analysed. If there's any question – or if you suffer blisters or injuries because of ill-fitting shoes – consult a podiatrist who specialises in treating runners.

⑤ REDUCE CANCER RATES

An American study found running women produce a less potent form of oestrogen than their sedentary counterparts. As a result, female runners cut by half their risks of developing breast and uterine cancer, and by two thirds their risk of contracting the form of diabetes most common in women.

⑥ SISTERS UNITED

Having another woman or a group of women to run with regularly will help keep you motivated and ensure your safety. It's also a lot more fun than running alone. Women runners become more than training partners; they're confidantes, counsellors and coaches, too.

PHOTOGRAPHY STUDIO 33. DIGITAL IMAGING PRE MEDIA

1

Warm up your
willpower

Focus on
the health
benefits

(7) TAKE ON THE RIGHT NUTRITION

The two minerals which female runners need to pay the most attention to are calcium and iron (iron is especially important if you've got your period). Good sources of calcium are dairy products, dark leafy vegetables, broccoli, canned sardines and salmon, while foods high in iron include liver, fortified dry cereals, beef and spinach. Vitamin C helps you absorb the iron, too.

(8) KEEP IT REAL

Women who run for weight control may lose perspective on what is an appropriate body size. A recent survey of thousands of women found while 44 per cent of respondents were medically overweight, 73 per cent thought they were.

(9) TALK TO YOUR GP

Women who train intensively, have been pregnant in the past two years or consume fewer than 2,500 calories a day may need more than the routine blood tests for iron status, since these test only for anaemia (which is the final stage of iron deficiency). Ask for more revealing tests, such as those for serum ferritin, transferrin saturation and total iron-building capacity.

(10) PERIOD GAINS

There's no need to miss a run or a race just because you're having your period. If you're suffering from cramps, running will often alleviate the symptoms, thanks to the release of pain-relieving chemicals called endorphins. Speedwork and hill sessions can be especially effective, but use a tampon and a towel for extra protection.

(11) SKIN WINS

Running helps keep your skin healthy. According to

dermatologists, running stimulates circulation, transports nutrients and flushes out waste products. All of this leads to a reduction in subcutaneous fat, making skin clearer and facial features more distinct.

12 DON'T OVERDO IT

If you run so much your periods become light or non-existent, you may be endangering your bones. Amenorrhoea (lack of a monthly period) means that little or no oestrogen, essential for the replacement of bone minerals, is circulating in your body. You can stop, but not reverse, the damage by taking oestrogen and plenty of calcium. If your periods are infrequent or absent, make sure you consult a gynaecologist.

13 STRONGER BABIES

If you were a regular runner before you became pregnant, you might have a bigger baby – good news, because, up to a certain point, larger infants tend to be stronger and weather physical adversity better. Researchers in the US found women who burned up to 1,000 calories per week through exercise gave birth to babies weighing five per cent more than the offspring of inactive mums. Those who burned 2,000 per week delivered babies weighing 10 per cent more.

14 IN THE INTEREST OF SAFETY

Women who run alone should take a few sensible precautions. Leave a note at home stating when you left, where you'll be running and when you expect to return. Carry a mobile phone. Stick to well populated areas, and don't always run the same predictable route. Avoid running at night and don't wear jewellery. Pay attention to your surroundings and recurring faces. Carry some ID,

but include only your name and an emergency phone number.

15 CHEST SUPPORT

No matter what your size, it's a good idea to wear a sports bra when you run. Controlling breast motion will make you feel more comfortable. Look for one that stretches horizontally but not vertically. Most importantly, try before you buy. A sports bra should fit snugly, yet not feel too constrictive. Run or jump on the spot to see if it gives you the support you need.

16 LATE PREGNANCY AND BIRTH

If you ran early in your pregnancy, then you might want to try switching to a lower-impact exercise during the latter stages and after you've had the baby. Because of the release of the hormone relaxin during pregnancy, some ligaments and tendons might soften. This will make you more vulnerable to injury, especially around your pelvis. Walking, swimming, stationary cycling and aquarunning are good choices.

RUNNING HELPS KEEP YOUR SKIN HEALTHY AND BOOSTS YOUR CIRCULATION

17 IGNORE TAUNTING

It's not much consolation, but men are sometimes verbally harassed and occasionally threatened while running, just as women are. Be sensible when you run, but don't let insignificant taunting limit your freedom.

18 MONTHLY MOMENTS

"That time of the month" (or even the few days preceding it) is not the time when women run their worst. The hardest time for women to run fast is about a week before menstruation begins (a week after ovulation). That's when levels of the key hormone progesterone peak, inducing a much-higher-than-normal breathing rate during physical activity. The excess ventilation tends to make running feel more difficult.

19 MAKE SURE YOU MAKE TIME

Just because you're married and have young children and a job doesn't mean you don't have time to run. Running is time-efficient and the best stress-reducer on the market. You need this time. Taking it for yourself (by letting your husband baby-sit while you run, for instance) will benefit the whole family.

20 BREAST-FEEDING

Though not conclusive, some studies have suggested that babies dislike the taste of post-exercise breast milk, because it is high in lactic acid and may impart a sour flavour. You may like to either express milk for later feeding, or breast-feed before running.

21 PERSPIRATION INSPIRATION

Women sweat less than men. Fact. And, contrary to popular belief, women dissipate heat just as well as their male counterparts. The reason: women are smaller and have a higher body-surface-to-volume ratio, which means that although their evaporative cooling is less efficient, they need less of it to achieve the same result. You'll still need to take on plenty of water to prevent dehydration, mind.

**Your baby will
be born to run**

BABY STEPS

Pregnancy and parenthood needn't spell an end to your running days. Use our guide to running with bump, baby and beyond to take it all in your stride

Not so long ago, the notion of a woman running during pregnancy was laughable, even shocking. These days the running community, at least, is supportive of its mothers-to-be, but elsewhere the idea persists that running with bump is irresponsible. If you or your partner is expecting, you'll be anxious to know what's best for both mum and baby. The good news is that running can keep you healthy during pregnancy, happy and slim post-pregnancy, and, thanks to the ever-increasing range of jogging buggies, you can get junior in on the act six months on. Whether you're an expectant mum or dad, or your eye's just started twinkling, you'll find everything you need to know about getting the most from your running pre- and post-bump over the following pages.

① WHAT TO EXPECT

You're pregnant – is it OK to keep running? And for how long? We've got the answers

Q I currently run three times a week. Is it safe to continue now that I'm pregnant – and for how long?

A "Yes, in fact medical professionals encourage women to exercise and maintain good fitness and a healthy weight," says GP, runner and mum Dr Gemma Newman. "Especially because obesity during pregnancy is a growing crisis. Many women will have been running for weeks before discovering they're pregnant, but don't worry that you've done yourself or the baby any harm – keeping active does you both good." Only run if you feel up to it, though. In the first trimester you may be too exhausted. The second trimester is usually when women 'bloom' and feel most energetic. By the third you may be feeling more uncomfortable, so consider cross-training. However, there's no reason you can't jog right into the maternity ward, if that's what feels right. "The most important thing is to listen to your body," says Dr Newman.

Q But are there any risks associated with running while I'm expecting?

A The main risk is you face overheating: there's a risk to your baby if your core temperature – which is already higher during pregnancy – rises further. But this is easily managed by limiting the intensity of your workouts. If you have a heart-rate monitor, stay under 75 per cent of your max. If not, "stick to a pace at which you can easily chat, remembering the speed may change depending on conditions or how tired you are," says running coach Karen Weir (runwithkaren.com). "Always make sure you keep hydrated and avoid tough sessions such as tempo or threshold runs, or training in the heat. And feel free to enter events for fun, but put racing on hold."

Again, always listen to your body. "If you experience bleeding, dizziness, palpitations or pain – or running just doesn't feel right – stop," says Newman. Seek and heed medical advice, "but contrary to some people's belief, exercise isn't a major risk factor for miscarriage, nor will your baby be shaken around and damaged".

From the second trimester, as your shape changes, bear in mind that your centre of gravity will shift and balance can go awry. "Choose safe routes – trails, for example, are out,' says Weir. Also remember that the pregnancy hormone relaxin is coursing through your body, loosening your pelvic (and other) joints and ligaments in preparation for the birth. This increases the risk of injury. "Be mindful of this and limit post-run stretches to a gentle 10 seconds," says Weir.

Q Are there any expectant mothers who should avoid running?

A This is not the time to take up the sport if you've never run before, or you haven't done for some time. "Your doctor may advise against it if you've had any bleeding or been diagnosed with an incompetent cervix," says

The Multi-use hydration system for new parents...

Newman. "If you experience any vaginal bleeding, abdominal pain or the baby stops its normal movements, stop running and see your GP straight away."

Q My partner's still not convinced about the benefits. What can I say?

A Numerous studies, including research published in *Clinics in Sports Medicine*, show that pregnant women who stay active have fewer delivery complications and shorter, easier labours.

In addition, research published in *Epidemiology* also found that women who exercised vigorously during pregnancy decreased their risk of premature birth, while another study in *The Journal of Obstetrics, Gynecologic and Neonatal Nursing* found it made them less likely to need a caesarean section. The study in *Clinics in Sports Medicine* also showed babies whose mothers do regular, moderate exercise have better neural development and are less likely to become overweight.

"Exercise can help get the baby in the right position, control pregnancy weight gain and boost your mood – especially important as antenatal depression is common," says Newman. A recent US study, published in *Medicine & Science in Sports & Exercise* also found aerobic exercise reduces pregnancy symptoms such as nausea, heartburn and cramps.

Q Will I need new kit to accommodate my changing body shape?

A Some maternity fitness clothing will help you look and feel the part once you've outstretched your standard Lycra. Many companies have yoga wear that will do the trick, or check out the range on fitnfabulous.co.uk. They have maternity running capris, T-shirts and vests. "Your bra size will change throughout pregnancy and breasts will probably become uncomfortable at some point," says Weir. "Get yours measured regularly and invest in an extra-supportive high-impact sports bra."

Freya Active and Shock Absorber both have very good high-impact ranges, and specialist running store Sweatshop has specially trained staff to measure you for style, size and fit. Some women find bump bands helpful – try the Fertile Mind Bando (£14.99, cheekyrascals.co.uk). Extra weight and postural changes coupled with relaxin can increase foot size and cause over-pronation. So ensure your running shoes still fit well, or consider a simple orthotic like Carnation Powerstep (from £30, powerstep.co.uk).

"Even if you don't normally run with water it's wise to when you're pregnant," suggests Weir. Use an ergonomic bottle such as the Hilly Hand Held (£3.99, lansonrunning. com). A simple heart-rate monitor can also keep your intensity in check (Polar FT2, £47.50, lansonrunning.com).

Q Running's becoming too uncomfortable now I'm bigger. How can I stay fit?

A Cross-training can help to keep you fit and strong for labour and maintain your fitness post-pregnancy. "In late-pregnancy, cycling is out, because of the risk of falling, and the elliptical trainer can over-strain the pelvis and hips," explains Weir. "Walking is always good, and swimming is a fantastic full-body workout which also keeps you cool and supports your joints. A simple, light free-weights routine can help stamina in late pregnancy and labour."

You should also be doing pelvic floor exercises throughout pregnancy (see After the Bump, *overleaf*) and look for local antenatal yoga or pilates classes, which are a fun way to keep yourself fit and active, prep your body for labour and, of course, meet other mums-to-be.

RUNNING MUMS

Zoe Folbigg, 36, Herts. Mum to Felix (2) and Max (6 months)

"I had to justify my decision to keep running during pregnancy. As my bump emerged and I took to the streets, I got disapproving looks, mainly from women, which upset me. At 23 weeks, I ran a 10K race and heard one horrified spectator say, "look, how awful". It was upsetting, but I was running with my dad who held my hand and kept me strong. As we crossed the line, I realised three generations had made it and felt a swell of pride. Ill-informed people will pass judgment, but with a thick skin you'll be fine."

2 AFTER THE BUMP
Running is a great way to get back in shape and ward off the baby blues. Here's the lowdown before you lace up

The standard medical advice is that you shouldn't think about exercising until after your six-week GP check-up. They may give you the green light then, but if you've had a caesarean section or stitches, then you may be advised to wait a little longer.

As in pregnancy, the mantra is 'listen to your body'. You don't have to start running at six weeks, and as a sleep-deprived new mum it may be the last thing you feel like doing. And it might not be the best thing for your body: Paula Radcliffe returned to running a fortnight after the birth of her daughter and ended up with a sacral stress fracture. And some experts advise waiting beyond the six-week minimum: "To get the most from running and look after your body, I advise waiting until 20 weeks before your first run," says pre- and post-natal exercise specialist Wendy Powell (mutusystem.com). "You still have relaxin in your body, and your ligaments, core and pelvic floor aren't ready for the impact." In the meantime there's walking (aka pram pushing, which you'll be very familiar with), and crucial conditioning to get your body run-ready.

"Now is the time to work on alignment and core restoration," says Powell. "In the immediate post-natal period, the postural change of pregnancy is still in evidence – slumped shoulders, exaggerated curve in the lumbar spine – so work on correcting it."

POSTURE AND PELVIC FLOOR EXERCISES

"Keeping good posture is all about connecting with your deep transversus abdominis muscles," explains Powell. "Exhale, slowly pulling your belly button to your spine. Don't tuck your pelvis under or pull your shoulders back. At the same time, work your pelvic floor muscles." This isn't just about squeezing the muscles you use when trying not to wee, the pelvic floor is a system of muscles that runs from the front of your pubic bone back to the base of your spine and you need to engage them all. Imagine you're trying to pick up a cherry tomato with the middle section. Then a raisin. Then a grain of rice. Do this exercise whenever you can.

Check out Powell's DVD MUTU Focus for a 12-week pelvic floor and 'mummy tummy' programme, or try the My PFF app, which guides you through a pelvic floor programme and sends reminders (lightsbytena.co.uk/mypffapp).

RUNNING MUMS
Anna Scally, 40, Surrey. Mum to Connor (3)

"Prior to my first pregnancy, aged 37, I ran for Wales and coached at my club Ranelagh Harriers. There was no question that I'd stop running, but I did lots of research on how to modify my training, and used my knowledge as a coach and my instincts. I ran with a heart-rate monitor to keep my speed in check. At 36 weeks, I switched to swimming. I'm convinced my fitness helped with childbirth – my labour was a swift six hours and I recovered quickly. I am now pregnant again, and I will continue to run this time as well."

Take motherhood
in your stride

RECTIS ABDOMINIS

These muscles may not come back together automatically after pregnancy, causing that soft 'mummy tummy' and, in extreme cases, hernias. "In the majority of cases surgery can be avoided through posture and pelvic floor exercises," says Powell. "You don't need to do specific ab exercises. Crunches, sit-ups, straight leg lifts and the plank can make it worse."

YOUR FIRST RUN

Don't make the classic mistake of too much, too soon. "Women tend to fall into two camps," says Powell. "Those who think motherhood has given them superpowers and those who lack the confidence to start again. You will get your old levels of fitness back; just start short and slow. Walk if necessary and, if something doesn't feel right, take it down a notch." Breast-feeding and running aren't mutually exclusive, however, you may prefer to feed or express before a run so your breasts are less heavy and uncomfortable. Wear breast pads to disguise leaks, and wear an extra-supportive sports bra. You might also consider a buggy-fit class where you'll meet like-minded mums and be taught by someone with a post-natal exercise qualification. Check out pushymothers.com and buggyfit. co.uk, or The Guild of Pregnancy and Post-natal Exercise Instructors (postnatalexercise. co.uk) for more info.

THE MOTHERHOOD EFFECT

Fancy a PBPB (post-bump personal best)? It seems risible when you feel whale-like, but post-bump you could be in the shape of your life. Your organs learn to work harder when you're pregnant, while blood volume increases by up to 60 per cent to transport oxygen to the womb. And those extra cells remain for months, improving stamina. There's also evidence that mental acuity sharpens and pain threshold increases post-labour. Research in the *Scandinavian Journal of Medicine* and *Science in Sports* found 11 per cent of women performed better in endurance events after having a baby. No wonder new mum Paula won the New York City Marathon.

WOMEN'S RUNNING

3 PUSHY PARENTING

Our favourite jogging buggies mean you can train while junior comes along for the ride

There are two golden rules when running with a buggy. One: your baby needs to be a minimum of six months old. Two: you need a running-specific buggy – your everyday McClaren won't cut it. The key difference is stability, which is why jogging buggies have three wheels for better weight distribution. Being able to fix the front wheel is essential for a smooth run and reduces the risk of the wheel being knocked off course by stones, bumps or holes in the ground. An adjustable handle ensures you have enough room to run without kicking the back axle; a handbrake helps control speed, while a wrist strap stops the buggy getting away from you.

OUT N ABOUT NIPPER SPORT

A handlebar-mounted brake lever and hefty wheels ensure a smooth, safe ride wherever you run. At under 10kg it's easy to haul in and out of the car (or over stiles) and the slightly smaller wheels and length mean this could easily double as your normal pushchair. **£250, practical pushchairs.co.uk**

MOUNTAIN BUGGY TERRAIN

For dads who want their wheels rugged, the masculine 'Flint' colour scheme and bump-absorbing steel-frame components positively shout 'outdoor parent'. At 13kg, you'll get some resistance training, too. Pricey, but they don't come much sturdier. **£499, preciouslittleone.com**

BABYJOGGER SUMMIT

Babyjogger has been making these for 25 years and it shows. A 12in front wheel and a massive 16in at the back make for a smooth and stable ride over any terrain. Its patented Quick-Fold system is a dream for weary limbs post-run, and this adjusts to be suitable from birth so you'll only have to fork out for one set of wheels. **£379.95, johnlewis.com**

BUMBLERIDE INDIE TWIN

This lightweight all-terrainer can double up as your everyday transport, too. The USP is it's available as a double, so parents with two can get in on the act. Make no mistake, though, it's hard work – pushing twins up any gradient gives new meaning to 'hill reps'. **£699 (for Twin), bumblerideuk.com**

YOUTH POLICY

4 So what happens when junior gets too big for the buggy?

With NHS figures showing almost a quarter of children are overweight or obese by the time they start school, maybe you should get them running, too. "As soon as they have control of their bodies – at about five – children need two to three hours of exercise a day, one of which should be high intensity, like running," says Mike Antoniades, performance director of The Running School (running school.co.uk). "At that age their bodies are designed for short bursts, but they don't have the necessary enzymes for running long distances. Stick to short distances, around 1K, until they hit 11 or 12." Parkrun welcomes youngsters, or find a local fun run. And finally, lead by example. Research at the University of Essex found kids of inactive parents were less fit themselves.

RUNNING MUMS

Liz Yelling, 37, double Olympic marathoner

"I really listened to my body when I was pregnant with my daughter Ruby, now three. I aimed to run for an hour each day, then if it didn't feel great I'd cut it short. My goal was staying fit but not training for performance. Once Ruby was born, a jogging buggy was a great investment – it means that, together with my husband, we can do Parkrun as a family."

COME BACK STRONG

This workout is specifically designed for a post-pregnancy return to form, but also makes a great any-time, full-body routine for women

Carrie Tollefson, a 2004 Olympian (1500 metres), ran all the way through her pregnancy – right up until two days before going into labour. By the time her daughter was three months old, Tollefson was back to logging an impressive 40 miles a week. Granted, Tollefson went into pregnancy being incredibly fit. But she says it was the weight lifting she did while pregnant – and now, postpartum – that got her back up to speed quickly and without injury. "It's all about the gym," says Tollefson, who at four weeks postpartum was given the green light to resume weight lifting up to three days a week.

"The first focus should not be returning to running," says Tim Hilden, physical therapist at the Boulder Center for Sports Medicine. "What's most important is rehabbing the post-delivery woman – or anyone who's gone through a setback of any sort – by strengthening the essential muscles that the body will need to recruit for running."

Tollefson's routine, shown here, is advanced – the modified versions are a good place to start. For each exercise, do three sets of 10; progress to five sets of 10. Try to do this routine three times a week – make sure you have your doctor's permission before commencing with the routine, of course.

Get on a roll on your way back to recovery

HAMSTRING CURLS

Strengthen glutes, hamstrings, lower back, oblique muscles, stabilising muscles of the hips and pelvis.

TOLLEFSON'S MOVE Lie on the ground with your feet on a Swiss ball (as above). Lift your pelvis up. Then, while maintaining that position, push the ball away with heels, then pull it back. Lower and repeat.

MODIFY IT Place your feet on a stable object. Lift up your pelvis, lower. Progress to placing both your heels on a ball.

PHOTOGRAPHY: SARA RUSINSTEIN. APPAREL AND SHOES: ADIDAS; LOCATION: COURTESY LIFETIME FITNESS

PRESS-UPS

Strengthen upper-body and abdominal muscles.

TOLLEFSON'S MOVE Place hands on a medicine ball and lower down into a press-up, keeping your back straight.

MODIFY IT The easiest way to do press-ups is by standing up and pushing off from a wall instead.

PLANKS

Strengthen abdominals, obliques and glutes.

TOLLEFSON'S MOVE Place your shins on a stability ball and your palms on the floor. Then lift one leg at a time.

MODIFY IT Rest on your forearms with your feet on the ground, and keep your back flat.

LUNGES

Strengthen hips, pelvis, quads, and core muscles.

TOLLEFSON'S MOVE Stand as shown above. Lunge down and touch a medicine ball to the floor in front of you.

MODIFY IT Do standard lunges on the ground, without balls. Progress to lunges with your back foot on a stability ball, while touching your hand to the ground in front of you.

STEP-UPS

Strengthen quads, glutes, calves, and core muscles.

TOLLEFSON'S MOVE Stand with your left foot on a stool. Hold a dumbbell in your right hand. Step up and bring your right foot up in the air and lift the weight overhead.

MODIFY IT Do the same motion on a lower step without a weight.

BICEPS AND TRICEPS

Strengthen biceps, triceps, and core muscles.

TOLLEFSON'S MOVE Do bicep curls and then overhead tricep extensions with dumbbells while you stand with both feet on a Bosu ball (a 'half' Swiss ball).

MODIFY IT While standing on one foot, do bicep curls. Then do tricep extensions.

Chapter
10

TRAIL RUNNING

Bored of the treadmill? Tired of the road? For a literal change of pace try forest tracks and muddy trails

240   **OFF TRACK**
The unique benefits of leaving the road

242   **TRICKS OF THE TRAIL**
How to master uneven terrain

244   **SUMMIT FOR THE WEEKEND**
A guide to the UK's best hill runs

250   **RACING HOME**
Why trail legend Scott Jurek loves running off road

MODEL DEAN ENNION
PHOTOGRAPHY GLEN MONTGOMERY

OFF TRACK

Even for committed road runners, there are benefits to be had from adding trail runs to your regime, says coach Ian Torrence

Hardcore road racers don't tend to consider trails as anything but a distraction from their real goal: speed. But that's a mistake, because sprinkling a little dirt into your race training programme can freshen up your motivation and make you a physically stronger, more well-rounded and, yes, faster runner. Whatever your level of ability – whether you're a newbie or a veteran – incorporating

some trail running will help, as long as you make some physical and mental adjustments. Most importantly, as you'll initially feel slow relative to your normal pavement pace, you need to ignore your watch and manage trail runs according to duration and fatigue, both of which will be significantly greater than you're used to.

The short-term payoff is that mixing trails into your regime will build your aerobic capacity, lessen

your risk of 'overuse' injuries and reduce recovery time by working different muscles at different times. Just running once or twice a week on mildly undulating terrain can help you to build extra strength and improve stability. Climbing steep hills strengthens the calves, hamstrings and glutes; jogging back down again will add strengthen to your quadriceps; and hopping over uneven surfaces improves mobility and lateral core

PHOTOGRAPHY: GLEN MONTGOMERY. MODEL: DEAN ENNION

Get on the trail of a new challenge

strength for stabilisation – and these are all movements rarely practised on the roads. Running on rocky terrain also encourages a shorter, more efficient stride. Use the training guide below to convert your existing road sessions and take full advantage of all of these benefits, plus the ultimate payoff of a slower pace on softer surfaces: longevity in the sport.

THE ROAD RACER'S TRAIL PLAN

Typical road and track sessions can be replicated on trails, but it does take some creativity to make the necessary adjustments. As your lungs and muscles will no doubt tell you, even a gently undulating trail can add a considerable amount of resistance to your effort. Add too much intensity and you can end up running yourself into the ground. So, stick to trails with easy gradients that won't compromise form, or fatigue your legs and lungs to exhaustion. In addition to the sessions below, it's easy to develop your own – just as long as you make sure you pick the right kind of trail to produce the desired effects, and you avoid running on very steep terrain too frequently.

LONG RUNS	Develop/ maintain aerobic endurance	At least once a week throughout race training	Flat, rolling, and/or hilly trails	As with the long runs prescribed in standard marathon plans, these should be slow. Even slightly rolling trails can spike your heartrate, so ease up to keep your pace steady. Try not to focus on the mileage, but rather think about the equivalent time you'll be on your feet.
SHORT EXPLOSIVE HILL SPRINTS	Develop muscular explosiveness	Once a week during the base-building phase of your race training	One with a short, steep section	To build power and strength, do this 6-8 times on the same stretch, or find places for each interval during a run. After a warm-up, attack short uphills for 15-25sec, bounding over roots or rocks and using your arms to help propel you. Recover at a gentle pace for the same duration in between.
LONGER INTERVALS	Up aerobic capacity at faster paces over longer distances	Once weekly during base training, up to about mid-training plan	Flat to slightly rolling trails	If those 5x1-mile repeats on the track get monotonous, head to the woods. Do 12x3-6min fartlek-style bursts of hard but controlled running, followed by rests of the same duration. Aim for consistency, regardless of the terrain. Recover by running easy on flat ground.
LONG PROGRESSION RUNS	Build late-race stamina	Once a week from midway to the end of your race training plan	Flat to moderately rolling trails	After warming up, go easy for the first 50-60 per cent of the run, then at your perceived marathon effort over the final 40-50 per cent. Start with a shorter overall workout duration (60-90min) until you've built an aerobic base, then slowly increase to longer durations (90min-3hr).
SHORTER INTERVALS	Clear lactate and develop strength and speed	Once a week during the second half of your race training plan	Moderately hilly trails	Do a 30-50min fartlek run with short bursts (45-90sec) of hard running, using the terrain as a guide. (This workout is similar to 12 x 200m or 10x400m on the track.) Proper form is more important than speed. Jog slowly to recover between hills. End with a few 50m strides.
YASSO 800S	Develop running economy and clear lactate	Once a week for the length of your training regime	Flat to gently rolling, with good footing	Warm up, then run at 5K race effort for the same time in minutes and seconds as your marathon finish time in hours and minutes (if you're in 3:30 marathon shape, run for 3.5min). Recover for the same amount of time. Do 6-10 intervals. Don't worry if you don't think you're covering 800m. Effort is key.

TRAIL RUNNING

TRICKS OF THE TRAIL

Get more out of your next trail-running experience by using these simple-to-follow expert tips to ensure you keep a spring, not a sprain, in your step

PRE-TRAIL PREP

"Always research the trail you're planning to run," says Nancy Hobbs, president of the American Trail Running Association. Carry a bottle of water, a mobile phone and a map, and check the weather conditions on the day. "Weather can change quickly out on the trails, and it's just not worth getting caught without another layer," says Matt Carpenter, 11-times winner of the US trail race the Pikes Peak Marathon in Colorado. "I always take a shell jacket with me."

DESCENTS

Stay upright with just enough lean to maintain forward motion without losing control. "Stepping on rocks can be jarring on descents, so choose the track," says Elinor Fish of *Trail Runner* magazine. However, when the trail is steep, rocks can serve as steps.

PASSING

'On your right' and 'Coming through' both work, but hikers are not often used to the notion of runners coming up from behind. "The most important thing is to be courteous," says Hobbs, who suggests adding a 'Thank you'.

STEEP CLIMBS

All trail runners, even pros, walk steep gradients. "If you can walk faster than you can run, always walk," says Fish. "It helps to conserve energy."

ROCKY ROAD

"On trails littered with obstacles, seek out clear sections," says Rob Shoaf, founder of Epic Running camp. Dirt is almost always a safer bet – even a flat rock can be unstable. "We tend to step where we look, so avoid staring at the rocks; aim for dirt," he says.

ILLUSTRATION: ROBERT L PRINCE

FORM TUTOR

On the trail, proper technique can be the difference between enjoying the scenery and face-planting in it

....

WATCH YOUR STEP

"A lot of people trip over because they want to enjoy the scenery, myself included. But the more challenging the terrain, the more you should pay attention to where your feet are landing," says Carpenter. Alternate between looking up and focusing about three to six strides in front of you.

BE CONSISTENT

"Learn how to run with the same effort over different types of terrain," says Carpenter. "I try to run with the same cadence and gait on the trails as I do on the roads. That means not pushing too hard on uphills and not relaxing too much on the way back down."

SHORTEN YOUR STRIDE

Don't move in leaps and bounds. "Taking smaller steps will help maintain your centre of gravity," explains Carpenter.

RAISE YOUR ARMS

"Like wings, they help you balance," says Fish. Relax your shoulders and hands to avoid tension.

TRAIL RUNNING

It was a bad
time to drop
his car keys...

SUMMIT FOR THE WEEKEND

It's never too soon to reach a peak, so test your mettle with our pick of the UK's greatest hill runs

When you're training, "hills are speed work in disguise" – so says marathon legend Frank Shorter. They may also be the stuff of your nightmares, but our lung-bursting, sinew-straining ascents are worth the effort: they offer wonderful rewards to those runners ready to trade guts for glory. *Runner's World's* panel of hill-running experts select the very best the UK has for you to tackle, whether you're looking for an unforgettable race day or simply a nice, upwardly mobile weekend away.

BEN MORE, CRIANLARICH HILLS

This is one of few hills in Britain where you can climb as-near-as-damn-it to 1,000m up a continually steep gradient, covering a mere 4K horizontally. Scotland's Ben More (it means 'Great Mountain') is the sixth-highest peak in the British Isles. "It's one tough climb," says hill-running legend Angela Mudge. "The gradient is very steep all the way, with no softening, and the views are incredible. Park your car on the A85 by Loch Lubhair (it's the hill to the south). It takes quick runners around 50 minutes. As you're climbing to just shy of 1,000m make sure you take some warm clothes to wrap up in so you can spend some time enjoying the well-earned reward of those spectacular views from the summit."

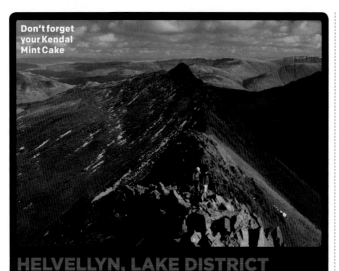

Don't forget your Kendal Mint Cake

HELVELLYN, LAKE DISTRICT

"Inmate of a mountain-dwelling, thou hast clomb aloft, and gazed, from the watch-towers of Helvellyn; awed, delighted, and amazed!" wrote William Wordsworth after his first Helvellyn ascent. England's third-highest summit, it's a must if you have a thirst for conquering hills – or you need inspiration for poetry. The terrain is a mix of paths, rocky sections and steep climbs. And if all that's not enough, consider Ironman-ing up for the terrifying Helvellyn Triathlon (trihard.co.uk).

MAKING THE GRADIENT

"Take small steps at a steady pace," says Tom Owens. "If it gets too steep, walk. Because this is a mental game as much as a physical one, you need to be able to switch off the pain."

ARTHUR'S SEAT HOLYROOD PARK, EDINBURGH

With the pedigree of hosting the 2008 World Cross-Country Championships and unparalleled views of the beautiful Scottish capital, this 250m peak offers a unique climb with a number of different routes to the summit. "It's a hill right in the city centre with steep sections and a flatter area near the top where the famous Hunter's Bog is."

Start at the southern side of the park if you are unfamiliar with the terrain, near the Royal Commonwealth Pool. Some of the multiple routes up are on well-trodden paths, but there are plenty of grassy areas, too. And you can vary the severity by going via the Salisbury Crags, Duddingston Loch or even climbing the 199 very steep steps of Jacob's Ladder, not one for the faint-hearted.

DUMGOYNE HILL CAMPSIE FELLS, GLASGOW

Having Dumgoyne on their doorstep could explain why so many strong fell runners hail from Glasgow. Nestled on the edge of the Campsie Fells, along the route of the West Highland Way, it's a grassy hill with a killer climb. "It may not be the biggest hill in Scotland, but it is seriously steep," says Owens.

Park near the Glengoyne Distillery and follow the path for half a mile through the forest. "After the stile, it's a 15-20-minute climb – if you run very hard," says Owens. "It's a challenge, and if you're brave, you could try reps on it... I never have."

THE RUNNER'S WORLD ALTITUDE EXPERTS

ANGELA MUDGE
A legend in hill-running circles, five-time British Fell Running Champion and co-author of *The World's Ultimate Running Races*.

TOM OWENS
International-class mountain runner and 2010 SkyRaid World Champion, Tom also won the Yorkshire Three Peaks Race.

CLAIRE GORDON
Scottish international-class runner and women's winner of the 273K GORE-TEX Transalpine Run in 2011.

NICK GRACIE
One of the UK's most experienced trail runners, his team have won five British Adventure Racing championships.

IMAGES: PREVIOUS PAGE - MARY SANSEVERINO; THIS PAGE: CHRIS UPSON, GETTY IMAGES, DARREN CLARKE

To be fair, you'll probably find kinder ascents

KINDER SCOUT PEAK DISTRICT

A classic for walkers and climbers, Kinder Scout is a moorland plateau that provides runners with an enticing challenge. There are plenty of routes, but we recommend the nine-mile option starting in Edale, which takes in over 600m of climb.

Head north out of the village, following Grinds Brook upstream towards Crowden Tower, then on to Crowden Head which, at 631m, is the highest point in the Peak District. Continue north-east from Crowden Head until you reach Kinder Downfall, a 30m waterfall. From there, head south towards Edale Cross and you'll hit the Pennine Way, which will take you back down towards Edale.

TRAIL RUNNING

Be careful you don't hit the wall ...

SLIEVE DONARD NEWCASTLE, N. IRELAND

On the coast of County Down, Northern Ireland's highest peak allows you to run from practically sea level to the 850m summit, where you're rewarded with views as far-reaching as Belfast and Dublin.

Park in Donard Park and follow the Glen River, travelling along forest and mountain tracks. Make sure you take extra layers for the summit, it can get a tad breezy. If you fancy racing up, the Slieve Donard Mountain Race takes place every July. The men's record stands at 54:33, and the women's at 1:05:26. Not that we think you're competitive in any way.

Will you make it home for nightfall?

HIGH WILLHAYS AND YES TOR, DARTMOOR NATIONAL PARK

Dartmoor National Park's harsh terrain has made it perfect for use as a training area for the British Army so you can rest assured it's not for the faint-hearted. But there are aesthetic and adrenaline rewards aplenty. We could have picked High Willhays as the highest point in England south of Kinder Scout, or the neighbouring Yes Tor for its spectacular views, but we decided to go for both.

Park at the northern end of Meldon reservoir and head south, handrailing the reservoir and head south, down hill to your right. Cross a footbridge, head south-east for the Black Tor, at which point High Willhays will loom into view.

BEN NEVIS, FORT WILLIAM

It's Britain's highest peak – what more do challenge-hungry souls need to know? William Swan made the first recorded running ascent back in 1895, making it from the old post office in Fort William to the summit and back in 2:41. A race inevitably followed, and has been in its current guise since 1937. The current men's record of 1:25:34 was set way back in 1984 by Kenny Stuart. Fancy your chances? Log on to bennevisrace.co.uk to enter.

Starting at New Town Park, the out-and-back 14K route along the main footpath takes in 1,360m of climb. "The Ben is a relentless gradient, with no respite as it never flattens out," says Mudge, who was first lady in the 2011 Ben Nevis

Race. "The bottom is on a rough man-made path with uneven steps breaking your rhythm." After Red Burn, either follow the race route, which is straight up on loose rock and very steep, or continue along the path, which is more runnable.

MAKING THE GRADIENT

"When running down, try to land on your forefoot," says Angela Mudge. "Look at least 10m ahead – looking down at your feet will slow you down."

PEN Y FAN, BRECON BEACONS

If you've ever harboured fantasies of being an elite member of the SAS, you can test yourself against part of their selection process on the infamous Pen y Fan. The would-be boys in black tackle a 24K route called the Fan Dance, which involves climbing 778m up South Wales's highest peak. Twice.

Starting at Storey Arms Mountain Rescue Centre, run to the top of Pen y Fan, down the other side, then up and down again to Storey Arms – army boots, 18kg rucksack and assault rifle are not necessary. If you fancy some fierce competition out there then sign up for the Fan Dance through Avalanche Endurance Events at thefandancerace.com.

Get there early to avoid the queues

THE BIG DIPPER, MERTHYR MAWR SAND DUNES

You don't need to enter the Marathon des Sables to battle a mighty dune. Trade the sweltering heat of Morocco for a more clement weather climb near Merthyr Mawr, a Welsh village a mile from a massive network of dunes that stretches along the coast towards Porthcawl and the Mumbles.

Smack-bang in the middle is the daddy of them all, the Big Dipper. The highest dune in the UK, and the second-highest in Europe, this mighty climb is well worth the effort. If you fancy making a day of the adventure, the dune forms part of the 10K Merthyr Mawr Christmas Pudding Race (runnersworld.co.uk/puddingrace), held every December by the Brackla Harriers and rightly regarded as a classic, not just because it might help you shift some festive pounds.

TRAIL RUNNING

RACING HOME

Race-winning ultra runner Scott Jurek shares the early inspiration that led to his success

I hated running. I was originally just doing to train for cross-country skiing. The best way to train for Nordic skiing when there's no snow is either by roller skiing or running. I couldn't afford roller skis, so we we'd go out and run with ski poles.

After I started doing these two- or three-hour trail runs, I started to enjoy the feeling of getting out there and doing something big. Part of it was that I was getting better and better, and I was able to see the fruits of my labour when I started competing in trail races.

But the other part of it was being able to reconnect with nature: we don't have huge mountains in Minnesota, where I grew up and started trail running, but it's pretty amazing when you're on the ridge of Duluth and looking out over Lake Superior. Any time you climb to a high point and get a bit of a vista, it's beautiful. It smells clean and there are birch, maple and even some old-growth

pines. By the time I got to college, I was in love with trail running.

I wouldn't be the runner I am today if I hadn't grown up running those trails around Duluth. They make you tough. The winters are brutal, with temperatures getting below -6°C. Then, when summer finally rolls around, it's 32°C with 85 per cent humidity. The bugs make you a better runner, too. Everywhere's thick with mosquitoes, but they're not the main problem – it's the horse and

THERE'S SOMETHING RUTHLESS ABOUT THE TRAILS IN DULUTH – THE TERRAIN REALLY TOUGHENS YOU UP

AS TOLD TO GORDY MEGROZ

**Scott conquers
a Minnesota trail**

deer flies that chase you, forcing you to run faster to find relief.

It's the terrain that toughens you up the most, though. I've travelled all over the world racing and running and there's still something ruthless about those trails in Duluth. I learned that after I'd spent four years in Seattle, then went back home and tried to run the Superior Hiking Trail again. I'd got so used to doing long climbs and descents out West that it was

hard for me to transition into the rapid changes in terrain of the Superior Trail.

It's very hard to get into a rhythm. One moment you're going through a rock bed, the next you're wading through swamps – it really forces a runner to become one with the trail. It created some excellent skills for me early on and has definitely helped me with my technical running abilities. That capacity to adapt and change

quickly is what prepared me more than anything to win races.

I trained for my first 100-mile Western States ultra on those trails in Duluth from December to April. I ran in the snow on snowmobile trails, and through ice by putting metal screws in my shoes for traction. It was the first time I ran through a winter instead of skiing, and it really set me up. I won that first race – and then went on to win it seven years in a row.

Chapter 11

TRAINING FOR RACING

Whichever distance you want to attempt, from a mile to a marathon, you'll find all you need to train for it here

254 **NATURAL SELECTION**
What's your ideal distance?

260 **YOUR BEST YEAR EVER**
Mix up your running over 12 months

266 **MILE IN A MONTH**
Try this classic distance for a challenge

268 **TRAINING PLANS**
For 5K, 10K, half an full marathons

282 **WHY LESS IS MORE**
All your tapering questions answered

284 **26 MILES LATER...**
How to recover from a marathon

NATURAL SELECTION

What distance were you born to run? Here's how to figure out what kind of runner you are – and realise your full potential

Success in some events comes more naturally than in others. In fact, few runners have the same potential to be outstanding at all distances. Some have the innate gift of speed, while others are natural-born long-distance runners. In the end, your physiology, temperament and priorities will determine the ideal racing distance for you.

You may be surprised to find out where your true strengths lie. "Everyone thinks the marathon is the Holy Grail, when a lot of people should really be doing the 5K," says Jason Karp, an exercise physiologist and running coach.

The physiology you're born with determines how well you'll perform your first time out, and how much improvement you'll be able to make in training. The good news is that with the appropriate training strategy, you can make the most of what you were born with.

So how do you determine whether you were meant to be a speed demon or a multiple marathon runner? You could turn to pricey lab tests, but that would probably be overkill. Your running habits reveal plenty about what distances you'll excel at.

Read on to learn which physiological factors help shape your running identity. Then examine your training, racing history and tendencies to find out which distances are perfect for you. Finally, learn how to tweak your training routine and set realistic goals to better match your newfound specialty.

MINI CONTENTS

A
KNOW YOUR PHYSIOLOGY

B
IDENTIFY YOUR TRUE CALLING

C
SET REACHABLE GOALS

D
TRAIN LIKE A SPECIALIST

Which distance were you built to run?

THE RUNNER

RACING

SPEED RACER
These athletes are built to go fast – not long. Consequently, the 5K and 10K are ideal events to target.

MIDDLE-DISTANCE
These people are best at sustaining a tough pace. So they're well suited to run strong 10-milers and half-marathons.

LONG-HAULER
These runners are meant to go the distance. Though they may lack speed, their true calling is the marathon.

A

KNOW YOUR PHYSIOLOGY

Four qualities that influence how fast and how far you can run

LACTATE THRESHOLD

pace is the fastest pace that you can sustain for an extended period (roughly 30 minutes or more) before lactate – a by-product of the fuel burned during hard exercise – starts building up in the blood. Marathon winners often have high lactate thresholds, which help them hold a strong pace for a long time. With specifically targeted training – maintaining a certain intensity over a distance – you are able to raise your lactate threshold.

MUSCLES are made of slow-

and fast-twitch fibres. An elite marathon runner's muscles might be 75 per cent slow-twitch; an Olympic sprinter probably has a high proportion of fast-twitch. Most runners are born with a modest mix of both. You can't change the muscle composition you inherit, but you can train your muscles for speed or to sustain steady paces over long distances.

VO2 MAX measures the

maximum amount of oxygen that can be consumed per minute while exercising. Runners with a naturally high VO2 max often find it easier to run faster because their hearts can deliver more oxygen to their muscles. There are many ways to boost VO2 max, including speedwork, which forces the heart to pump blood around the body at a much higher rate. Beginners can improve it by about 20 per cent. Fit runners can only fine-tune it.

RUNNING ECONOMY

measures the amount of oxygen you need will need to run at any pace. It reflects how efficiently you are running. Other physical factors can have an impact on your running economy – if you're overweight or have a sloppy gait, for instance, you're going to need to use more oxygen than a leaner person with a cleaner stride would. As you train by running more, and improve factors like your VO2 max, weight and biomechanics, you'll develop a considerably better running economy than you had before.

B

IDENTIFY YOUR TRUE CALLING

Learn what kind of running will give you the best performances

1 HOW MANY HOURS A WEEK CAN YOU DEVOTE TO TRAINING?

A. 2 to 3
B. 4 to 5
C. 6 or more

2 HOW WOULD YOU DESCRIBE THE PERFECT TRAINING RUN FOR YOU?

A. It brings a big surge of adrenaline and power channeling right through your body – like kicking into high gear.
B. Running right at the edge of your abilities – not backing off, but not pushing so much that you could run out of steam.
C. It's getting into a meditative rhythm, where you can zone out or get absorbed in your thoughts, a conversation or your just the scenic surroundings.

3 IF YOU COULD SKIP ANY SESSION EACH WEEK, WHAT WOULD IT BE?

A. Any run that takes more than an hour. It's just too exhausting and far too boring.
B. Workouts that don't feel long enough or fast enough.
C. Any run where there's pressure to hold a very fast pace. It ceases to be enjoyable.

4 WHEN YOU'RE OUT ON A GROUP RUN, YOU STAND OUT FROM THE PACK BY:

A. Surging to the finish – no matter how hard the rest of the group has been running.
B. Managing to stick with the lead group, no matter how much they're pushing it.
C. Feeling pretty fresh at the end of a long run – no matter how far you've gone.

5 WHEN YOU GET INJURED, WHAT USUALLY CAUSES THE PROBLEM?

A. Total mileage. Overdoing it always seems to trigger some ailment – like plantar fasciitis or a screaming IT band.
B. A muscle pull, a tendon tweak or something that got twisted or torn while trying to keep up or dash to the finish.
C. No major injuries.

6 HOW DO YOU FEEL ABOUT SPENDING MONEY ON RACING?

A. With all the races I do, it's hard to justify shelling out more than £20 on just one.
B. Spending £35 or so on a race is okay, as long as there aren't a lot of other costs for travel and logistics.
C. No one likes to part with hard-earned cash, but for a few big events each year, it's not an issue to spend £70.

PHOTOGRAPHY: AARON GOODMAN. MODEL: CHRISTI MARRACCINI

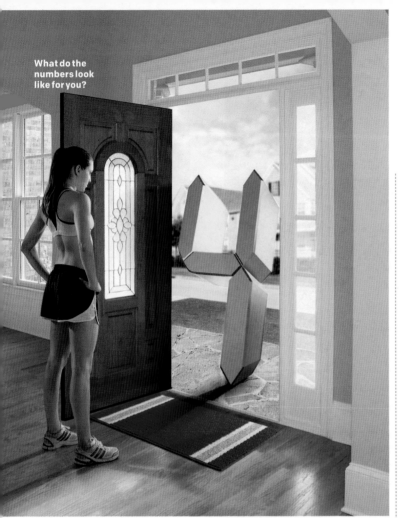

What do the numbers look like for you?

HOW TO INTERPRET YOUR SCORE

Your tally says a lot about you – your strengths, the distances you were born to run and your ideal training strategy.

10 TO 18 POINTS: YOU ARE A SPEED RACER

You may not have thought about 5Ks and 10Ks since you first started running, but as you seem to be able to pick up speed with ease, that maybe the place to stand out. You can put your all into it without feeling like it compromises your life to any degree.

19 TO 26 POINTS: YOU ARE A MIDDLE-DISTANCE SPECIALIST

It may feel like the world revolves around the marathon, but you don't have to go that far: 10-milers and half-marathons could be for you. By running them, you'll find out how far and fast you can run. And as 13.1-milers become the most popular races, many have taken on the big-league feel of the famous marathons.

27 TO 34 POINTS: YOU ARE A LONG-HAULER

While some people could never imagine 'looking forward' to several hours pounding out the miles, you savour the long, slow distance running that let you spend long stretches of time outside whatever the elements maybe. The marathon is your race. You may get left behind in a 5K by those quicker off the mark, but that shouldn't matter. Remember the tortoise and the hare.

---

7 **WHEN YOU'RE CHOOSING A RACE, WHAT MATTERS MOST?**

A. Convenience. Running shouldn't take time away from family, work or other important commitments.

B. Getting a decent workout – and a good test – from it without having to deal with a lot of travel or other race-day logistics.

C. It should feel like a big deal. Whether the race is a large, well-known event or is in a beautiful location, it should be something to circle on the calendar and look forward to, and it should feel like a reward for all the hard work of training.

8 **WHAT ARE THE RACE DISTANCES WHERE YOU HAD YOUR BEST FINISHING TIMES?**

A. 5K
B. 10 miles or half-marathon
C. Marathon

Answer Key
(Give yourself points as noted)

	A	B	C
1	A=2	B=4	C=6
2	A=1	B=2	C=3
3	A=1	B=2	C=3
4	A=1	B=2	C=0
5	A=1	B=2	C=0
6	A=2	B=4	C=6
7	A=2	B=4	C=6
8	A=2	B=4	C=6

RACING

It's time to find out what kind of runner you are

⊕ DON'T KNOW YOUR PACE?

Your 5K pace is a good benchmark to help you assess your fitness and set goals – whether you're running 3.1 miles or 26.2. If you haven't raced before (or for a while), this time trial, developed by exercise scientist Bill Pierce, will give you a good estimate.

❶ At a track, run 3 x 1,600m (four laps) at a challenging pace, and time each segment. Jog for two minutes between intervals to recover. The goal is to run each segment at an even pace.

❷ If the times of each of the three segments are similar (within 10 seconds of each other), work out your average pace per mile, then add 15 seconds. If not, try it again another day.

❸ So if your segment times were 6:00, 6:04 and 6:08, your average pace is 6:04. Then add 15 seconds to get 6:19 – that time is a good estimate of your 5K pace per mile.

Ⓒ SET REACHABLE GOALS

Online tools help you find the right pace and best race

THE BEST ONLINE PREDICTION TOOLS

Runners have lots of questions. Is the marathon really for me? Is a 25-minute 5K realistic? Prediction calculators can provide some answers. These tools forecast how fast you can run one distance based on a time for another. Say you ran a 3:30 marathon, and the 5K time the calculator shows is five minutes faster than your PB. That's a clear sign that you are more likely to perform better over long a long distances race.

The predictions are based on algorithms that include factors such as race statistics and the natural tendency to run slower at longer distances. They're only accurate if you've trained for each distance.

RUNNER'S WORLD

Runnersworld.co.uk/calculators is loaded with resources that can help you gauge how fit and fast you are – and figure out how to make your mark. It also links to SmartCoach, a tool that lets you tailor a training plan to your ability and goals.

Our race-time predictor will predict how fast you could run 11 different distances based on your performance at one race distance, and suggests training paces based on your results.

The Runner's World race-pace band shows the pace you need to maintain at various distances to reach your goal. Then you can create your own marathon pace band listing your splits for race day.

OTHER SITES

Mcmillanrunning.com has a tool that converts any race time to equivalent distances.

Fetcheveryone.com allows you to build a portfolio of past and future races. The site calculates your PB times over a variety of different distances.

Jeffgalloway.com has a site calculator that's especially helpful for beginners or anyone who hasn't raced before.

D

TRAIN LIKE A SPECIALIST
Target your strengths to maximise your training gains

Once you know your strong suit, you can develop the traits that will help you excel. Of course, with focused training, you can fulfil your potential at any distance. "Our bodies are remarkably adaptable," says exercise scientist Bill Pierce. Work out with purpose and, he says, and "you can reach your goals". Here's how...

BE A SPEED RACER
(Run fast 5Ks and 10Ks)

➡ **YOUR GOAL** Improve VO2 max, fast-twitch muscles and running economy.

➡ **YOUR STRATEGY** Get lots of practice running fast. Intervals, which involve working near maximum heart rate, force the heart to move as much oxygen as it can to the muscles, which boosts VO2 max. The bursts of speed get your fast-twitch fibres firing. And as your legs and feet turn over at a quicker rate, you'll shed sloppiness and run more efficiently.

➡ **KEY WORKOUT** Speedwork. Run intervals about 10 seconds faster than 5K race pace, or the quickest pace you can sustain and repeat. At a track, run 400-1,600m intervals, or on the road, run fast for up to five minutes. Between intervals, jog for two minutes. Start with three intervals.

➡ **HOW TO IMPROVE** Work your legs. You'll need leg strength to make powerful strides and avoid injury. Twice a week, try moves like squats and lunges to strengthen your leg muscles.

BE A MIDDLE-DISTANCE SPECIALIST
(Run 10-milers to half-marathons)

➡ **YOUR GOAL** Raise your lactate threshold (LT).

➡ **YOUR STRATEGY** Master the art of running comfortably hard. Hold an intense pace for 20 to 45 minutes – this delays the time it takes for lactate to start building up in the blood and for fatigue to set in. It also builds mental stamina; you'll have more confidence in the hardest moments of the race. Don't drop speedwork and long runs – they make tempo work feel more manageable.

➡ **KEY WORKOUT** Tempo run. Start with 15 to 20 minutes at a pace that's 15 to 45 seconds slower than your 5K pace. Build up to 30-to-45 minutes. As you get more comfortable, gradually increase the pace.

➡ **HOW TO IMPROVE** Learn to breathe and relax – even during maximum effort. When you're pushing your pace, it's natural to tense up, which steals energy your heart and legs need. Running on a treadmill in front of a mirror helps you evaluate your own form and identify when you're tensing up.

BE A LONG-HAULER
(Run a strong marathon)

➡ **YOUR GOAL** Improve your running economy.

➡ **YOUR STRATEGY** The more you run, the more economical your form will become, and you'll feel stronger on your feet for longer. Also, your body will become more efficient at preserving energy for later in the race. Don't slack on the speedwork and tempo runs though – a strong heart and higher lactate threshold will help you stay strong for the final miles.

➡ **KEY WORKOUT** The long run. Start with a one-hour run and gradually build up to three hours. Aim to run about 30 seconds slower than your goal marathon pace. As you get more comfortable, work on picking up the pace in the middle miles. Then, shift into a higher gear in your last segment.

➡ **HOW TO IMPROVE** Build a strong core, and your form will be less likely to fall apart when you're fatigued. Being at your ideal weight can help, too – the lighter you are, the less oxygen you'll need.

Do you feel the need for speed?

YOUR BEST YEAR EVER

For improved fitness and more fun, mixing it up is the name of the game. The rules are simple: run a race distance on every terrain over the next 12 months

Your road map to running success

Even if you feel like you've ticked most of the 'must-do' boxes in your time as a runner (milers to marathons, maybe with the odd adventure race thrown in), chances are there are still things you'd like to try. Perhaps you've never attempted cross-country or donned fancy dress. Maybe you'd like to run a European city marathon or brave a fell race. "Many of us get stuck in a pattern of doing the same training and the same races, year after year," says Keith Anderson, running coach at Full Potential. And while this may give you a very accurate performance record, it is unlikely to yield the best results – or the most enjoyment – from your running.

"If you don't mix up the distance and type of event you're working towards, your training can become stale," says Anderson. So this year, why not let your running take you on a journey of exploration? Below is 12 months' worth of races to aim

for, designed to challenge your speed, stamina, strength and skill. Whether you pick and mix or take on the whole challenge is up to you. But one thing's certain: follow these training guidelines and this will be your fittest year yet.

CROSS COUNTRY
JANUARY

Why now? Cross-country can help lay the foundation for the year ahead, according to Urban Bettag, a UK Athletics Level 3 endurance coach (runurban.com). "It's a great way to develop endurance, good technique, muscular strength and the ability to change pace, making you a more versatile runner," he says. Commonwealth Games bronze medallist Liz Yelling agrees, and likes to factor in some cross-country races in the build-up to a marathon. "I have a real passion

for the mud and the hills," she says. "I believe cross-country running makes you strong and really teaches you to race – for once, you're not just chasing times."

Training It is essential to find your "off-road feet" if you plan to take on cross-country races, but Yelling advises easing yourself in gently. "If you aren't confident about running off-road, start with grass and a firm trail before heading to less well-trodden paths," she advises. And don't do all your off-road work at a slow pace – introduce faster bursts through fartlek training, or run intervals on grass instead of track.

Race strategy Choose your first race carefully, advises Tim Wright, captain of Orion Harriers, a cross-country running club (orionharriers.co.uk). "If you have time, it's worth looking at the course to locate any obstacles such as stiles, choose the best route through a boggy patch or prepare for difficult climbs or descents," he says. At the very least, check how many laps there are and where the finish line is. "If you are not ready for spikes, then trail or fell shoes will give you plenty of grip, but make sure your laces are tight so you don't lose a shoe in the deep mud!"

HILLY RACE
FEBRUARY

Why now? To develop the strength, endurance and mental toughness that will fortify you for the year ahead. "When you're running uphill, there's no respite – your heart and lungs are working much harder than on a comparable run on the flat," says W40 world mountain running champion Angela Mudge. On an incline of just five per cent, energy expenditure is about 20 per cent higher than it would be at the same speed on flat ground. "It makes you stronger,

both physically and mentally," says Mudge. "You also learn skills such as how to survive the elements."

Training "To succeed in hill racing, you must be able to break your rhythm: varied terrain and gradient means always having to adjust your stride length and pace," says Mudge. That's why you need to get some practice in on the kind of terrain you'll be encountering in a race. "On the descents, learn to disengage your brain and let yourself go." Not tempted to take on a fell race? "Hill training is a valuable component of any training schedule," says British athlete and *RW* contributing editor

Jo Pavey. "Hilly runs or structured hill sessions build leg strength and speed, and improve aerobic capacity." And what goes up must come down: "A gentle descent is a great place to work on increasing your leg turnover, which will carry over into your road running later in the year," says Anderson.

Race strategy For your debut race, choose a user-friendly course – something that resembles a hilly trail race rather than a fell race and lasts 30-40 minutes, advises Mudge. Hill and fell races are grouped into three categories, denoting the steepness of the climbs and the proportion of the course that is off-road. "Novices should look for B or C category races," she says, where more than 20% of total distance is on-road.

10 MILES
MARCH

Why now? After building a strong aerobic base over the winter, it's time to test yourself on the roads. The 10-miler is far less frequently raced than the 10K or half-marathon, but it's a great challenge of your ability to maintain a fast pace for a prolonged period. "Newer runners often find there's a big gap between a 10K and half, so a 10-mile race offers a great interim distance to aim for," says Stella Bandu, a UK Athletics Level 3 coach.

Training You'll need endurance to cover the miles comfortably, so aim to include at least a couple of overdistance runs (runs over 10 miles) in your build-up. "Threshold or tempo training will help to teach your body to resist fatigue and prevent you slowing down as the miles pass," explains Bandu. Alternate weekly between a continuous tempo run for 20-40 minutes and intervals of five to 15 minutes with a recovery jog equal to 20 per cent of the length of the effort. The pace should feel 'comfortably hard', which usually equates to around 25-30 seconds slower than your 5K pace.

Race strategy Set off at half-marathon pace (or a little quicker, if you're a speedier runner), and if you feel able to pick up the pace a bit, then great, says Bandu. A 10-mile race can work well as part of your marathon build-up. "It's not so far that you'll be too fatigued to tag a few more miles on at the end or to do another run later in the day," says Bandu.

MARATHON
APRIL

Why now? A spring marathon gives you something to focus on through the long winter months – and there are lots of races to choose from, both home and away.

Training While most budding marathoners faithfully put in the long easy runs, many neglect to train at the pace they plan to race at. "Introducing running at marathon pace is very important, especially for those who have a specific target time in mind," says Bettag. "Getting the body accustomed to the target pace – and rehearsing it – is key." Bettag recommends running the bulk of your long runs 20 per cent slower than your target marathon pace, but with a fast finish (for example, the last 20 minutes of a two-hour run). "This teaches you to pick up the pace towards the very end of the run, when you might normally be fading," he says. Yelling

⊕ A FIRST-TIMERS' GUIDE

If you're new to running or you've simply never raced before, here are the best distances to aim for – and how to prepare for them

SUMMER GOAL: 5K

1 Run three to four times a week with a day off between each run.

2 Consider including some strength training and core stability work in your weekly programme to avoid injury.

3 Build up one of your weekly runs to 45-60 minutes so you have the confidence to know you can comfortably cover the race distance.

4 Once you can comfortably run 30 minutes continuously, introduce some tempo-paced training to help build your pace. Warm up for 10 minutes, run for 10 minutes at your comfortably hard pace, then run easy for 10 minutes. Do this three or four times a week.

5 Include one session every other week on a track, treadmill, or road, in which you run at a hard effort for two to three minutes. Jog/walk to recover for the same time in between efforts. Repeat five to six times in total.

AUTUMN GOAL: HALF-MARATHON

1 Run three to five times a week, giving yourself at least one day off after each of your harder sessions.

2 Consider including some strength and core stability work in your weekly programme to help resist injury.

3 Start building up your long run 12 weeks prior to race. Aim to get six to nine long runs in during this period, starting at eight miles and adding one mile on every one to two weeks to reach at least 13 miles – ideally a little more.

4 Schedule a 10K race into your 12-week training plan. Multiply your time in minutes by 2.22 to get an idea of what your half-marathon time will be.

5 Include tempo training and intervals in your programme. If you are running three or four times per week, alternate between the two. If you are running five times, include both.

Become an urban pace setter

try a few 'brick' sessions, where you tag a run on to a bike ride to get your legs accustomed to the change.

Race strategy When choosing your race, find out how challenging the leg of your weakest discipline is to give yourself the best chance of a good experience. The great thing about triathlons when you're a runner is that the best bit comes last – if you pace yourself properly. Keep your effort level steady during the bike and swim, and leave something in the tank for the run.

1-MILE RACE
JUNE

Why now? With the curtain up on the outdoor athletics season, now is the time to up the pace. "Training for a miler breaks up the monotony of distance training as well as improving your running economy," says US coach Greg McMillan (mcmillanrunning.com).

Training The bread and butter for mile training – or at least, the type that you probably don't already do – is short reps, around 200-400m. "Short intervals at mile race pace are a key component in enhancing your VO_2 max, leg speed and functional strength," says McMillan. But you don't have to hit the track. "A sports field is fine, and don't get too hung up on the distance being exact," says Bandu. "The important thing is that you're running faster than you're accustomed to." Make your recovery jog twice as long, time-wise, as your effort – but gradually reduce it as you get fitter.

Race strategy Racing over such a short distance, it's essential that you warm-up – you don't want to spend half the race trying to get into your stride. "Do a 10-15-minute warm-up jog, and then perform four to six strides to remind your legs to move faster," advises Bandu.

recommends scheduling in some faster-than-marathon-pace work. "Tempo training and interval work will help make your marathon pace feel easier on the day," she explains.

Race strategy So you've made it to the start line, injury-free and raring to go. "Regardless of whether it's three and a half hours or six hours, you need to have an idea of how long the race is likely to take, so you can pace it accordingly," says Yelling. Research shows that when marathon runners begin the race at a pace that is just two per cent faster than their practised race pace, they're more likely to flounder later on. "Steady pacing is the best strategy," says Yelling. And what if you're feeling remarkably good mid race? "If you have the energy, you could try increasing your pace at 20-22 miles," says Yelling. "But I wouldn't risk doing it earlier."

TRI/DUATHLON
MAY

Why now? "Entering a triathlon or duathlon gives you a new goal to work towards and challenges you to learn new skills," says triathlete and coach Richard Allen, who has a 10K PB of 30:30. If you're recovering from the rigours of a marathon, swimming and cycling give your joints a break, without letting those hard-earned fitness levels slip.

Training Long bike rides can replace long runs if you are in a post-marathon phase. You'll already have a great endurance base and the running component of your event is likely to be 5K (sprint distance) or 10K (Olympic distance) tops. Swim little and often to improve your 'feel' for the water and hone technique. As the event draws near,

Track your progress

5K
JULY

Why now? Revving up your pace with mile training will have had a significant effect on your PB potential over 5K – and three miles isn't too much to tackle, even if it's a scorching summer.

Training "The 5K and 10K have many similarities, but there are also differences," says Pavey. "Both require good speed endurance, but repetitions for 5K training may be faster, with slightly longer recoveries than for the 10K". Your VO_2 max (maximal aerobic uptake) is the most important determinant of your 5K performance, so schedule in some sessions designed to raise it. According to French scientists, the optimal way to develop VO_2 max is with intervals of three minutes with a two-minute recovery jog between. Aim for four to six efforts at current 3-5K race pace. Pavey recommends speedwork amounting to 3,000m in volume for 5K training.

Race strategy Good pacing is vital, says Bettag. "Many inexperienced runners tend to set out too quickly and accumulate lactate, which forces them to slow down during the later stages," he explains. "For the best outcome, try to go for even pace, or set off a bit slower in the early stages and progress through the race midway with a final push over the last 800m."

10K
AUGUST

Why now? The recent speedwork and VO_2 max training will help set you up for a fast 10K, which in turn lays the foundations for a good half-marathon next month.

Training "There definitely needs to be more of a focus on endurance when preparing for a 10K, compared with a 5K," says Pavey. "To work on specific 10K endurance, I would use longer repetitions at a slower pace and with a shorter recovery." Physiologically, a high aerobic capacity and lactate threshold are equally important determinants of your performance in a 10K race – demanding a balance of VO_2 max sessions and tempo runs. And, says McMillan, don't neglect race-pace training. His favoured 10K training session is three lots of two miles at goal pace with five-minute jogs in between – but you need to work up to it. Start with six one-mile reps with three-to four-minute recoveries, eight to 10 weeks away from your race.

Race strategy Don't under-estimate the distance and go off too fast, like a number of those around you will. Yes, it's only 6.2 miles, but setting off at your 3K pace is sure to backfire. To get an idea of your potential performance, double your 5K time and add one minute.

1/2 MARATHON
SEPTEMBER

Why now? Instead of always using it as a stepping stone or measuring stick for a full marathon, give the half all the attention it deserves, and race it in its own right. With a year of varied training behind you, you should have the perfect combination of speed and endurance to set a good time.

Training "When training for a half-marathon, sessions should be focused on achieving staying power, but also have the aim of making race pace feel comfortable," says Pavey. Malcolm Balk, running coach and author of *Master the Art of Running* (Collins & Brown), likes to include some race-pace work. "Race-pace intervals, starting with 1K and working up to 5K per repeat work well, as do long runs with up to 5K at race pace at the end." Balk is also a firm believer in including short, hard efforts. "Even marathoners and half-marathon runners should use strides and short hill efforts (under 10 seconds) to build power and prevent injury," he says.

Race strategy If you're running for 90 minutes or more, opt for sports drinks instead of water to top up fuel stores. Start further back in the pack if you know you'll be tempted to set off too fast. "Even pacing is the smartest way to a good time," says Balk, who achieved a half-marathon PB of 1:20 at the age of 56.

TRAIL RACE
OCTOBER

Why now? It's nice to get off the roads again and see autumn in all its glory. Plus, your legs will welcome the change of terrain. "Running off-road boosts your fitness while reducing impact, cutting down on the risk of injury," says Pavey. While it's kinder on the joints, the uneven surface and undulations make you work harder than when you're on firm terrain, challenging your balance and core stability, as well as building knee strength.

Training Forget about trying to maintain the same speed on off-road terrain as you do on the road. "It's about effort rather than pace," says Anderson. "So throttle back where necessary. And relax – you won't run naturally if you're tense."

You may need to tweak your technique. "Pick your knees up a bit higher and shorten your stride," Yelling advises. If you are going to be hitting the trails regularly, invest in some trail shoes. "They offer extra support, cushioning and grip," says Natalie White, a member of the Salomon Trail Team.

DEAR DIARY...
Log your miles as you progress. Studies show it will keep you motivated

Many runners keep a training journal – but what do you do with it, come the end of the year? Does it get consigned to the bottom drawer, or do you spend time reading through it? "I don't think we look back on our training often enough," says Anderson. "Reflecting on what you have achieved enables you to build on your strengths, address weaknesses and find ways to become a more rounded athlete. Recording information is only worthwhile if you use it." With so many challenges to take on this year, there will be plenty of learning opportunities. Record – and reflect.

Race strategy With such a variety of routes and race distances, you can forget about chasing PBs on the trails and enjoy the scenery instead. "You have to approach trail races differently," says White. "Don't worry about your minutes-per-mile-pace. If you're a first-timer, start with something manageable that will give you a feel for the trails."

PACE SOMEONE
NOVEMBER

Why now? So far, all your training has been geared towards improving your own fitness and achieving new goals. Now it's time to help someone else achieve theirs. "It's so rewarding to share the passion you have about running," says Pauline Beare, chief executive of the Women's Running Network, which runs nationwide female-only groups for all abilities. "If you can

get someone out of the door, you will help them take a step towards doing their first event."

Training Share your knowledge about training to help your protégé progress, but try to remember what it felt like to be a beginner, and make sure the goal you're working towards is theirs, and not what you think they are capable of.

Race strategy "Pacing someone is not easy," warns Beare, who recently paced a member of her training group through the Goofy Challenge – a 39.3-miler consisting of a half-marathon and full marathon on two consecutive days. "It's easy to think you're following when actually you're setting the pace. Hold a step back so that they genuinely have the lead."

ADVENTURE
DECEMBER

Why now? You've got a solid base of miles in the bank, but perhaps you're getting a little weary of road racing. Or maybe you just need to take your eye off the clock. "A non-standard race distance or novel event can be refreshing," says Balk. "You have no preconceived ideas of how you should perform."

Training Do your research about your chosen adventure race and make sure you are prepared for its unique challenges. In training for the Marathon des Sables, 34-year-old stockbroker Andrew Kocen hit the gym as well as the roads. "I'm sure the core training and free weights work I did left me with fewer injuries than I would have had otherwise," he says.

Race strategy Whether you are dressed as a banana, racing a train or battling your way through an obstacle course, enjoy it. This part is all about reminding yourself what fun running can be.

Prepare for the ultimate sprint test

MIRACLES IN A MILE

Odds are you've never considered training for the mile, but this classic test will boost all-round performance

Even if you only take four weeks out to do it, shifting your focus away from long distances can provide benefits in droves. And it's surprisingly enjoyable. Racing a mile – there's a variety of open events to get stuck in to up and down the country – is about as close as most of us will come to feeling like an elite athlete.

However, there are a few key points to consider before you start your mile training.

① QUALITY SESSIONS

Being of a shorter duration and a higher intensity, miling requires a greater amount of anaerobic work than races of 10K or longer.

This means you need to train your body to cope with the rapid onset of fatigue, which results from faster anaerobic work. The best way to do this is to run interval sessions – preferably on grass, which is more forgiving than the track. The duration of the repetitions should be short, because you will be running at

the hamstrings, gluteals, calves, groin and quadriceps areas. Hold stretches for at least 30 seconds. Do the stretches before and after a session, because the increased intensity of the exercise will lead to muscle tightening and stiffness. Self-massage will also help to counter this tightening.

3 DOWNHILL RUNNING

Increasing your stride rate will also help to boost your running speed. The most effective way to increase your stride rate is to do some downhill running, where you are almost forced to move your legs quicker. It is important that you do this in a safe manner to avoid the obvious injury problems. Find a suitable location that consists of a stretch of grass with a very gentle down slope. It makes sense to do this sort of workout when you are relatively fresh and warmed up; so following a 20-30 minute run will be better

than after your longer Sunday morning effort. A good way to structure the run is to stretch, and then to do six to eight strides at a fast pace with a walk-back recovery. The emphasis should be on a fast pick-up of the legs.

4 STRENGTH WORK

There is a strong association between muscle strength and speed, which is partly why most sprinters are bulky creatures and marathon runners are of a slighter build. Improving your strength will help to improve your miling but you need to work on the right muscles. As you will be on your toes more in the mile than in a long-distance race, it will help to strengthen the calves with a series of calf raises. You will also need driving quads, and half squats will strengthen those. Initially your bodyweight alone will provide sufficient resistance, but you may start holding weights when you want to progress.

a speed equal to or faster than your mile time. Your session should be preceded by a good warm-up and some stretching exercises (it's preferable to stretch before an interval session rather than afterwards) and followed by a cool-down. It's best to build up to the pace at which you run the reps in successive sessions, rather than simply increasing the volume, because you are, after all, training your body to go faster.

2 FLEXIBILITY

Running speed is dictated by two factors: stride length and stride rate. Developing flexibility of the correct muscles will help you to increase your stride length without the risk of overtraining. Concentrate on stretching the muscles in

+ SET YOUR GOAL

This table will give you a basic idea of what mile time you should be capable of on the basis of your fastest 10K. If you run it much quicker than the predicted time, you clearly have talent for miling!

+ 10K TIME		+ MILE PREDICTION
34:00		4:41
36:00		4:57
38:00		5:13
40:00		5:31
42:00		5:49
44:00		6:07
46:00		6:25
48:00		6:42
50:00		7:01
52:00		7:19
54:00		7:37
56:00		7:55

5 THINK LIKE A MILER

Running, or indeed racing, on the track may be a completely different experience for you, but you have to think in a positive way and attack the track rather than being scared of it. It might be a refreshing change to have a bash at the mile, but your attitude must change to meet the new demand. Things happened very quickly – whatever the standard – in a race over this distance. You have to think about what you are doing. Decide in advance what pace you want to run at and calculate your desired 400m splits. Don't get carried away at the start if everyone else goes off at a fast pace, be disciplined and run at the pace that suits you. That said, if you feel good with a lap to go, don't be afraid to take a risk and make a bold strike for home.

TRAINING PLANS

With the right advice, any runner can become a racer, no matter what distance they choose. These plans will see you over the finish line in style

YOUR FIRST 5K

If you're new to running the idea of doing a race has probably crossed you mind. It's a very good idea – it will give you focus to your training and a sense of achievement once you complete it. But there's no need to overstretch yourself in the process. While a marathon might be the most high-profile race it's a challenge you should build up to. For starters, how about a simple 5K instead? It's a perfect distance: 3.1 miles require relatively little build-up for most runners, the training doesn't take over your life, and the race itself is over fairly quickly. And by simply logging only three or four runs per week, you could be ready to toe the line of your first 5K in just five weeks.

Top coach Chris Carmichael (trainright.com) encourages all runners to try a 5K. "People run for a variety of reasons, but they get more out of it when they're working towards something specific," he says. "And a 5K race is an attainable goal for any runner." Plus, there's the 'fun factor', says US running guru Jeff Galloway, author of *Running: Getting Started*. "My favourite thing about 5K races is the atmosphere. Almost everyone there is in a good mood. How many other events in your life are like that?"

FIVE WEEK PLAN

In the five weeks leading up to your first 5K, most coaches agree that you need to run three or four days a week. During one of those weekly runs, you should focus on increasing the amount you can run at one time until you build to at least the race distance, or the equivalent amount of time spent running. "I encourage runners, particularly beginners, to focus on time and effort, rather than becoming obsessed with miles and distance," says running coach, Nick Anderson. "Thinking in minutes is more gradual and self-paced, it will help to make sure you don't get injured by doing too much too soon." Completing the equivalent of the 5K distance in training gives you the strength and confidence you need to finish the race. And if you increase your long run up to six miles (or twice the amount of time it should take you to cover the 5km), you'll run with even greater strength (or speed, if you prefer).

ILLUSTRATION: JONATHAN BARTLETT

RACING

Most of your running during the week should be at a comfortable pace. This is especially true for runners who simply want to finish the race. But because adding some faster training to your schedule is the best way to improve your speed and endurance, even novices should really consider doing some quicker running. "Intervals are not reserved for elites," says Carmichael. "Running three one-mile intervals with recovery in between will do more to increase your sustainable running pace than running three miles at once."

First-time racers can do some faster running one or two days a week, but these sessions don't have to be regimented. Anderson recommends adapting one session per week to include about 10 minutes of speedwork, made up of two five-minute runs at a faster pace, each framed by five minutes of jogging. Once this becomes easy, try one 10-minute interval at threshold pace – this is about 85 per cent of your maximum heart rate, where you can utter a few words but not hold a conversation. Always bookend harder runs with easy warm-up and cool-down jogs.

THE BIG DAY

The greatest challenge of running your first 5K is maintaining the correct pace, says Anderson. Start out too fast and you might struggle to even cross the finish line. That's why Galloway recommends that all first-time racers (including veteran runners) should settle at the back of the pack when at the starting line. This prevents any chance of an overzealous start and allows you to gradually build up speed during the race, ideally running the final mile the fastest. But how fast should you expect to run come race day? While Carmichael says the main goal really should be to just have fun, he tells experienced runners who are new to racing that they can expect to race about 30 seconds per mile faster than training pace. So, runners training at a nine-minute-per-mile pace should finish in around 26:25; those training at a 10-minute-mile pace should finish in 29:31; and those training at an 11-minute-mile pace should expect to finish in around 32:39.

Galloway has a very different way of predicting race times. Every two weeks, his clients run a mile around a track as fast as they possibly can. Then he uses a pace calculator, like the one that can be found online by visiting runnersworld.co.uk, to predict their times for longer distances. In general, he finds that most runners slow down about 33 seconds per mile when they go from a one-mile run to 5K race.

However, most experts will discourage first-timers from setting themselves strict time goals for race day. "Make it a race against yourself," says Carmichael, "because it's your progress that will be most valuable to you." Galloway seconds that. "If you enjoy it, you'll do it again." And probably faster.

FIVE WEEKS TO YOUR FIRST 5K

It's training time. New runners who need to build up to the distance should follow this beginner plan

BEGINNER'S 5K PLAN

WEEK	MON	TUE	WED	THU	FRI	SAT	SUN
1	WALK/XT 20 min or day off	RUN 10 min	WALK/XT 20 min or day off	RUN 15 min	WALK/XT 20 min or day off	Rest	RUN 2 miles
2	WALK/XT 20 min or day off	RUN 15 min	WALK/XT 20 min or day off	RUN 20 min	WALK/XT 20 min or day off	Rest	RUN 2.5 miles
3	WALK/XT 30 min or day off	RUN 20 min	WALK/XT 30 min or day off	RUN 25 min	WALK/XT 30 min or day off	Rest	RUN 3 miles
4	WALK/XT 30 min or day off	RUN 25 min	WALK/XT 30 min or day off	RUN 30 min	WALK/XT 30 min or day off	Rest	RUN 3.5 miles
5	WALK/XT 30 min or day off	RUN 30 min	WALK/XT 30 min or day off	RUN 30 min	WALK/XT 30 min or day off	Rest	5K Race

INTERMEDIATE 5K PLAN

WEEK	MON	TUE	WED	THU	FRI	SAT	SUN
1	3 miles plus 5 x strides	Rest	4 miles plus 5 x strides	Rest	4 miles plus 5 x strides	2 to 3 miles; 15-min core workout	Rest
2	**3 miles plus 5 x strides**	**Rest**	**4 miles with 2 x 5 min at SS intensity; 15-min core workout**	**Rest**	**3 miles plus 5 x strides**	**5 to 6 miles; 15-min core workout**	**Rest**
3	3 miles plus 6 x strides	Rest	4 miles with 3 x 5 min at SS intensity; 15-min core workout	Rest	3 miles plus 6 x strides	6 miles with the last 15 min at SS intensity; 15 min core workout	Rest
4	**3 miles plus 6 x strides**	**Rest**	**4 miles with 2 x 10 min at SS intensity; 15-min core workout**	**Rest**	**3 miles plus 5 x strides**	**6 miles with the last 15 min at SS intensity; 15-min core workout**	**Rest**
5	3 miles plus 4 x strides	Rest	3 miles; 15-min core workout	Rest	2 miles	2 miles plus 3 x strides	5K RACE

Keep watch for your best time

⊕ BEGINNER PLAN KEY

WALK/XT You can walk or cross-train (swim, bike, elliptical trainer, etc) at a moderate intensity for the stated amount of time, or take the day off.
Weekday runs All weekday runs should be at a steady pace.
Weekend long run This is measured in miles, rather than minutes, to ensure you increase the distance you cover each week. Long-run pace should be two or three minutes per mile slower than the pace you can run one mile flat-out. Feel free to take walk breaks.

⊕ INTERMEDIATE PLAN KEY

Weekly mileage Except where noted, weekly mileage should be run at a perceived effort (PE) of 6/10.
Strides After completing the run, run hard for 20 seconds and recover with easy jogging or walking for 45 seconds; repeat as instructed.
Core workout Do a series of basic exercises to strengthen the core muscles and improve posture.
SS intensity Intervals at Steady State intensity should be run at a PE of seven or eight.

RACING

YOUR 10K PLAN

It's the nation's favourite distance – long enough to test your personal endurance, short enough for you to switch on the afterburners. You'll be glad to hear that 10K training forms the ideal foundation of almost all types of running performance. That's because it includes ample amounts of the three core components of distance training: strength, stamina and speed. Obviously, you can use it to train for your goal 10K, but with certain adjustments you can also use it to prepare for everything from the 5K to the marathon. This is the classic distance, made famous by Ethiopian legends Haile Gebrselassie and Kenenisa Bekele. So read through the runner profiles below, and decide which of our six-week plans is best for you, but remember that these are not one-size-fits-all plans. If you can't complete a given session, you don't have to, rearrange your training days to fit your schedule.

WHO AM I?

➡ BEGINNER

You're a notch above novice. You've been running at least six months, and may have done a 5K or two. You run three to five miles, three or four days a week; have done a little fast running when you felt like it; and now you want to enter – and finish – what you consider to be a real distance race.

➡ INTERMEDIATE

You've been running a year or more, have done some 5Ks and maybe even a 10K, but you've always finished feeling as if you could or should have gone faster. You consider yourself mainly a recreational runner, but you still want to make a commitment, and see how fast you can go.

⊕ BEGINNER

If you are a beginner, your 10K goal should be less about achieving a personal best (PB) than an LDF (longest distance finished). You want to run the whole 6.2 miles, so

your main aim is endurance, because it's likely to take you an hour. "Basic aerobic strength is every runner's first need," says running coach Bud Baldaro, so you should aim to do most of your running at a steady, moderate pace.

However, we're also going to add a dash of pseudo-speedwork into your endurance stew for flavour. This will put some added spring into your step, give you a brief taste of what it feels like to run a little faster, and hasten your progression to the Intermediate level. So, every week, in addition to your steady running, you're going to do two extra things:

➡ AI = AEROBIC INTERVALS

In these, you push the pace on a bit – until you breathe just a little harder than usual – followed by slow jogging until you feel rested enough to resume your regular speed, and you always stay well short of going anaerobic (simply stated that means squinty-eyed and gasping for breath). Treat these runs like play. When you do

BEGINNER'S 10K SCHEDULE

WEEK	MON	TUE	WED	THU	FRI	SAT	SUN	TOTAL
1	Rest	2 miles, 4 x 1 min AI, 2 miles	3 miles or rest	4 miles + 3 GP	Rest	5 miles	Rest	16-20 miles
2	Rest	2 miles	3 miles or rest	4 miles + 3 GP	Rest	5.5 miles	3.5 miles	18-21 miles
3	Rest	2 miles, 4 x 90 secs AI, 2 miles	3 miles or rest	4.5 miles + 3 GP	Rest	6 miles	4 miles	18.5-22 miles
4	Rest	2 miles, 6 x 90 secs AI, 2 miles	3 miles or rest	4.5 miles + 6 GP	Rest	6.5 miles	4.5 miles	20-24 miles
5	Rest	2 miles, 4 x 2 mins AI, 2 miles	3 miles or rest	5 miles + 6 GP	Rest	7 miles	5 miles	21.5-26 miles
TAPER	Rest	2 miles, 3 mins, 2 mins, 1 min AI, 2 miles	2 miles	2 miles + 2 GP	2 miles + 2 GP	Rest	10K race	

them, try to recreate that feeling you had as a child when you ran to the park, excited to get there.

➡ GP = GENTLE PICK-UPS

With pick-ups, you gradually increase your pace over 100 metres to about 90 per cent of all-out, hold it there for 10–20m then gradually decelerate. Walk to full recovery before you do the next one. Nothing big, nothing stressful – just enough to let your body go. (After a few AI/GP weeks, your normal pace will feel more comfortable, and you'll get race fit more quickly this way.)

➡ RACE-DAY RULES

Have a drink and an energy bar or bagel two hours before the race, and arrive early enough to make your way to the start without stress. Walk around for 10 minutes before the start; maybe even do a few minutes of slow jogging. Start off at a slower pace than you think you should, and work gradually into a comfortable and controlled pace. Let the race come to you. If there is a water station, stop to drink and relax for 10 seconds.

⊕ INTERMEDIATE

Here's the two-pronged approach that will move you from up from recreational runner to the cusp of competitive athlete. First, you'll be adding miles to your endurance-building long run until it makes up 30 per cent of your weekly mileage. Second, you'll now be doing a substantial amount of tempo running aimed at elevating your anaerobic threshold, the speed above which blood lactate starts to accumulate in the system. You can avoid this unpleasantness with regular sustained sessions at just below 10K pace; that is, tempo-run pace. This will significantly improve your endurance and running efficiency in just six weeks.

So your training will include weekly 10-10 sessions as tempo work, along with a mix of intervals and uphill running, all of which strengthen running muscles, heart and related aerobic systems.

Running fast requires effort and discomfort. But be conservative. If you can't maintain pace throughout a given session, or if your body really starts to complain, call it a day and think about adjusting your pace next time you run.

Plan your training using the chart overleaf (plus you're going to need a stopwatch and a running track or known distances). Here's what the abbreviations mean.

➡ PI = PACE INTERVALS

Run at target 10K pace to improve your efficiency and stamina, and to give you the feel of your race pace. For 10-minute/mile pace (a 1:02:06 10K), you need to aim to run 400m in 2min 30sec (2:30); 800m in 5:00; 1,200m in 7:30.

For nine-minute/mile pace (55:53), aim to run 400m in 2:15; 800m in 4:30; 1,200m in 6:45

For eight-minute/mile pace (49:40), run 400m in 2:00; 800m in 4:00; 1,200m in 6:00.

With these pace intervals and with speed intervals (below), you should slow jog half the distance of the interval to recover.

➡ SI = SPEED INTERVALS

Run these at 30 seconds-per-mile faster than race pace. 10-min/mile pace run 400m in 2:22; 800m in 4:44; 1,200m in 7:06. Nine-min/mile pace 400m in 2:08; 800m in 4:16; 1,200m in 6:24. Eight-min/mile pace 400m in 1:53 800m in 3:45; 1,200m in 5:38.

➡ 10-10

These are 10 x 10-minute tempo repetitions at 30 seconds per mile slower than 10K goal pace, with three- to five-minute slow jogs after each.

Learn how to set your goals in stone

ILLUSTRATION: SIMON BRADER

RACING

➡ TUT = TOTAL UPHILL TIME

Run repetitions up the same hill, or work the uphill sections of a road or off-road course.

➡ S = STRIDES

Over 100m, gradually accelerate to about 90 per cent of all-out, hold it for five seconds, then smoothly decelerate. Walk to full recovery.

➡ RACE-DAY RULES

"Many intermediate runners have a tendency to run too fast in the first half of the race," says Baldaro. "That's just about as close as you can ever get to a guaranteed way of running nothing but a mediocre time, way below your goals. Even pace is always the best way to go, which means that the first half of the race should feel really easy." Divide the race into three two-mile sections: easy in-control pace for the first two, push yourself a bit over the middle two, then go even harder over the last two and, finally, sprint for all your worth when you see the finish line.

+ KEY TO PERCEIVED EFFORT (PE)

5 (out of 10) or 50% maximum heart rate (max HR) This is a brisk walk, never a jog.

6 (out of 10) or 60% max HR Recovery running. This is a very easy running pace that allows you to maintain a conversation with a running partner without gasping for breath.

7 (out of 10) or 70% max HR Steady running. A little harder than recovery pace, but you should still be able to hold a conversation.

8 (out of 10) or 80% max HR Threshold running and target half-marathon pace. You should only be able to say a few words.

YOUR HALF MARATHON

The half-marathon really does have something for everyone, despite its daunting distance. Whether you're a beginner looking to stretch yourself for the first time or a marathoner who wants to stay in tune, a 13-miler could fit the bill. You might not think it, but training for a half is within reach for all runners. Our three-day-a-week beginner's and improver's schedules, devised by coach Nick Anderson (runningwithus.com), will show you how.

The beginner runner's training schedule lets you run by measuring time spent and your own effort levels, rather than counting out the miles. It's designed for those who have never competed in a half-marathon before and allows them to build from 30-minute run/walk sessions to competing on race day over a 12 week plan.

The improver's programme is, of course, somewhat more advanced. It's designed specifically

INTERMEDIATE'S 10K SCHEDULE

WEEK	MON	TUE	WED	THU	FRI	SAT	SUN	TOTAL
1	Rest	2 miles, 1-2 x 10-10, 2 miles	4 miles	400m, 800m, 1,200m, 800m, 400m PI	Rest	4 miles + 4 x 100m S	6-7 miles	24 miles
2	Rest	6 miles inc 6 mins TUT	4 miles	1,200m, 2 x 800m, 4 x 200m PI + 4 x 200m SI + 4 x 100m S	Rest	4.5 miles + 5 x 100m S	7-8 miles	26 miles
3	Rest	2 miles, 2-3 x 10-10, 2 miles	4 miles	800m, 1,200m, 800m PI + 2 x 400m SI, 4 x 100m S	Rest	5 miles + 6 x 100m S	7-8 miles	27.5 miles
4	Rest	6-7 miles inc 8 minutes TUT	4 miles	1,200m, 800m, 2 x 400m, 2 x 200m SI + 4 x 100m S	Rest	5 miles + 6 x 100m S	8-9 miles	29 miles
5	Rest	2 miles, 3-4 x 10-10, 2 mile	4 miles	800m, 4 x 400m, 4 x 200m, 800m SI, + 4 x 100m S	Rest	6 miles + 6 x 100m S	8-9 miles	31 miles
TAPER	Rest	800m, 2 x 200m, 400m, 2 x 200m SI + 6 x 100m S	4 miles	4 x 200m SI + 4 x 100m S	Rest	3 miles easy + 3 x 100m S	10K RACE	

for runners who have already competed in at least a few half-marathons, but are looking to make a marked improvement on their personal best time. It's also a good training plan for anyone eager to maintain marathon fitness when they have six months or more between races.

"Improvers should certainly be looking at sub two hours, specifically 1:50, but I've actually coached runners who have been able to run under 1:30 for a half-marathon just by training with this three-day-weekly schedule," says Anderson. You should gauge your effort using your rate of perceived exertion, as described on the opposite page, or keep a track of your heart rate using a monitor.

BEGINNER'S HALF-MARATHON SCHEDULE

WK	MON	TUE	WED	THU	FRI	SAT OR SUN
1	Rest	30 mins: 5-min walk/5-min run, repeat 3 times. PE: 5/7	Rest	30 mins: 1-min walk/1-min easy jog/1-min run, repeat continuously. PE: 5/6/7	Rest	30 mins: 5-min walk/5-min run, repeat 3 times. PE: 5/7
2	Rest	**30 mins: 4-min walk/6-min run, repeat 3 times. PE: 5/7**	Rest	**30 mins: 2-min walk/2-min easy jog/2-min run, repeat continuously. PE: 5/6/7**	Rest	**30 mins: 4-min walk/ 6-min run, repeat 3 times. PE: 5/7**
3	Rest	30 mins: 2-min walk/8-min run, repeat 3 times. PE: 5/7	Rest	30 mins: 2-min walk/2-min easy jog/2-min run, repeat continuously. PE: 5/6/7	Rest	30 mins of 2-min walk/8-min run, repeat 3 times. PE: 5/7
4	**Rest**	**30 mins: 2 x 10 mins of continuous easy running. Have a 5-min walk between blocks. PE: 5/7**	**Rest**	**45 mins: 3-min walk/3-min jog/3-min threshold run, repeat continuously. PE: 5/6-7/8**	**Rest**	**50 mins: 2-min walk/ 8-min run, repeat 4 times. Have a 5-min brisk walk warm-up & cool-down. PE: 5/7**
5	Rest	20 mins continuous running with 5-min walk warm-up and cool-down. PE: 5/7	Rest	Repeat above session	Rest	60 mins: 3-min walk/12-min run, repeat 4 times. PE: 5/7
6	**Rest**	**25 mins continuous running with 5-min walk warm-up and cool-down. PE: 5/7**	**Rest**	**5-min walk/5-min easy run/5-min threshold run, repeat 3 times. PE: 5/6-7/8**	**Rest**	**Repeat above session**
7	Rest	30 mins easy-pace run with 5-min walk warm-up and cool-down. PE: 5/7	Rest	45 mins: 5 x 5-min threshold/ 2-min walk & 5-min warm-up and cool-down. PE: 5/8	Rest	75 mins: 3-min walk/12-min run, repeat 5 times. PE: 5/7
8	**Rest**	**40 mins easy pace with warm-up and cool-down walks. PE: 5/7**	**Rest**	**5-min threshold/5-min easy run, x 2 with warm-up walk/jog and cool-down. PE: 5/8**	**Rest**	**Repeat above session**
9	Rest	45 mins easy pace with warm-up and cool-down walks. PE: 5/7	Rest	30 mins: 5-min easy/5-min threshold. Add a 5-min warm-up and cool-down jog. PE: 5/6-7/8	Rest	90 mins: 3-min walk/12-min run, repeat 6 times. PE: 5/7
10	**Rest**	**45 mins easy. PE: 6-7**	**Rest**	**40 mins: 5-min easy/5-min threshold. Add a 5-min warm-up and cool-down jog. PE: 5/6-7/8**	**Rest**	**100 mins: 18-min easy run/2-min walk, repeat 5 times. PE: 5/6-7**
11	Rest	30 mins: 10 very easy jog/ 10 steady/10 threshold PE: 6/7/8	Rest	40 mins easy pace: 2 x 10 mins threshold. Have a 5-min jog between efforts. PE: 6/8	Rest	60 mins: 25 mins easy pace/5 min walk, repeat 2 times PE: 5/6-7
12	**Rest**	**30 mins: 5-min easy/5-min threshold, repeat 3 times PE: 6/8**	**Rest**	**20 mins easy relaxed run. PE: 6-7**	**Rest**	**Race Day 15-20 mins easy pace/walk 5 mins. Drink while walking. PE: 5/6-8**

Have your eyes
on the prize come
race day

+ **KEY TO PERCEIVED EFFORT (PE)**

6 (out of 10) or 60% max HR Recovery running. This is an easy running pace that allows you to maintain a conversation.

7 (out of 10) or 70% max HR Steady running. A little harder than recovery pace, but you should still be able to hold a conversation.

8-8.5 (out of 10) or 80-85% max HR Threshold running and target half-marathon pace. You should only be able to say a few words.

8.5+ (out of 10) or 85%+ max HR This is just below your maximum effort and you won't be able to speak. Use for intervals and speedwork.

IMPROVER'S HALF-MARATHON SCHEDULE

WK	MON	TUE	WED	THU	FRI	SAT OR SUN
1	Rest	10 mins easy/8 mins @ threshold pace, repeat 2 times. PE: 6-7/8-8.5	Rest	10 mins easy, 2 x 5 mins of continuous hills (approx 45 secs up/45 secs down), 10 mins easy. PE: 6-7/8-8.5	Rest	60 mins easy PE: 6-7
2	Rest	10 mins easy, 10 mins @ threshold pace, repeat 2 times. PE: 6-7/8-8.5	Rest	10 mins easy, 2 x 7 mins of continuous hills, 10 easy. PE: 6-7/8-8.5	Rest	70 mins easy. PE: 6-7
3	Rest	7 mins easy, 7 mins @ threshold, repeat 3 times. PE: 6-7/8-8.5	Rest	10 mins easy, 3 x 5 mins of continuous hills, 10 easy. PE: 6-7/8-8.5	Rest	75 mins easy PE: 6-7
4	Rest	36 mins: 6 x 3 mins, with 3 mins easy in between Reps 1, 3 & 5 @ PE: 6-7; reps 2, 4 & 6 @ PE: 8-8.5	Rest	40-min hilly run. Easy but faster up hills PE: 6 if easy, PE: 7-8 if hilly run	Rest	60 mins easy or 10K race. PE: 6-7 or 8-9
5	Rest	45 mins relaxed. PE: 6-7	Rest	10 mins easy, 2 x 10 mins of continuous hills (approx 45 secs up/45 secs down), 10 easy. PE: 6-7/8-8.5	Rest	80 mins easy PE: 6-7
6	Rest	5 mins easy, 2 x 12 mins @ threshold/HM race pace with 4 mins easy recovery, 5 mins easy. PE: 6-7/8-8.5	Rest	10 mins easy, 3 x 7 mins of continuous hills, 10 mins easy. PE: 6-7/8-8.5	Rest	80 mins with last 20 mins @ HM race pace. PE: 6-7/8
7	Rest	45 mins: 15 easy, 15 steady, 15 threshold. PE: 6/7/8	Rest	40 mins hilly run. Attack the hills, relax rest of run. PE: 6-7/8-8.5	Rest	60 mins easy. PE: 6-7
8	Rest	5 mins easy, 3 x 10 mins @ threshold/HM pace, 5 min easy. PE: 6-7/8-8.5	Rest	10 mins easy, 3 x 8 mins of continuous hills, 10 mins easy. PE: 6-7/8-8.5	Rest	90 mins easy with 20 mins @ HM race pace. PE: 6-7/8
9	Rest	10 mins easy, 25 mins @ HM/threshold pace, 10 mins easy. PE: 6-7/8-8.5	Rest	10 mins easy, 2 x 6, 4, 2 mins @ HM, 10K, 5K pace with 2-min easy between sets, 10 easy. PE: 6-7/8-9	Rest	100–110 mins easy. PE: 6-7
10	Rest	10 min easy, 5 x 2 min hard/2 min easy, 10 min easy. PE: 6-7/8-9	Rest	45 mins hilly run or 40 mins easy if racing Sunday. PE: 6/7 or 8	Rest	75 min easy OR 10K race. PE: 6-7 or 9
11	Rest	48 mins: 3-min threshold/3-min easy, repeat 8 times PE: 6-7/8-8.5	Rest	15 mins easy, 5 x 3 mins @ 10K pace with 2-min easy recovery between each rep, 15 mins easy. PE: 6-7/9	Rest	60 mins easy. PE: 6-7
12	Rest	30 mins: 5 mins easy/5 mins @ threshold, repeat 3 times. PE: 6/7	Rest	20 mins easy. PE: 6	Rest	Half-Marathon Race. PE: 8

ILLUSTRATION: DOUGLAS FRASER

RACING

Reach race day ready for the challenge

YOUR FULL MARATHON

You can conquer your first 26.2 mile race with this thorough training plan that uses a combination of gradual build-up, speedwork, and goal-paced runs to get you fit and raring to go. Follow each stage carefully and judge how well you are doing by the times and distances provided. Keep your perceived effort in check as going too hard or too easy at the wrong point in the plan could hinder your training. Ready for a challenge? They don't come much bigger than a marathon.

✚ KEY TO BEGINNER'S MARATHON SCHEDULE

EASY Run or cross-train at a conversational pace (40 to 60 seconds slower per mile than your marathon pace).

LSD Long, slow distance run that builds endurance. Run at a conversational pace. LSDs are rehearsals for race day – use them to determine your gear choices and strategies.

MP Marathon goal pace. After warming up properly for at least one mile, practise the speed you hope to hit at the race. Cool down by slowing your pace to easy running.

REST Ideally, do no exercise. Non-impact cross-training like stretching, yoga, or swimming can be beneficial instead.

YASSO 800S Warm up with one to two miles Easy running, then run 800 meters in the time that's "equal" to your marathon goal time. So for example, if you're targeting a 4:30 marathon, run each 800 in four minutes and 30 seconds. Jog 400 meters between repeats. Cool down with Easy running.

BEGINNER'S MARATHON SCHEDULE

WK	MON	TUE	WED	THU	FRI	SAT	SUN	TOTAL
1	Rest	4 miles EASY	4 miles EASY	4 miles EASY	Rest	3 milesEASY	10 miles LSD	25
2	Rest	4 miles EASY	5 miles EASY	4 miles EASY	Rest	3 miles EASY	12 miles LSD	28
3	Rest	3 miles EASY	5 miles EASY	3 miles EASY	Rest	5 miles EASY	14 miles LSD	30
4	Rest	3 miles EASY	4 miles EASY w/2 miles @ MP	4 miles EASY	Rest	3 miles EASY	10 miles LSD	24
5	Rest	3 miles EASY	6 miles EASY w/2 miles @ MP	4 miles EASY	Rest	3 miles EASY	16 miles LSD	32
6	Rest	5 miles EASY	4 miles EASY w/4 x 800	Yasso 800s 5 miles	Rest	3 miles EASY	18 miles LSD	35
7	Rest	5 miles EASY	7 miles EASY w/3 miles @ MP	5 miles EASY	Rest	3 miles EASY	20 miles LSD	40
8	Rest	5 miles EASY	8 miles EASY	3 miles EASY	Rest	3 miles EASY	13 miles LSD or half-marathon	32
9	Rest	7 miles EASY	8 miles EASY w/5 miles @ MP	7 miles EASY	Rest	5 miles EASY	16 miles LSD	43
10	Rest	5 miles EASY	3 miles EASY w/6 x 800	Yasso 800s 7 miles	Rest	5 miles EASY	18 miles LSD	38
11	Rest	4 miles EASY	7 miles EASY w/5 miles @ MP	5 miles EASY	Rest	4 miles EASY	20 miles LSD	40
12	Rest	7 miles EASY	7 miles EASY w/4 miles @ MP	6 miles EASY	Rest	4 miles EASY	18 miles LSD	42
13	Rest	7 miles EASY	3 miles EASY	7 miles EASY	Rest	3 miles EASY	20 miles LSD	40
14	Rest	5 miles EASY	6 miles EASY w/8 x 800	Yasso 800s 8 miles	Rest	3 miles EASY	13 miles LSD	35
15	Rest	5 miles EASY	7 miles EASY	5 miles EASY	Rest	5 miles EASY	10 miles LSD	32
16	Rest	6 miles EASY	Rest	5 miles EASY	Rest	1–3 miles EASY	EASY RACE DAY	40.2

RACING

Follow the road
to successful
running

THE PLAN: BREAK 4:00

The Runner's World race-tested marathon-training programme will get you across the finish line in 3:59:59 – or better! – with early hill work, later tempo sessions and strategic goal-pace runs

⊕ KEY TO INTERMEDIATE MARATHON SCHEDULE

HILLS Run the mileage for the day on the hilliest course you can find. Focus on sustaining an even effort as you climb and descend each one. If you live in a flat area then run intervals (also known as speedwork) instead.

TIME TRIAL Go to a local 400-metre track or any one-mile stretch of road. After 10 minutes of walking and jogging, run one mile, or four laps of the track. Over the course of training, your fitness gains will be reflected in your time trials.

MP Marathon goal pace. Practise the speed you're hoping to hit in the race. Warming up and down.

TEMPO RUN Run Easy for one to two miles as a warm up. Then dial into the pace that's given. Run Easy for two miles to cool down.

YASSO 800S Warm up with two miles of Easy running, then run 800 metres at the given pace that's "equal" to your marathon time.

LONG RUNS Later in the programme, pick up the pace in the last two to three miles for a fast finish.

INTERMEDIATE MARATHON SCHEDULE (SUB-4:00)

WK	MON	TUE	WED	THU	FRI	SAT	SUN	TOTAL
1	Rest	4 miles Easy (10:04/mile)	Hills: 4 miles	Rest	4 miles Easy (10:04/mile)	4 miles Easy (10:04/mile)	9 miles Easy (10:04/mile)	25 miles
2	Rest	4 miles Easy (10:04/mile)	Hills: 5 miles	Rest	5 miles Easy (10:04/mile)	5 miles Easy (10:04/mile)	9 miles Easy (10:04/mile)	28 miles
3	Rest	3 miles Easy (10:04/mile)	Hills: 5 miles	Rest	5 miles Easy (10:04/mile)	5 miles Easy (10:04/mile)	12 miles Easy (10:04/mile)	30 miles
4	Rest	4 miles Easy (10:04/mile)	Hills: 5 miles	Time trial	4 miles Easy (10:04/mile)	4 miles Easy (10:04/mile)	11 miles Easy (10:04/mile)	28 miles
5	Rest	4 miles Easy (9:58/mile) with 4 strides	Hills: 7 miles	Rest	4 miles with 2 miles @ MP (9:09/mile)	4 miles Easy (9:58/mile)	13 miles Easy (9:58/mile)	32 miles
6	Rest	5 miles Easy (9:58/mile) with 5 strides	Hills: 6 miles	Rest	4 miles with 2 miles @ MP (9:09/mile)	6 miles Easy (9:58/mile)	15 miles Easy (9:58/mile)	36 miles
7	Rest	6 miles Easy (9:58/mile) with 6 strides	Hills: 7 miles	Rest	5 miles with 3 miles @ MP (9:09/mile)	5 miles Easy (9:58/mile)	16 miles Easy (9:58/mile)	39 miles
8	Rest	5 miles Easy (9:58/mile) with 5 strides	Hills: 8 miles	Rest	Time trial	4 miles Easy (9:58/mile)	14 miles or half marathon	32 miles
9	Rest	3 miles Easy (9:52/mile) with 3 strides	Tempo: 8 miles with 3 miles @ 8:30/mile	Rest	9 miles with 7 miles @ MP (9:09/mile)	3 miles Easy (9:52/mile)	18 miles Easy (9:52 pace) fast finish	41 miles
10	Rest	4 miles Easy (9:52/mile) with 4 strides	Yasso 800s: 9 miles with 6x 800s at 3:57	Rest	10 miles with 8 miles @ MP (9:09/mile)	Rest	20 miles Easy (9:52 pace), fast finish	43 miles
11	Rest	4 miles Easy (9:52/mile) with 4 strides	7 miles Easy (9:52/mile)	Rest	10 miles with 8 miles @ MP (9:09/mile)	4 miles Easy (9:52/mile)	20 miles Easy (9:52 pace), fast finish	45 miles
12	Rest	7 miles Easy (9:52/mile)	Tempo: 9 miles with 5 miles @ 8:30/mile	6 miles Easy (9:52 /mile)	Time trial	8 miles Easy (9:52/mile)	15 miles Easy (9:52/mile)	45 miles
13	Rest	5 miles Easy (9:46/mile) with 6 strides	Yasso 800s: 10 miles with 8x 800 at 3:57	Rest	6 miles Easy (9:46/mile)	5 miles Easy (9:46/mile)	22 miles Easy (9:46/mile)	48 miles
14	Rest	8 miles Easy (9:46/mile) with 8 strides	Tempo: 8 miles with 4 miles @ 8:20/mile	Rest	7 miles Easy (9:46/mile)	7 miles Easy (9:46/mile)	15 miles or half marathon	45 miles
15	Rest	5 miles Easy (9:46/mile) with 5 strides	Tempo: 5 miles with 3 miles @ 8:20/mile	Rest	5 miles Easy (9:46/mile)	5 miles Easy (9:46/mile)	12 miles Easy (9:46/mile)	32 miles
16	Rest	Tempo: 5 miles with 3 miles @ 8:30/mile	Rest	5 miles Easy (10:04 /mile)	Rest	3 miles Easy (10:04/mile)	Race Day (9:09/mile)	39.2 miles

RACING

WHY LESS IS MORE

To race your best, you need to get enough rest beforehand.
But can you have too much of a good thing?

Tapering – scaling back your miles to allow your muscles to repair and your body to simply rest – is the critical last phase of training before a race. It's no less important to achieving the time you want than, say, long runs. But consider this: trimming your mileage right back abruptly might not be the best move. In fact, maintaining a higher volume during the taper period can give you a better chance of hitting peak performance on the big day.

"The problem with a big cut in mileage is that your body gets used to being on holiday," says exercise physiologist Greg McMillan. Top running coach Jack Daniels puts it more bluntly: "You can taper too much."

Just as you can add miles too quickly (and get injured), cutting them drastically can lead to a sluggish or sickly feeling. It's not uncommon even for elite athletes to come down with a stinking cold the week before a big race. One possible reason is that a major mileage cut could send signal to the immune system that it's OK to ease up. By maintaining volume, however, your immune response will remains consistent.

McMillan not only maintains more of his runners' miles in the days leading up to a race, he also shortens the taper (two weeks for a marathon, seven to 10 days for a half). He says today's recreational runners simply don't need as much rest as those of 30 years ago. That's because they generally log 30- to 40-miles per week instead of 70, making a heavy taper unnecessary. In addition, he says, "we understand the recovery cycle better." Today's training programmes have rest and recovery built into them, so runners are less likely to overtrain.

NECESSARY CUTBACKS

Tapering correctly is critical to keeping your fired up and injury-free on race day. Use this guide before you toe the line, adding easy days where needed

5K or 10K	7 days before	4	2 or 1
	Reduce weekly mileage by 10 to 20%. Do 3 to 5 x 3min at your goal 5K or 10K pace, with 1min rest in between	Rest or run according to your schedule	Rest or run according to your schedule

½ marathon	10 days before	7	4	2 or 1
	Reduce your weekly mileage by 10 to 20%	10 miles, with the last 2 to 3 miles at half-marathon pace	5 x 3min at your target half-marathon pace, with 1min rest in between	Rest or run according to your schedule

Marathon	14 days before	12	10	7	4	2 or 1
	Reduce your weekly mileage by 10 to 20%	10 x 400m at your 5K pace, with 1min rests	3 x 2K at 10K pace, 2-3min rests	Reduce mileage by another 10 to 20%; 12-mile run with last 6 at race pace	4 x 3min at 10K pace, 1min rests in between	Rest or run according to your schedule

Sometimes a drop-off can be beneficial

So what's the key to a successful taper? Some cutback in total mileage combined with a little quality work. McMillan suggests reducing your volume by 10 to 40 per cent, depending on race distance and your fatigue level. A 5K, of course, requires less of a reduction and a shorter taper than a marathon (see Necessary Cutbacks, *left*). Similarly, low-mileage runners need less taper time than long-haulers.

It's best to reduce volume by eliminating miles from each of your weekly runs. Do a shorter long run, fewer miles on easy days, and less higher-intensity work (instead of eight 800s, run four; instead of four tempo miles, do two). Just don't cut out quality

+ TAPER YOUR DIET

Tweaking your food intake is key to your pre-race prep. Use this guide to help you fuel up right

⊕ 7 DAYS BEFORE
For marathon runners only: reduce your intake by 100 calories for every mile you knock off your training.

⊕ 4 DAYS BEFORE
For all distances: start carb-loading now. Aim for 500g per day. Wholegrain pasta or bread is ideal.

⊕ 2 DAYS BEFORE
Start fluid-loading. Sports drinks are good, but water will do.

⊕ NIGHT BEFORE
Eat a high-carb meal containing 800-1,000 calories. Stick to what you know – your stomach doesn't want any surprises on race day.

⊕ RACE DAY
Eat 800 calories of low-fat carbs up to two hours before.

altogether – multiple studies show some fast-paced running is critical to keeping your lungs and legs sharp.

Keep in mind that every athlete is "an experiment of one," says Daniels. Percentages and time lines are guides – use them as a place to start, and adjust according to how you feel. Test your fatigue level a week or two before your taper by doing a two- to six-mile run at race pace. If you feel sluggish or just don't run the time you want, you might need to extend your taper by a few days or reduce your mileage by another five to 10 per cent. Do what feels comfortable. "Part of a taper is physiological; part is psychological," says Daniels. "If it doesn't settle in your mind, it interferes with the benefits come race day."

RACING

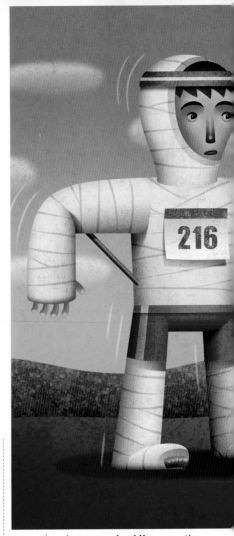

26 MILES LATER...

So you've completed your first marathon? How you recover is as important as how you trained

Congratulations: marathon done! But running 26.2 miles places high demands on the body and you're likely to end up with low fuel stores, fluid in the muscles, dehydration and perhaps some damaged muscle tissue. So, not surprisingly, you will be susceptible to injury and infection after the race. You may also be feeling disorientated, or even depressed, in the come-down after achieving such a significant goal.

There's no formula for working out exactly how long your body will take to recover. A seasoned marathon runner can expect to bounce back quicker than a marathon novice, for example. What you can do though, is make sure you know exactly what your body needs. Here's how to deal with the most common post-marathon ailments, how to combat the blues and, of course, top advice on when and how to resume running.

HEALTH AND NUTRITION

Delayed onset muscle soreness (DOMS) can begin eight or more hours after the race and may linger for up to a week after the marathon. For the first 24 hours after the race, apply ice (wrapped in a cloth) frequently to any painful parts of your legs, keeping it on for about 12 minutes at a time. Elevate your feet and legs for at least an hour after the marathon and for 30 minutes a day for a week.

In the days after the race, take ibuprofen or aspirin to calm muscle inflammation. Rub salicylate anti-inflammatory creams into skin over aching joints or throbbing tendons – these penetrate deeply enough to limit discomfort.

BLISTERS

The best advice for dealing with blisters is leave them be. If they've broken open during the race, your main concern should be preventing infection. Twice a day, soak your feet for up to 20 minutes in water containing iodine solution. Gently dry your feet, and cover the blistered area with a sterile gauze or plaster. Continue this process until the blister no longer oozes.

COLDS AND FLU

The stress of running a marathon can depress your immune system, leaving you susceptible to colds, flu and other infections in the days immediately following the race. Self-care is the best way to reduce your risk, so get plenty of sleep, eat well-balanced meals and drink lots of water. You might also want to try

ILLUSTRATION: EMILIANO PONZI

normal. Try to eat meals that are 50-60 per cent carbohydrate to replenish your glycogen reserves, and foods rich in protein to assist your body in repairing muscle. Indulge any cravings you might have – these could be your body's way of telling you what it needs.

Eat foods rich in iron – including meat, spinach, beans, peaches, parsley and peas – and promote iron absorption by drinking orange juice or consume other rich sources of vitamin C.

WEIGHT GAIN

Some runners complain of weight gain immediately after a marathon. This is most likely due to water retention as your muscles repair and rebuild. Don't be tempted to diet – your body requires a full complement of nutrients to recover from the stress of the race. If you're still gaining weight after the first week, adjust your calorie intake to suit your new activity levels.

FIGHTING THE POST-MARATHON BLUES

You've spent several months training hard and thinking about little else but your marathon, and now it's all over. And you're depressed. Luckily there are

HOW TO RESUME TRAINING

Now the big question: how do you pick up your training afterwards? For many years, exercise scientists have debated whether it is best to rest completely or jog lightly during the days that follow a marathon. The argument could go either way: light jogging should stimulate blood flow to the muscles, reduce tightness and preserve fitness. On the other hand, total rest allows the leg muscles to devote all their energies to the rebuilding process.

To gauge the relative values of rest and running, scientists in the USA recently studied a large group of marathon runners. About half of them refrained from running for a week following a marathon, while the other group jogged lightly for 30 minutes each day. Both sets of runners were stiff and sore during the week after the race, but the resting runners recovered more quickly. Leg-muscle endurance returned to normal after three days for the inactive runners, but was still below par after seven days for the light joggers. So take a one-week rest from training after your marathon. You deserve the break, and your muscles will return to normal more quickly.

During this one-week respite, you can do some light walking to burn off a few calories, keep your leg muscles loose and satisfy your desire for exercise. Once you're ready to get back to your favourite sport, prudence is the word. Remember that it takes four weeks for your muscles to really return to normal, so run only 30-60 per cent of your usual mileage.

Heart-rate monitoring is another good way of gauging when you are ready to resume training. A resting heart rate of 10 beats per minute or more above your pre-race rate is a sign that your body has yet to fully recover. So listen to it, and take it steady.

YOU SHOULD TAKE A ONE-WEEK REST FROM TRAINING AFTER A MARATHON

herbal remedies such as echinacea, or nutritional supplements such as zinc and vitamin C.

LACK OF ENERGY

A general lack of energy in the week following a marathon is perfectly

plenty of ways to combat the post-marathon blues.

Set new running goals and try shorter distances, or join a club for some company. Try something new, such as cross-training. Most importantly, give yourself a treat such as a holiday. You've earned it!

WHAT ARE YOU WAITING FOR?

With trails like this spectacular one to be found the length and breadth of the country, you've got little excuse to be sat here still reading this. Get out there and start running!

LOCATION Hadrian's Wall, Northumberland
PHOTO Steve Bateson **RUNNER** Balazs Somogyi

INDEX

A

Abdominals, **153**
Achilles tendonitis, **169**
Alexander Technique, **93**
Anaerobic exercise, **224**
Aqua running, **176-179**

B

Babies, 228-233
Ball half squats, **165**
Barefoot running, 191-199
Bent-leg calf lowering, 168
Bras, 44
Breast-feeding, 227
Bridge, 87

C

Cadence, **196**
Caffeine, **110**
Calculator, **258**
Calf, **21**
Cancer, **224**
Cheese, **132**

Chest
    burning, **152**
    female, **227**
Circuits, **94-95**
Clubs, **72-74**
Compression kit, **42**
Core
    anatomy, **84**
    fitness, **84-89**
Coughing
    post run, **153**
Cravings, **146**
Cross training, **78-97**
Crunches, **87**
Cycling, **81**

D

Donkey kicks, 163
Downhill running, 266

E

Exercise
    ball half squats, 165
    bridge, **87**

calf lowering, **168**
crunches, **87**
lying leg lift, **165**
metronome, **87**
olympic, **236-237**
plank lift, **88**
self-lowering, **168**
side-clamshell, **163**
straight-leg calf, **168**
side plank, **88**
superman, **87**
toe flexes, **171**

F

Fartlek, 59
Flexibility, 266
Food
    guide, 132-137
    junk, 144, 145
    tips, 114-119
Foot turns, 165
Footroll, 171
Form, 182-189
Fruit, 134

G

Gait, **93**

H

Half marathon, 274
Hamstring, 89
Headache, 153
Hill
    guide, 244-249
    running, 62-65
    starts, 64
Hydration, 111
Hydrotherapy, 113
Hyponatraemia, 112

I

Iliotibial band syndrome, **162**
Injuries, **161-171**

J

Jackets, 41

K

Kit, **40-44**
Kneeling stretch, **167**
Knees, **89**

L

Lactate threshold, 258
Leggings, 40
Long run, 56-57
Lower back, 89
Lunge and twist, 90
Lying ITB stretch, 163
Lying leg lift, 165

M

Marathon, **277**
Memory, **218**
Metronome
    exercise, **87**
Mile, **266**
Milk, **132**
Minimalism,
    see barefoot running
Motivation, **206-211**
Mountains, **63**

N

Nutrition, 98-129

O

Outdoor circuits, **94-95**

P

Pace, 287
Period
    menstrual, 226
Perspiration, 227
Phone
    apps, 145
Pilates, 92
Plank lift, 88
Plantar fasciitis, 170
    stretch, 171
Prams, 234-235
Pregnancy, 224
Preparation, 18
Pyramid, 90

Q

Quad
    stretch, **21**

R

Recipe
    Bangers & Mash, 128
    Chilli Con Carne, 128
    Fish & Chips, 129
    Fruit Crumble, 129
    Macaroni cheese, 128
    Pizza, 129
Recovery, 154-159, 236-237
Rehabilitation, 163, 165, 167, 168, 171
Reverse table, 90
Runner's knee, 164

S

Seated stretch, **167**
Shin splints, **166**
Shoes, **136-139**
Shorts, **40**
Short sprints, **77**
Side-clamshell, **163**
Side plank, **88**

Sleep, **172-174**
Socks, **41**
Speed
    sessions, **140**
    tips, **60-61**
Standing stretch, **167**
Standing wall stretch, **168**
Straight-leg calf lowering, **168**
Stretching
    calve, **21**
    footroll, **171**
    hamstring, **20**
    kneeling, **167**
    lying ITB, **163**
    quad, **21**
    seated, **167**
    standing, **167**
    standing wall, **168**
Strength work, **266**
Superman, **87**
Sweat-rate, **112**
Swimming, **81**

T

Taper, 282-283
Tea, 132
Tempo runs, 66-67, 140
Throat
    burning, 152
Timing, 22-25
Toe flexes, 171
Trail running, 240-243
Training
    essentials, 48-50
    disciplines, 76-77
    plan, 52-53, 268-277
    tips, 76-77
    watches, 43
Treadmills, 68-71
T-shirts, 40

W

Walking, **27-29**
Water, **108-113, 176-179**
Weight-lifting, **81**
Weight-loss, **138**
Women's health, **222-223**
Workouts, **84-89, 236-247**

Y

Yoga, 90-93

INDEX

UNLOCK YOUR TRUE MARATHON POTENTIAL

Got the runinng bug? Ready to take on the ultimate challenge of a marathon? Then the *Runner's World Coach: Marathon Training Guide* will answer all your questions and help you to avoid injury, increase stamina and improve times. With the latest science from the best experts, you'll soon be ready to race

▷ **Marathon-specific training tips** ▷ **How to avoid hitting the wall**

▷ **The secrets to a sub-3:30 marathon** ▷ **The best races in the world**

▷ **How Olympians run the 26 miler** ▷ **The best gels and supplements**

ON SALE NOW IN WHSMITH FOR £7.99